Joan Smith is a novelist, columnist and human rights activist. She has been involved in campaigns for free expression, authors' rights, and literacy in Sierra Leone. She currently speaks for Hacked Off, the organisation which represents victims of phone hacking. She is an honorary associate of the National Secular Society and supports Republic, the campaign for an elected head of state.

http://politicalblonde.com/
@polblonde

THE PUBLIC WOMAN

JOAN SMITH

The Westbourne Press

Published 2013 by The Westbourne Press

The Westbourne Press
26 Westbourne Grove, London w2 5rh
www.westbournepress.co.uk

A full cip record for this book is available from the British Library.

ISBN 978-1-908906-04-5
eISBN 978-1-908906-05-2

Printed and bound by Bookwell, Finland

CONTENTS

INTRODUCTION

How are women supposed to make sense of the world today? The hugely popular TV series *Sex and the City* reminded us that we enjoy unprecedented freedom, compared with previous generations: we can have sex when and with whom we like, live with a partner or on our own, have children when and *if* we want to, and get further in our careers than any women in history. The series was American but a lot of other women identified with it, loving its playful combination of sexual pleasure, female friendship and high heels. The main characters talked about things – how hard it is to make equal relationships, professional rivalry and the pain of break-ups – which are part and parcel of a modern woman's life. Obviously I'm thinking mainly about secular Western culture here, even if I'm writing shortly after *Cosmopolitan* launched in the Middle East for the first time. But it's easy to forget how recently women's lives have changed even in Europe and the US, allowing us to pursue dreams and ambitions our grandmothers could scarcely have imagined.

Only a century ago, in the run-up to the First World War, life was very different: British women didn't have the vote, couldn't stand for Parliament, were not allowed to graduate at Oxford and Cambridge, had to pass stricter tests to get a divorce and were barred from a number of professions including the law and accountancy. The home was a safe place, as long as you obeyed the rules laid down by husbands and fathers, but marital rape was legal and domestic violence never talked about. A woman's reputation was fragile, and a woman who divorced or had children outside marriage faced a lifetime of ostracism and shame. The process of radical change, of opening up the public world to the other half of the human race, was begun by brave and far-sighted women who campaigned on one front after another: for the vote, for women to be allowed to enter the professions, for an end to the economic discrimination which kept women dependent on men. In terms of recorded history, the citadels fell remarkably fast, but it often didn't feel like that for individual women; when I applied for my first mortgage, women were still being told that their salaries didn't 'count' because they were only working until they became pregnant.

All of that's gone now. In the UK, women have got to the very top in politics, business and the judiciary; we've had a woman prime minister, foreign secretary, a couple of female home secretaries and the first woman Supreme Court judge. More women than ever are becoming doctors, lawyers, journalists and company directors; girls have been out-performing boys in A levels and female applicants to university dramatically outnumbered males (393,096 girls compared to 307,065 boys) in 2011.[1] Offices have as many women working in them as men, forcing slow but visible changes in the culture of work, where employment conditions have changed to ensure that women (and to a lesser extent men) can take time off to have families. Some battles are still to be won, notably equal pay, but there's never been a better moment in Western history to be born female.

So why doesn't it feel like that? Why is it still so uncomfortable to be a woman? What is it about this public world that makes us feel anxious, marginal, unwelcome? There's plenty of evidence that that *is* how we feel, from cries of outrage about sexism on social networking sites to a new wave of political campaigning. The SlutWalks movement started in Canada but was quickly taken up in other countries because young women feel threatened by and blamed for sexual violence, just like an earlier generation who went on Take Back the Night marches. From Toronto and London to Cairo and Tunis, public space still isn't as safe as it should be for women, who suffer everything from routine harassment on the street to forms of sexual violence including rape. In the West, we live in societies which have made a legal and ethical commitment to equality, and the UK has dedicated institutions – a government minister for women and equality, and an Equality and Human Rights Commission – which are supposed to guarantee it. Yet something has gone wrong in practice, creating a chasm between what we expect and actual experience.

In the wake of the 2008 economic crisis, British women are faring much worse economically than men, bearing the brunt of the Coalition government's expenditure cuts and suffering record levels of unemployment. Women still do most of the caring, whether it's for children or elderly relatives, but are the number one target for right-wing politicians who like to blame struggling single mothers for 'broken Britain'. Education is more important than ever – girls like 15-year-old Malala Yousafzai in Pakistan have risked their lives for it – but celebrity magazines present a bland catalogue of Wags, royals and singers as role models.

Why is there such a dearth of alternatives, sending the message that girls can be clever *and* proud of their bodies? How are they supposed to develop healthy forms of self-esteem when huge billboards advertise lap dancing clubs, showing young women as sex toys? We know that paying for sex is more popular than ever among British men, and the demand is so great that foreign women from the ruined economies of Eastern Europe and the slums of West Africa are being trafficked into the country to work as sex slaves. Meanwhile, in the north of England, child prostitution rings have been exposed in one town after another.

No wonder women are angry, all over the world. They're lobbying Parliament in the UK, holding demonstrations against sexual harassment in the Middle East and creating innovative forms of protest in Russia. (I couldn't have written this book without raising a cheer for the punk collective Pussy Riot.) In India, thousands of women took to the streets to protest against male violence after a horrific case – the rape and fatal torture of a medical student on a bus in Delhi in December 2012 – exposed the state's abject failure to ensure safety and equality. The internet has played a vital role in a new wave of feminism, enabling women in different countries to connect and compare experiences of campaigns and activism. In the UK, young women are rejecting hostile stereotypes on websites such as www.ukfeminista.org.uk, while The Vagenda (www.vagendamag.blogspot.co.uk) provides a space to respond to sexist articles in the media. Hollaback! (www.ihollaback.org) and the Everyday Sexism Project (www.everydaysexism.com) encourage reporting of sexist abuse and street harassment. Two Facebook campaigns, *No More*

Page 3 and *Turn Your Back on Page 3*, attracted thousands of signatures in a matter of weeks. Instead of having to plead for attention from the mainstream media, the founders of these campaigns have found themselves courted by editors who've suddenly realised they need to take them seriously.

We're living in an age in which feminism has returned in new and exciting forms, and I've written this book to add to the argument I made almost a quarter of a century ago in *Misogynies*. When I began writing that book, I thought – I hoped – that woman-hating was a historical phenomenon. I was documenting attitudes that had been around for thousands of years, teasing out links between misogynist literature in the Roman republic and the crimes of the Yorkshire Ripper. Misogyny was ubiquitous, but it had flourished in unequal societies and I didn't think it was inevitable. In traditional cultures, boys spent their early years with their mothers, growing up to realise later that women had low status and were even despised, with disastrous effects on relations between adult men and women. I believed that the development of more equal societies, an aspiration which many men supported, would change all that. Adults would be able to create new relationships, based on respect and mutual pleasure, and I still think that's happened to some extent. What's also happened, however, is a backlash against gender equality of staggering viciousness.

Let me list some of the manifestations: women who say they've been raped are abused – and have their identities revealed – all over the internet. Disbelief of victims is so reflexive that men who evidently pose a danger to girls and women, such as the Soham murderer Ian Huntley or the serial killer Levi Bellfield, who abducted and murdered

Milly Dowler, are able to carry out assaults with impunity for years. Domestic violence affects one woman in four and we're becoming familiar with the dreadful phenomenon of 'family annihilation' in which angry men slaughter their entire families. Across the world, women are being tricked and coerced into prostitution, and – as the story of 'Crystal' reveals in this book – forced to work for little or no pay as domestic servants. Even when women get to the top, they often do it by adopting the behaviour and values of the most sexist men, as I argue in a chapter on the former *Sun* and *News of the World* editor, Rebekah Brooks. Then there is the return of religious extremism, probably the most overt of all the attempts to reassert patriarchal values, which tries to persuade women that they don't have the same right to enjoy public space. The incidence of 'honour-based' crime is increasing in the UK, exemplified by the horrific rape and murder of Banaz Mahmod, whose killing was planned by her own relatives. At the same time, in one Middle Eastern country after another, the Arab Spring has brought conservative religious parties to power, threatening women's hard-won rights across the region. As I was writing the book, I thought many times of the great Egyptian feminist Hoda Shaarawi, and how astonished she would be to see the return of the veil in her own country.

I don't think any of this is an accident. I see it as a warning, a message that if women insist on living in the public world, we're on our own: the *female eunuch* has become the *public woman*, but the price of giving up the protection of patriarchy is that we have to take our chances in a harsh world. How true that is was brought home to me during the writing of this book, when the Jimmy Savile scandal sent shock waves across the UK. In a matter of days, a supposedly 'much-loved' TV presenter was exposed as a narcissistic sexual predator who had been targeting teenagers, most of them girls, for decades. His illegal activities apparently went undetected by a series of institutions, including Broadmoor special hospital and the BBC, whose journalists were stopped from exposing his activities even after his death in 2011. Some of Savile's victims *had* complained, either at the time they were assaulted or when they were older, but they were not believed until the revelations turned into a torrent in 2012.

The scandal marked a huge failure of child protection in the workplace but it also did something unexpected, creating a space in which alleged victims suddenly felt able to talk publicly about the sexual abuse and harassment they'd experienced as children and adults. It became clearer than ever that a sexist culture existed in many organisations, not just the BBC, which allowed much worse behaviour to flourish – and it was not merely a historical phenomenon. In the 1970s and 1980s, employers did not have to produce codes governing accusations of sexual harassment and in any case it was often senior executives who were the worst offenders. But even in 2013, when such codes are common in both the public and private sector, victims still have to weigh up the likely damage to their careers if they make a formal complaint. Indeed, the argument of this book is that sexual harassment is one of the ways in which women are made to feel uncomfortable – outsiders and interlopers – in the workplace. It's not always conscious but there's an elision here of two ideas which has dire consequences for women: if a woman insists on her rightful place in the public world, some men will assume that she's publicly *available*.

I've written this book as a challenge to that notion. The public woman is a *sexual* woman but on her own terms, not those dictated by misogynist bosses, politicians and clerics. She's a lot of other things as well: smart, educated, independent, sexy – if she chooses, of course – and open to equal relationships with other adults. While this book may seem dark at times, and I found some of it gruelling to write, I end on an optimistic note. The principle of gender equality is widely supported in the modern world but it requires new ways of thinking if it's going to be achieved on the ground. Women are first and foremost human beings and we have the right, like men, to move freely between the public and private worlds. Contemporary notions of human rights fail to address women's *specific* experience, and I've tried to remedy that with my own declaration of women's rights for the 21st century.

Finally, I would like to mention several people who were always willing to discuss ideas with me and encouraged the writing of this book: Sarah Green, Caroline Coon, Annajoy David, Lucy Popescu and Natasha Lewis. I'm grateful to the Poppy Project for introducing me to 'Crystal' and 'Sonya', and I'd like to thank both women for talking to me about their experiences. I also have to thank my inspirational publisher Lynn Gaspard, who needed only a single conversation to grasp what I wanted to do. Her belief in me and the book has been invaluable.

Joan Smith
London, January 2013

DISPLAY

BRITAIN'S GOT NARCISSISM

Once upon a time, little girls dreamed of marrying a prince and living happily ever. Now it seems they aspire to have breast implants, date a footballer or two, marry an Australian crooner and a transvestite cage-fighter – not at the same time, obviously – date an Argentinian male model and launch a range of pink-themed accessories. Katie Price, formerly known as the glamour model Jordan, has done all of these things by her mid-30s and fans flock to her public appearances. She easily fills bookshops when she signs copies of her autobiographies (four to date), selling her dream of celebrity to other women. It's not hard to see that Price represents a very modern kind of success: she is a former Page 3 girl who has made millions by branching out into 'reality' TV shows, appearing in celebrity magazines and newspapers – including writing a column for the *Sun* – and promoting her own line of cosmetics. She isn't shy about what she's achieved, boasting in her first memoir *Being Jordan*,[1] which was published when she was 26, that she owns two houses 'with a fair bit of land', two flats, several 'very nice' cars including a Range Rover and a Bentley, and three horses. Price is, in other words, the quintessential media personality and her success is inextricably linked to her willingness not just to incarnate fantasies – markedly different ones for men and women

– but to act as an inexhaustible source of stories. In the relatively recent circumstances of a 24-hour media cycle, supported by a raft of publications parasitic on TV shows, she has provided one drama after another. Since her late teens, her private life has been lived out in public and it hasn't all been roses and tiaras: in a nod to the late Princess Diana, Price's narrative is also about overcoming adversity, from her struggle as a single mother to her repeated disappointments in relationships. At the beginning of her career as a glamour model, a single date with the footballer Teddy Sheringham was considered sufficiently big news to be reported on the front page of the *Sun*; later she had a longer relationship with another footballer, Dwight Yorke, who is the father of her disabled son Harvey. Other famous boyfriends have included a couple of pop stars, Dane Bowers and Gareth Gates, and the Formula 1 driver Ralf Schumacher. She met her first husband, Peter André, during an appearance on the 'reality' TV show *I'm a Celebrity … Get Me Out of Here!* and the rights to their wedding photographs were sold to *OK!* magazine. The couple had two daughters together and an acrimonious divorce, after which Price married Alex Reid, a cross-dressing cage-fighter whose female *alter ego* goes under the name Roxanne. For her second wedding, Price opted for a 'private' ceremony in Nevada where the happy couple was reported to have celebrated by visiting pole-dancing clubs in Las Vegas. Back in the UK, Price's ex-husband André broke down on Sky News when the presenter, Kay Burley, asked him how he'd feel if Reid wanted to adopt his two daughters. In the midst of this roller-coaster narrative of passion, jealousy, recriminations, TV confessions and sponsorship, Price's marriage to Reid lasted a year. When it ended, she began stepping out with male model Leandro Penna, while Reid enjoyed a brief relationship (and had a child) with a former winner of *Celebrity Big Brother,* Chantelle Houghton.

Price no longer does glamour modelling but that hasn't reduced her public profile. The case for her as a role model is rooted in the notion that she has achieved something which has almost sacramental status in modern culture: she makes choices. Choice is the holy grail of unfettered individualism, so much so that it doesn't actually matter if someone's choices are spur-of-the-moment or downright unwise. Contemporary scepticism about Freud's ideas has had the unfortunate effect of banishing the concept of the unconscious, to the point where celebrities are insulted by the suggestion they might be doing something for motives they don't fully understand. There are few better examples of this than Princess Diana, who made catastrophic choices about men and showed not a glimmer of insight into why her relationships kept going wrong. Diana exemplifies a species of female narcissism which is repeatedly misread in popular culture, glamourising stunted ambition – wanting fame and admiration – and erasing any requirement for personal responsibility. Since her death, one woman after another has followed in her footsteps, seizing the opportunities offered by the entertainment industry, 'reality' TV and talent shows. Like Diana, they're known by their first names – Katie, Cheryl, Jade, Alesha, Kerry, Victoria, Tulisa – and like her they tend to come from backgrounds where education isn't valued. In her first memoir, Price is adamant that this is the life she always wanted:

I'd always wanted to be a model; either that or a pop star – or both! I can almost hear you thinking, She must think a lot of herself. But I don't. I've just always been a bit of an exhibitionist. I love showing off and being the centre of attention.[2]

Price's insistence on the importance of choice is evident in her repeated excursions into cosmetic surgery. She became a Page 3 model with perfectly natural breasts but she wasn't satisfied with them; she went ahead with the first operation even though it meant she could no longer appear on Page 3, which had a rule banning models with implants. She insists her decision had nothing to do with an ex-boyfriend who told Price her 'boobs' weren't big enough and boasted about his previous girlfriend who'd appeared on Page 3. She writes:

But, when I saw his ex, I thought, Stuff it, if she can make it so can I. She was attractive, but nothing special, and I didn't think her boobs were that impressive. I tried to ignore Gary and kept my dreams alive.[3]

This episode could stand as a catalogue of the illusions and insecurities of female celebrities. It speaks volumes about self-deception, low self-esteem – often a trait of self-confessed exhibitionists – and corrosive rivalry with other women. The popular press loves the latter, reporting celebrities' feuds over husbands and boyfriends with relish; the 'cat fight' is a staple of tabloid culture, confirming age-old stereotypes about women, and the resource they're fighting over is usually men. The message for anyone outside the charmed circle of celebrity is that other women can't be trusted, and even teenage girls need constantly to measure themselves against their friends and make sure they come out on top. It's a world which exists outside modern value systems which stress altruism and equality, and it's so divorced from reality that repeated bouts of unnecessary surgery are treated merely as proof that a woman is an agent in her own life. Add to that a distortion of feminist ideas in popular culture – the personal has replaced the political – and it's easy to see how Price has achieved a weird form of cultural domination. 'Some people want designer clothes. I want a designer body,'[4] she once said. It's as simple, and artificial, as that.

For millions of girls and young women who avidly watch MTV or shows like *I'm a Celebrity*, *The X Factor* and *Britain's Next Top Model*, the conclusion is straightforward: academic qualifications don't matter and looks are everything. They bring famous boyfriends, celebrity husbands, expensive cars, big houses and (eventually) large families in their wake. Nor is it difficult to know what to aim for, for the women who inhabit this world look pretty much the same; regardless of their ethnic background, they are all young and boyishly slim with flat stomachs, small waists, big breasts and big hair. At a time when almost 60 per cent of the female population of the UK is overweight or obese, what they don't look like is the average British woman, and the bodies which fill pages of celebrity magazines are bound to inspire envy and anxiety. Getting and maintaining the look is hard work, demanding a great deal of exercise and a severely restricted calorie intake, but the primary purpose isn't better health. It would be no bad thing if women thought more about diet and exercise, reducing the risk of conditions associated with excess weight and inactivity, but that is emphatically not what the celebrity lifestyle is about. The desirable body shape is that of a pubescent girl with large breasts, a species of girl-woman who barely exists in real life, and Price understands that fact very well. In *Being Jordan*, she singles out a famous woman who's never admitted to having breast augmentation and observes:

> You only have to look at her – skinny all over except her boobs … I cannot believe she achieves that big-cleavage, boobs-standing-to-attention look with tit tape alone: it's good, but it's not *that* good.[5]

There's an unnerving combination here of professional scrutiny – the anecdote emerges from a 'you-show-me-yours' session in a ladies' lavatory – and rivalry. To be clear, Price *isn't* suggesting there's anything wrong with cosmetic surgery. In the book she treats it almost casually, joking about the possibility that she might have a fourth 'boob job', and the numbers of women following her example are growing. Well-known women who *haven't* had implants, such as the singer Rihanna, are frequently the target of speculation: why does she put up with small breasts when she could easily afford a new pair? *Not* having surgery is the oddity, as though getting a new pair of 'boobs' is no more momentous a decision than buying a new winter coat.

Of course there are several unspoken words in Price's narrative, and one of them is class. The big-breasts, big-hair, tiny G-string look she incarnated at the beginning of her career appeals to the aspirant working class: *Sun* readers, natural Tory voters who may have turned to New Labour briefly in 1997, and their values are based on hard work and self-interest. Price's narrative, which is all about personal ambition and acquisition of material goods, is perfect for them but it isn't received so warmly elsewhere. There's an undeniable snobbery behind 'Essex girl' jokes but there is also a problem about a system of values based on little more than unquestioning admiration for youth, beauty and wealth. The first attribute in that list is often the prerequisite for the other two, something that isn't always appreciated by people who behave as though getting older is merely a poor lifestyle choice. But it also means there's a disjunction between working-class notions of beauty and what middle-class women aspire to, exacerbating pre-existing class divisions. It's evident in the contrast between celebrity magazines, whose heroines are singers, models and veterans of 'reality' TV shows, and glossy fashion magazines such as *Vogue*. It isn't that the world of high fashion offers healthier role models for women: far from it. High fashion regards big breasts with disdain, to the point where some of the most successful catwalk models barely have them at all. The large-breasted girl-woman of celebrity culture has no place in the twice-yearly fashion shows staged in London, Paris and Milan by the big couture houses, where a very different body type is in the ascendant. Here the boy-woman is in demand, a young and slender model with angular cheeks and jutting hip bones, in effect an adrogyne who looks – and in some cases is – starved by comparison. The fashion industry has often been accused of promoting eating disorders but the quest for thinness became ever more extreme in the first decade of the 21st century, culminating in the notorious cult of 'size zero'. The sinister symbolism of the phrase – it suggests a vogue for women who weigh nothing – seemed lost on top designers, who had come to regard a healthy size 12 as seriously overweight. A series of tragedies ensued on the international circuit, where three models died within the space of a year after suffering eating disorders. Ana Carolina Reston from Brazil was 21 when she starved herself to death on 15 November 2006; she was 5ft 8ins tall, weighed 40 kg, and had been living on a diet of apples and tomatoes. The Uruguayan model Luisel Ramos was only a year older when she died on 2 August 2006, just after coming off stage at Montevideo fashion week; Ramos was 5ft 9ins tall, weighed 44 kg, and hadn't eaten for several days before the show. Six months later her younger sister Eliana, aged 18 and also a model, died from a heart attack brought on by malnutrition. It should have been a wake-up call to the fashion industry, but to this day many catwalk models continue to have a body mass index which would put them in the anorexic category. Not much hope, then, of high fashion providing more attainable standards of female attractiveness than the celebrity-obsessed entertainment industry.

When Simone de Beauvoir wrote in *The Second Sex* that 'one is not born, but rather becomes, a woman',[6] she wasn't thinking about silicone implants and liposuction. She was suggesting that what girls were encouraged to aim for as they approached adulthood in the middle of the 20th century was inauthentic. They had to suppress feelings and ambitions to concentrate on fulfilling male ideals of womanliness, and the result was the female eunuch that

Germaine Greer would go on to write about. (Beauvoir's own formula, by the way, framed women as 'intermediate between male and eunuch'.) Beauvoir was thinking chiefly about social characteristics, the behaviour women felt they had to adopt to please fathers and husbands, but there was already a literal aspect to the process. For at least a century, women had been wearing corsets and other garments to achieve more womanly figures, and tight-lacing had been blamed for fainting and other health problems. At least corsets could be removed with a sigh of relief at the end of the day, but the desirable body shapes of the 21st century have permanent effects. An aversive attitude to food affects hormone cycles and weakens bones, while the insertion of silicone bags into tender flesh has long-term consequences. (In 2011, a scandal about sub-standard French implants fitted by private clinics sent hundreds of women to their GPs, pleading to have them removed.) It's as if the Greek myth of Pygmalion – the artist who sculpts a statue of a perfect woman and brings her to life – has been read literally, persuading girls that the body they're born with is simply raw material in need of extensive alteration. Becoming a woman has never been such hard work, a fact that's obscured by a popular culture which normalises and celebrates various forms of artificiality. When Kate Moss, Victoria Beckham, Cheryl Cole and Katie Price appear endlessly on posters, websites, book and magazine covers, most women are going to feel abnormal.

In the 21st century, that's feminism, surely? These women are famous, rich and successful, and they enjoy lifestyles which are widely envied. In fact, Price is open about the extent to which her assumptions about gender belong in a pre-feminist age. Writing about her glamour-modelling days in *Being Jordan*, she enthuses about how much she much she enjoyed adopting 'provocative positions' that 'look naughty'. She loves wearing 'girly' colours – pink, white, baby blue – and hot pants, cropped tops, G-strings, high heels and ankle socks.[7]

It's disturbingly close to a Lolita fantasy, but then Price was only 13 when she did her first modelling assignment for a jeans company. Not long afterwards, she had a narrow escape from a photographer who was arrested and charged with a string of paedophile offences. She was 18 when she embarked on her career as a Page 3 girl, appearing every day for a week to promote *Striptease*, a new movie starring Demi Moore. Price had been determined to have surgery on her breasts from the age of 16, when a clinic turned her down on grounds of age, but she managed to persuade a surgeon to take her on when she was 20. Her natural bra size was 32C but she didn't think her breasts were big enough for glamour modelling:

> I believe bigger breasts are sexier, more womanly and I think I suit them. I've never been one for the 'natural look'. I like the 'fake' look: big hair, big make-up, big boobs.[8]

Her surgeon performed two operations but declined to carry out a third, so she found someone else who was willing to do it. Gradually Price was becoming Jordan, a young woman with freakishly large breasts which turned her into a caricature of extreme femininity. I once saw her walk into a waiting area at Broadcasting House in central London when we were both guests on the Radio

4 programme *Woman's Hour*, and I didn't immediately recognise her. She was wearing tight jeans and stilettos but it was impossible to look at anything but her breasts, which jutted so far forward from her torso that she looked as though she might over-balance at any moment. On air, *Woman's Hour* presenter Jenni Murray asked Price who had given her the huge sparkling ring she was wearing. She replied – sadly, I thought – that she'd bought it herself, like most of her jewellery. It seemed an uncomfortable admission for a woman who believes unquestioningly in romance, describing herself as 'quite old-fashioned'. Price has sufficient self-awareness to know that not everyone admires the path she's chosen but she's defensive about her choices, angrily rejecting the accusation that she's addicted to cosmetic surgery. She insists there's 'a person' inside her surgically enhanced body, making a distinction which seems to echo the Jordan/Katie Price dichotomy. But it's clearly more complex than that: she is groping towards the idea that her highly sexualised external persona co-exists with an ungendered internal consciousness. No matter how many physical changes Price puts herself through – cosmetic surgery, hair extensions, denying herself food to make her stomach look flat – she feels there is an internal self that remains untouched by it. It is perhaps the part of her which is desperate to be loved, something she mentions more than once in *Being Jordan*, and the book ends with her unshakable conviction that she's finally got what she's always wanted. Peter André is 'the one' and she can't imagine life without him: 'He's my best friend, my lover and my soul mate. And I can't wait to say that he's my husband!'[9] Of course we know how that story ends but

Price's happy-ever-after fantasy is integral to the lure of the celebrity lifestyle.

When Freud wrote about narcissism, he distinguished between the infant's primary narcissism, which he regarded as an essential survival mechanism, and the species found in adults. His essay on the subject, published in 1914, is controversial because of his views on gender and homosexuality, but his recognition of unhealthy forms of adult narcissism remains important. There is nothing wrong with self-esteem or taking pleasure in the body, whether it comes in the form of wearing beautiful clothes, enjoying passionate sex or eating dark chocolate (I enjoy all three). But celebrity culture encourages something else, grandiose expectations of love and success which actually militate against it. Narcissistic fantasies are rife, encouraging a relentless pursuit of fame and popularity, but the impact on women is more extreme. I'm not talking about narcissistic personality disorder, although there has been a disturbing failure to recognise it in individuals like Jimmy Savile, but the effect of encouraging unrealistic expectations. Popular culture and 'reality' TV in particular foster a form of 'magical thinking' – Freud used the term in a slightly earlier work, *Totem and Taboo* – which leads individuals to believe they can get whatever they want if they just try hard enough (it's called 'living the dream'). Boys and young men are not immune, pursuing fame and success in sport and the entertainment industry, but they're not as vulnerable to romantic fantasies. They're also more likely to work on their bodies in the gym than undergo cosmetic surgery.

At school, even the best teachers have to compete with the constant promotion of perfect female bodies and material success in celebrity magazines and autobiographies. In a disturbing development, some teenage girls are so gripped by the fantasy that they allow boyfriends to film them on camera phones, suffering agonies when the footage is posted on social networking sites. (This is what happened to Tulisa Contostavlos, a judge on *The X Factor*, who sued an ex-boyfriend after a video made when she was in her teens was posted online.) Price says she was 'a fairly good student' until the age of 15 but then she got her first boyfriend and 'went off the rails completely'. For a woman born eight years after publication of *The Female Eunuch*, she displays a perplexing attachment to traditional ideas about romance, but she's far from alone among her generation. Cheryl Tweedy's marriage to the Chelsea footballer Ashley Cole took place amid an orgy of romantic display – the couple were photographed in matching white outfits, with a white limousine in the background – and ended in accusations of infidelity, acrimony and divorce. What is sold to young women as a way of feeling good turns out to be its opposite, bringing disappointment and low self-esteem. And pursuing a 'career' in the world of celebrity is often done at the cost of education, which is much more likely to provide lasting achievements and long-term stability.

The other unspoken word in Price's story is age. The standardisation of women's bodies in popular culture leaves no space for ageing gracefully, let alone comfortably. On the contrary, well-known women are minutely scrutinised for crows' feet and cellulite, and there is an assumption that at some point they will start finding it hard to hold onto their current partners. In this highly unnatural world, some forms of biological determinism remain unquestioned, none more so that the notion that it is 'natural' for older men to seek out younger women – but not the other way round. The end of Madonna's marriage to the film director Guy Ritchie, who is 10 years younger, was treated as inevitable, while the singer's failure to suffer an emotional collapse – she took up with an even younger man instead – infuriated her critics. Demi Moore, one of the most beautiful film stars of her generation, followed the script much more closely when her marriage to the actor Ashton Kutcher collapsed. Photographs of an obviously miserable Moore were plastered all over the tabloid press and celebrity magazines, accompanied by articles describing Kutcher's alleged infidelity with a younger woman. In reality, the 15-year age difference between Kutcher and Moore was as nothing compared with the 37 years dividing the newspaper tycoon Rupert Murdoch and his third wife Wendi Deng, but the rules are tougher for women. In tabloid terms, Moore's marriage was even more of a delicious disaster-in-waiting than Madonna's, and the star was mocked for supposedly following the prescriptions – teeth whitening, manicures, pelvic floor exercises, sun block – that readers of celebrity magazines are urged to adopt. Why would anyone go to such lengths to stay young – 'viable and fresh, like a lovely frosted cupcake in the bakery of life',[10] according to Jan Moir in the *Daily Mail* – if she hadn't been fed non-stop stories about the horrors of getting old? But the paper had waited quite long enough for Moore's marriage to fall apart, insisting she had always been 'asking for trouble' when she dated a man who was likely to leave her for a younger woman 'in her physical peak'.

It's rare to see disgust towards older women expressed so frankly, but it goes some way towards explaining the trap that women of Price's generation have begun to see looming ahead of them. In 2012, she appeared in a poster campaign for a charity which raises money for children who have genetic conditions similar to the one which affects her son. Riding an escalator on the London Underground, I caught sight of one of the posters and for a second time I didn't recognise her: Price's hair was scraped back in a ponytail, she was wearing a simple white t-shirt and jeans, and her facial expression was tentative. Most striking, however, was the fact that her breasts looked almost natural, which seemed to confirm suggestions that she'd had surgery to reduce their size. The poster campaign coincided with reports of a curious episode in a London club during a footballer's birthday party, when Price was said to have broken down in tears, asking why everyone was staring at her. Then she answered her own question: 'I'm plastic. I've got a fake nose, fake teeth and fake tits – only my arse is real.'[11]

Price's bout of self-revulsion came at the age of 34, by which time she had been a public figure for almost half her life. She was hardly old by any rational standard but the cult of celebrity is interested only in youth and novelty. Its products are left with divided selves, forced into a false choice between body and brain, beauty and intelligence. A few weeks after the posters appeared, Price broke up with her boyfriend Leandro Penna and appeared in public with her breasts restored to their old prominence. She also revealed what she was prepared to endure to get the body shape she wanted: during her fifth bout of surgery, the wound became infected and she had to rush to A&E for emergency treatment.[12] It was a vivid warning of how a narcissistic culture eats up young women, but the next generation of wannabes is already queuing outside TV studios.

POLAR DISORDER

In these hard economic times, women are constantly looking around for job opportunities. For students and single mothers, shift work is an option because it can be combined with lectures, course work and being around for children after school. In the first decade of the 21st century, young women began to hear about a new type of job which offered flexible working hours and the chance to earn much more than they'd get waitressing or doing arduous work in a care home. Stories circulated about women who were earning hundreds of pounds in a single night, enjoying a lifestyle beyond the reach of most students and anyone on the minimum wage. Here's what the job involved:

- freelance work in glamorous locations, and the chance to meet a wide range of people

- wearing fabulous outfits, including full-length evening dresses and stiletto heels

- being treated like a 'lady', and receiving generous tips

Magazine articles extolled the benefits of this type of work in terms of health and self-esteem, suggesting it was sexy, glamorous and great exercise. Celebrities endorsed it, and the singer Britney Spears incorporated it into one of her videos. What's not to like? In this atmosphere of hedonistic celebration, it seemed churlish to point out that the job also involved some or all of the following:

* top-to-toe grooming, including hair styling, make-up and removal of pubic hair, at your own expense

* providing a range of costumes, including evening wear and lingerie, at your own expense

* dancing on stage and at tables, in six-inch heels, for shifts that last 10 or even 12 hours

* no contract, no salary, no rights, no guarantee of earnings or future employment

* paying the boss a fee, typically £65 at an upmarket London venue, and a percentage of your earnings

* paying fines for lateness or infringing a strict dress code

* persuading customers to accept 'private' dances at their table, typically £10 for a dance with bare breasts or £20 fully nude in a London club

* providing 'private' dances or 'lesbian' shows with other dancers in a 'VIP' room

* posing for souvenir photographs with customers on a 'stag' night package

+ providing free nude dances for the boss's friends on request

+ groping and verbal abuse from customers

+ in some establishments, agreeing to have sex with customers for payment

Despite these drawbacks, the job I'm talking about – variously described as pole, table or lap dancing – was tirelessly promoted across popular culture. (Pole dancing is usually done on stage, by one or more dancers, giving customers a chance to look for a woman they like; table and lap dancing are performed for individual customers at their table or in a private room.) Club owners had spotted a loophole in the 2003 Licensing Act which allowed them to apply for a licence in the same way as a pub or restaurant, rather than as 'sex encounter' establishments. The number shot up to around 300 by 2009, according to the campaign group Object; it was far from being a metropolitan phenomenon, with clubs appearing in Aylesbury, Bournemouth, Harrogate, Scarborough, Doncaster, Rotherham and Luton. Pole and lap dancing scenes became common in movies, while DVDs and how-to guides told women how to teach themselves at home. Books spread the message that this was something the modern woman should include in her list of accomplishment: titles ranged from *Pole Power* and *Lap Dancing: The Naughty Girls' Guide* at the popular end of the market to weightier volumes such as *Pole Story: Essays on the Power of Erotic Dance*, and *Pole Dancing, Empowerment and Embodiment*.

'Pole dancing is revolutionising the way in which women relate to sex and their bodies,' according to the 'product description' for one of these books on Amazon.

It should be obvious that there is a significant difference between a woman signing up for pole dancing classes at home or in a gym, and doing it as a job in a club with male customers. This point is often missed in breathless articles about the popularity of pole dancing, which fail to recognise that women sign up for all kinds of dance classes – from salsa and tango to flamenco – without treating it primarily as a form of sexual display. The exercise angle sanitises something that might otherwise have a sleazy reputation, just as owners of men's clubs and magazines in the 1960s sought to link the commercial exploitation of women's bodies with exciting new ideas about personal and political freedom. Hugh Hefner, founder of the Playboy empire, tried to make an alliance with liberals by financing protests against the Vietnam war at the same time as he opened his first nightclubs in the US, but he didn't have things all his own way. In March 1970, around 50 people staged a demonstration outside the Playboy Club in Boston; a month later, 200 protesters picketed an anti-war fund-raising event at his Chicago mansion. The demonstrators, most of whom were women, aimed to 'expose the hypocrisy of Hefner's stated opposition to an unjust war abroad while profiting from his own unjust exploitation of women at home'.[1] They had a point: in a period of political and social turmoil, when feminism was challenging traditional gender roles, the USP of Playboy clubs was the presence of waitresses wearing tight corsets, rabbit ears and tails. Rules were rigorously enforced, as the *Bunny Manual* from 1968 makes clear:

> Your public and Playboy expects [*sic*] you to be a beautiful, well groomed young lady who projects warmth and graciousness at all times. Therefore, you will always want to look your best and be the perfect personification of 'Bunny Image'. 'Bunny Image' is so essential in your role that failure to meet and maintain the standards of this Image can result in dismissal.[2]

Bunnies were expected to arrive at clubs looking their 'loveliest' with styled hair, manicured nails and a clean costume. 'Costume offences', such as not wearing bunny ears in the centre of the head or displaying an 'unkept [*sic*] tail', attracted black marks or 'demerits'. Bunnies were allowed to smoke on duty but holding a cigarette was forbidden; they were expected to 'take a puff' and place lighted cigarettes on an ashtray. The management was at pains to highlight the international profile and varied background of its 'girls', who included former schoolteachers, secretaries, dancers and models. Some, it pointed out, were bright young women who worked part-time as bunnies to put themselves through college.

The parallels with today's pole and lap dancing clubs, with their equally strict dress codes, are obvious. What's different in the first decade of the 21st century is that the clubs began to flourish in a society where the principle of gender equality, far from being new and controversial, had long been established; laws banning various forms of sex discrimination started to be introduced in the UK in the

1970s, leaving the notion that women exist to serve men as the province of a few fringe politicians. Pole dancing clubs are an obvious violation of the equality principle, which is one of the reasons why they encountered such sustained opposition; people who lived near clubs, local councillors and feminist organisations argued that they were unsuitable for residential areas, demeaning to women and should be treated as 'sex encounter' establishments. As a consequence, licensing rules were tightened in 2010, making it harder to open a pole dancing club and forcing existing venues to reapply for a licence. Clubs closed up and down the country but their supporters, including a handful of academics, continued to emphasise their role in *female* empowerment. 'Natasha', a teacher who became a lap dancer, had this to say:

> The girls! What amazing young women. These girls are businesswomen. They plan from beginning to end. They earn the money most of the time, they go home and live. Any person who depicts the lap dancer as a powerless woman does not know what they are talking about.[3]

Brooke Magnanti, author of the *Belle de Jour* blog and books, has been a cheerleader for this form of 'empowerment', caricaturing critics of pole dancing as puritans who want women to return to being 'prim and proper'. It's a false opposition – it's entirely possible to love sex *and* equality – but it has confused and on occasion silenced critics of the commercial sex industry. Nor should anyone be surprised that these tactics work, up to a point; many young women are so terrified of appearing prudish that they've lost the ability to distinguish between liberation and libertinism. The latter is a way of looking at sex solely in terms of power and predation: the strong, who are almost always men, exploit the weak on the assumption that they exist to be exploited. Of course the modern libertine has to pretend that his fantasies are benign, which is why the commercial sex industry emphasises the supposed autonomy of pole and lap dancers. In addition, there's a generation of young women who have grown up with the cultural phenomenon of lads' mags – soft porn in an 'ironic' modern guise – and they've come to believe that exaggerated sexual difference is the route to success. That doesn't mean we have to take any of these claims at face value, so here is the one thing you really need to know about pole dancing: it's what used to be called 'striptease' in a sanitised modern form.

Women in bras, thongs and stockings beckon you (assuming you're a man) into a fantasy world. It's a dark place, tricked out with crystal chandeliers and velvet drapes, where women pout, lick their lips and move like big cats; they're sinuous as animals, but animals which have been trained to accentuate their breasts and buttocks. Welcome to the website of a typical pole dancing club, which offers head-and-shoulders shots of women in bikini tops, and perhaps one of a couple of women apparently enjoying a lesbian encounter. (According to a former dancer, 'lesbian shows are possibly the worst part of the whole dancing experience … The lesbian show in the private room involved me and probably someone I would call a friend fondling each other and pretending to be lesbians in front of a fully-clothed man'.[4]) Here's a club in Surrey, laying out its attractions frankly, if ungrammatically:

Brazil, China, USA, Thailand, Russia, UK and on and on …

An exclusive selection of jewels flown in from all over the world who dance … entertain … tease and send pulses racing.

Without a shadow of a doubt The Diamonds Gentlemans club is an evening you owe to yourself, and one you do not want to miss out on.

With the girls special training and our unique philosophy, every client experiences the night they desire.

We are constantly changing the themes to which the girls work. On different evenings different music and maybe maids outfits or school girls or even uniforms …

We have bikini nights/lingerie nights/fetish nights – something for everyone, including the ladies![5]

If there's one constant in the world of pole dancing clubs, it's that the men are always 'gentlemen' and the dancers 'girls'; customers' egos are stroked, the dancers infantilised. Another club, in a residential area of West London, invites women to attend auditions in full make-up and instructs them to make sure that their nails are painted: 'Please wear lots of "bling" jewellery … Remember, the business of being a Table Dancer is a very glamorous one!'[6] The reality of the job is rather different, as several studies have established: pole dancing is an insecure form of employment, offering an unstable income and exposing women to arbitrary fines and high levels of abuse from customers. A study by researchers at the University of Leeds, titled *The Regulatory Dance: Sexual Consumption in the Night Time Economy*,[7] found that:

- Dancers paid commission to the clubs, usually 30 per cent per dance

- High overheads meant that 70 per cent reported having finished a shift without making any money at all

- Without contracts, many dancers felt unable to complain about working conditions and feared dismissal

- Just over 60 per cent had been fined for breaches of the club's code, including chewing gum, using a mobile phone, incorrect clothing and being late. The highest fine was £100 for missing a shift

- Just over half of the dancers reported being harassed 'lots of times' or 'a few times'. Almost half reported frequent verbal harassment and unwanted touching by customers

- Private booths and VIP rooms made dancers feel vulnerable

Two of the pioneers in the pole/lap dancing business were Peter Stringfellow, who had owned clubs in London for years, and the Spearmint Rhino chain. Both are at the top end of the market, offering luxurious surroundings, while Stringfellow encourages celebrities – boxers, footballers, film stars – to visit his flagship club in Covent Garden. Spearmint Rhino, which has an American parent company, lost £1.6m in 2009 but then the business began to look up and the American head of its UK operation, John Specht, boasted of taking almost £500,000 in January 2011. Specht turned the company round by cutting costs, including staff salaries which had included £100,000 for a barman.[8] Stringfellows did even better, until the economic crisis began to impact its business; in the year to June 2006, gross profits of the Covent Garden club rose from £2.98m to £5.06m.[9] The business enjoyed its best year in 2008 but Stringfellow acknowledged that it was likely to feel the impact of the banking crisis. 'We are connected to the financial world and bonuses in a big way,' he said in 2009. 'This year we could see a difference, but I like to think we will still have the cream on the cake even if we've lost a few of the cherries.'[10]

Six months earlier, a dancer called Nadine Quashie was sacked from his Covent Garden club for alleged drugs offences. Quashie, who had worked for the club for 18 months, not only denied the accusation but tried to sue for wrongful dismissal. A tribunal ruled against her in 2010, saying she was self-employed, but a year later another tribunal granted her leave to appeal. Lawyers for Stringfellows contested her claim, arguing that her case was constructed on 'lies', but the tribunal was offered a vivid insight into the finances of lap dancing. Quashie said she was not allowed to accept cash from customers, having to accept pre-paid vouchers issued by the club and known as 'heavenly money'. Twenty-five per cent of her earnings over £300 were deducted by the club, and she also had to pay an £85 fee each night; she had to perform free dances once an hour, each time a particular song was played, and she said she was fined £50 if she was in the changing room at the time. She claimed she was even threatened with fines if she failed to attend meetings with Stringfellow or his deputy, even though she had to find a baby-sitter.[11] Her lawyer, Shah Qureshi, told the tribunal that dancers were often exploited because of their lack of employment status. 'The clubs insist on them [sic] being self-employed despite the fact that they have obligations like any other employee including the provision of services, set working hours and financial penalties for not working.'[12] Quashie lost her case in December 2012 when the Appeal Court ruled that she had been self-employed.[13] But the ruling appeared to confirm evidence from academic studies, in which the absence of legal rights underlines the vulnerability – and expendability – of dancers.

Throughout the existence of lap and pole dancing clubs, there has been anecdotal evidence of links to prostitution. It is furiously rejected by the industry, which points to the existence of a no-touching rule in most clubs. Even so, undercover police operations have discovered instances of the rule being breached and have on occasion ended in detectives being told that sex was available for payment. In 2002, officers were offered sex with two dancers in a private room at a branch of Spearmint Rhino at a price of £500 for half an hour;[14] in 2003, a former employee of the chain claimed at an employment tribunal that he was sacked after complaining about dancers offering sexual services.[15] A female City trader, interviewed for a Fawcett Society report on the commercial sex industry's successful targeting of the workplace, said her male colleagues spent 'thousands of pounds' entertaining clients in lap dancing clubs. She said:

They would discuss the strippers back at the desk and how they paid them to provide 'extra services'. The way they talked was like all women were just there for sex. It was very uncomfortable to hear these discussions between the men I had to work with.[16]

Some of this may have been exaggeration and bravado, but an academic study carried out for Glasgow City Council in 2004 included interviews with customers who went to clubs specifically looking for an opportunity to buy sex:

> Approximately half the customers in Glasgow came to the club looking for sex. Four of the regular visitors claimed they had had sex with a dancer on the premises, and a further two said they had arranged liaisons outside of the club with the dancers by swapping mobile telephone numbers.[17]

The Glasgow study focused on four lap dancing clubs in the city and two in London. Some of the dancers reported pressure from management to create an impression of 'sexual availability' even if they weren't actually expected to sell sex, while researchers saw the following in one club:

> Every dancer, during their performances, displayed the inside of their genitalia by spreading their legs above the customers' heads. This seemed to be an established part of the routine. As one customer put it: 'What's the point of seeing a strip show and not getting a bit of fanny? The fun part is seeing her cunt. You can open the *Sun* if you just want tits.'[18]

A former lap dancer, Jennifer Hayashi Danns, collected testimony from dancers for her book *Stripped: The Bare*

Reality of Lap Dancing. A student who worked as a dancer in a topless bar described the change in the working atmosphere when a number of dancers arrived from a successful pole dancing club. She said:

> They had a much slicker style, with Ann Summers-style outfits, breast implants, pre-arranged routines, headstands, doing the splits – we looked like poor relations by comparison. I vividly remember one woman putting her finger in her vagina, drawing it out again and waving it under the customer's nose so he could smell it; this happened often, and a number of the women did it.[19]

When this kind of behaviour is permitted in clubs, it puts pressure on other women to join in. Another dancer whose account appears in *Stripped* did not want to touch or display her genitals while she was dancing, and she found herself embroiled in frequent arguments with customers: 'They would touch and grab me, and one even bit me during a dance. I did not feel safe.' One of the women interviewed for *Stripped* described the attitude of customers as 'carefully drink-hidden disdain, begrudgingly mixed with awe'. She said:

> There were men who held the attitude that they should never have to pay for a woman. There were those who only wanted a woman they'd paid for, and those that believed the women really fancied them …
>
> Everyone is different. But to explain the main attitude above – 'drink-hidden disdain, begrudgingly mixed with absolute awe' – I would say they subconsciously or consciously resented the fact that these women wouldn't

be talking to them if they weren't paying. That made them feel small and inferior.[20]

It isn't difficult to understand why the prospect of drunk, aroused and quite possibly resentful men emerging from a club at all hours of the day and night goes down badly with local people. But the relationship between dancers and customers goes to the heart of the problem with pole and lap dancing clubs: it is based on a fragile illusion in which the dancers pretend to be attracted to the customers, and they pretend – unless they're drunk or very stupid – to believe it in return. A London club owner admitted as much in a newspaper interview, observing that rival clubs were 'all about cash and alcohol-induced expenditure. It taps into that male insecurity that you can mask by flashing the cash and making yourself feel good about the "quality" of the girls who are pretending to be attracted to you.'[21] It's an unusually frank acknowledgement that the superficial glamour of the clubs is a cover for suspicion and a fear of being exploited on both sides. But there is an imbalance of power in the transaction and it's exposed by the fact that the groping is one way, especially when men pay to have a woman dance in a private booth or VIP room: they do it because they *can*.

This is a far cry from the rhetoric of female empowerment used by supporters of pole and lap dancing. It's clear that if the dancers have power, it's the age-old one of sexual arousal, which simply confirms all the anxieties insecure men have about women in the first place. They're paying not just to look at a woman's body but for the simulacrum of desire, trying to persuade themselves and their mates that the woman is genuinely excited, but both sides know it's really about money. It's a breeding ground for misogyny, harking back to the worst gender stereotypes, and entirely at odds with modern notions of equality; in that sense, perhaps the strangest thing of all is the way it's been misinterpreted in popular culture and by some academics. But I think we can allow the central transaction – a naked woman pretending to feel desire for a fully clothed man she regards with indifference or secretly despises – to tell its own unpleasant truth.

PERFORMANCE

Drug abuse, self-harm, assault charges, domestic violence, eating disorders, alcoholism: Amy Winehouse packed them all into her short life. When she died suddenly on 23 July 2011, she had recently given the worst performance of her life, leading to her being booed off stage in Belgrade on the first night of a catastrophic 'comeback' tour. She was reported to have spent the previous few months in an alcohol rehabilitation programme, and her last-known appointment was with a doctor at 8.30pm on the night before her death. Returning home to her house in North London, she spent the rest of her final evening alone except for a bodyguard. He recalled that she drank vodka until the early hours, singing and playing the drums until he asked her to keep the noise down. Next morning, he looked in on her and didn't realise that she wasn't just sleeping off a hangover. It was only in the afternoon, realising that she hadn't moved, that he tried to rouse her and discovered she was dead. Winehouse was 27.

It was a lonely end for the most successful female singer of her generation. A few months later, another international singing star died in similar circumstances, also after struggling to cope with multiple addictions. Whitney Houston was found dead on 11 February 2012, having drowned in a hotel bathroom in Los Angeles after suffering a massive heart attack. She was 48, and a stellar career in the 1980s had long been eroded by drug problems, allegations of domestic abuse and erratic performances. The public's appetite for pitiable women is well-established but in both cases the effect was dramatic: sales of Houston's music soared while Winehouse's second album, *Back to Black*, became for a time the UK's biggest-selling album of the 21st century. Sudden death was judged to be a shocking but unsurprising finale to lives lived on the edge, evoking romantic (and Romantic) notions about fierce spirits burning too fiercely and consuming themselves in their own flames. Winehouse's friend and producer, Mark Ronson, expressed this idea in an article in the *Observer* a few months after her death. He wrote:

> There are people on this earth (they certainly don't have to be famous) and they're just a bit more magical than the rest of us. And you want to be around them because the magic rubs off a bit, and you feel a bit more special when they're around. My best friend, Max, died about five years ago. And he had that same effect on people. Maybe the magical ones burn a bit brighter than the rest of us, so they don't get to be here as long.[1]

Winehouse's funeral took place in North London and the private ceremony was attended by friends, family and a few fans but not her ex-husband, Blake Fielder-Civil, who was serving a jail sentence (his second) at Armley prison in Leeds for burglary and a firearms offence. Houston's funeral in New Jersey turned into a spectacle, with her ex-husband Bobby Brown walking out after an argument over the seating arrangements. Houston was buried in a purple gown, wearing such an array of jewellery – more suitable for a party than a funeral – that guards were reportedly posted beside her grave.

That there was nothing inevitable about either death was easy to miss. So was the fact that both women, far from having a death wish, were actually very sick; Winehouse's mother Janis said her daughter's body couldn't cope with periods of not drinking at all followed by a sudden massive intake of alcohol, while Houston's post-mortem showed that she was suffering from advanced heart disease caused by 'chronic' drug use. The pressure to perform, some of it self-imposed, exposed both women to public humiliation: in 2009, Houston gave a halting performance on British television, looking dazed as she sang a new song on *The X Factor* and struggled to answer questions coherently in the interview that followed; Winehouse's disastrous Belgrade concert was preceded a few months earlier by a performance in Dubai when she was visibly drunk – not for the first time – on stage. Even so, Winehouse's bruised and emaciated appearance – she was just over five feet tall and weighed less than seven stone – did not prevent her self-destructive tendencies being celebrated by some of her fans. Immediately after her death, admirers left flowers, photographs and handwritten messages outside her house in Camden, following a tradition that started with the death of Princess Diana; more sinisterly, some left half-empty wine glasses and bottles of vodka in a defiant tribute to the addiction that killed the singer.

In the mawkish atmosphere that follows celebrity deaths, there was much talk about the 'eerie' coincidence that Winehouse had died at exactly the same age as a number of pop stars going back over decades – all members of the so-called '27 club'. Websites speculated that a '27 curse' was striking gifted performers, adding Winehouse's demise to the 'mysterious' deaths of Brian Jones, Jimi Hendrix, Janis Joplin, Jim Morrison and Kurt Cobain. In fact, there is nothing eerie about the number of pop stars who die in their 20s or 30s, destroyed by a lifestyle that's superficially attractive but inflicts huge physical and emotional damage. Jones was a heavy drug user who drowned in his swimming pool, Joplin died of a drug overdose, Hendrix choked on vomit, Morrison was a heavy drug user and drowned in a bath in Paris, while Cobain suffered from depression and shot himself. A study published in the journal *BMJ Open* confirmed all these points, finding a higher mortality rate among pop stars than the general population; it highlighted the fact that solo artists like Winehouse are twice as likely to die early, suggesting that the camaraderie of being in a band may have a protective effect in some cases. The authors speculated that people who have had difficult or unhappy childhoods may be attracted to a career in music, but they also pointed out that a successful pop career can feed a predisposition to unhealthy and risky behaviour.[2]

What's obvious to a detached observer is that, while famous people continue to be rewarded for taking risks and ignoring boundaries, more casualties from overdoses, accidents and self-harm are likely. But in Winehouse's case there was an additional element: the infantilising effect of a very particular species of femininity is integral to her tragedy. Winehouse was only 20 when she was hailed for her first, jazz-inspired album *Frank*, but it was *Back to Black*, three years later in 2006, which turned her into a huge commercial success. According to her family, she wrote most of the tracks in a burst of creative energy which followed a period of depression triggered by the death of her grandmother, Cynthia, who was also a singer. From an early point in her career, Winehouse cultivated an image which combined nostalgia for the girl singers of the 1960s – the Supremes, the Ronettes, the Shangri-Las – with the glamour of a sexual rebel. These elements fused on the cover of *Back to Black* in a photograph which was to become instantly recognisable around the world: Winehouse in a strapless white dress with red polka dots, a wide red belt and little-girl jewellery. (After her death, the dress was auctioned to raise funds for the charity set up by her father, and raised £43,200 when it was bought by a fashion museum in Chile.) On the album cover, Winehouse sits hunched on a stool in what appears to be a classroom. Her long dark hair is lustrous and she looks coltish enough, with her hands clasped between long bare legs, to be in her teens. Her lips are parted and she looks directly at the camera, at once submissive and defiant, as though she's been kept back after class to answer for breaking an unknown rule. It's a disturbing image, inviting endless speculation: who is this beautiful child-woman and what has she done wrong? If the intention was to suggest a kind of bad-girl glamour, it was both hugely successful and way off the mark, for it would soon become apparent Winehouse's transgressions were anything but minor. At this point in her career, Winehouse was slender but healthy; within two years, she would be rushed to hospital coughing up blood, and given a stark warning that she was at risk of developing the lung disease emphysema – a devastating diagnosis for a singer – if she did not stop chain-smoking and using crack cocaine. Discharged from hospital a few days later, she appeared gaunt as she lit a cigarette in the street, showing how difficult she would find it to act on doctors' advice.

The most powerful thing about Winehouse was her voice, which was equally at ease in jazz standards or belting out songs she'd written herself. Her vocals were more forceful than the lead singers of the girl bands she admired and she was unlike them in another way as well: tomboyish and streetwise in a way that would have been unimaginable in the 1960s. But the despair and yearning of tracks like 'Back to Black' harked back to a time when men had more power than women, and expressed a disturbing fatalism about sex and relationships. Winehouse's appearance seemed a physical manifestation of this confused identity: as her behaviour became more disordered, her unsteady beehive began to seem like a parody, while a sudden change in the size of her breasts shortly after her divorce prompted speculation that she'd had implants. (Fielder-Civil, who had his own problems with drugs and self-harm, started divorce proceedings in 2009 and refused to halt them despite emotional appeals from his wife. The divorce became final in August that year.) Winehouse was more ladette than torch singer and she spent her spare time with mates, such as the Libertines/Babyshambles singer Pete Doherty, who embraced the role of grown-up children in popular culture. Some of her friends acknowledged her childlike qualities, regarding them as part of her charm and aware that they were disarmed by it even when they could see that her behaviour was self-destructive. Mark

Ronson recalled visiting Winehouse at the private London Clinic, where she used to check herself in to dry out, and watching episodes of a TV show called, appropriately enough, *Arrested Development*: 'I would hang out in her room there for hours and not ever want to leave, like a sleepover at your best friend's house when you're 13 years old.'[3] He also remembered keeping an eye out while she smoked an illicit cigarette behind a fire door. How little time she spent in recording studios is reflected in the few finished tracks she recorded between *Back to Black* and her death five years later.

Winehouse's problem with addictions had a long history. Pain was never officially included among them but self-inflicted injuries, physical and emotional, are a recurrent theme in her biography. As an adult, her forearms still bore the scars from when she started cutting herself at the age of nine; she once talked about them, without displaying much insight, in an interview with *Q* magazine: 'It's a funny thing, a morbid curiosity. What does that feel like? "Ow, that fucking hurts". It's probably the worst thing I've done.'[4] The tabloid press discussed the tattoos that bloomed on her arms and body, speculating on their possible meaning, but almost always missing the point. It's very clear that Winehouse's 'body art' was another form of self-harm, as she acknowledged in *Q* magazine: 'It's a way of suffering for the things that mean a lot to you. Actually, I like the pain. To me, it relieves you.' It also served an exhibitionist function: in 2007, Winehouse used a shard of broken mirror to carve Fielder-Civil's first name into her stomach while she was doing an interview with an American magazine. This is alarming behaviour, suggesting a fragile if not disintegrating personality, but the tabloid press tracked Winehouse's multiple problems in lip-smacking detail. Some of the coverage was inevitable, given her arrests for alleged drugs offences and other brushes with the law: in 2006 she admitted punching a fan in the face and kicking Fielder-Civil when he tried to restrain her; in 2008 she was cautioned after admitting that she slapped a man's face; in 2009 she was cleared of punching a woman in the eye, but later in the same year she admitted common assault and disorderly behaviour and was given a conditional discharge. But the tabloids were just as interested in her weight loss, disintegrating marriage and physical injuries after a series of accidents, even sending photographers and reporters to spy on her when she was on holiday. Here are some typical headlines: 'Amy's not-so-glamorous poolside display of tattoos and scars' (*Daily Mail*, 2007); 'Amy Winehouse struggles to put on weight despite junk food addiction' (*Daily Mail*, 2007); 'Bloodied and bruised Amy Winehouse standing by husband who "saved her life"' (*Daily Mail*, 2007); 'Stricken Amy could have TB' (*Sun*, 2008); 'Amy's "pasta burn" shows no sign of healing as she continues Caribbean holiday' (*Daily Mail*, 2009); 'Amy Winehouse bruises boobs in "boozy" fall' (*Metro*, 2010); 'Amy Winehouse on crack' (*Sun*, 2011); 'Bruise that girl: Amy Winehouse displays nasty leg injuries as she hangs out by the pool' (*Daily Mail*, 2011); 'Sad Amy Winehouse's 3 drunk blackouts in one week' (*Sun*, 2011). The final headline appeared just two weeks before her death, above a piece which announced chillingly that 'star is boozing herself to death'.

In November 2011, four months after Winehouse's death, a public inquiry presided over by a High Court judge in London began to hear from individuals who had suffered from sustained press intrusion. Actors, authors, singers and victims of crime, including the parents of the murdered schoolgirl Milly Dowler, appeared at the Leveson Inquiry to describe the impact on their lives of intense media scrutiny. Some of the most compelling testimony came from J. K. Rowling, author of the *Harry Potter* novels, whose witness statement summed up what she and her family had to endure when her novels became bestsellers. Rowling said:

> The effect on me, and our family life, truly cannot be overstated. We were literally driven out of the first house I had ever owned … because of journalists banging on the door, questioning the neighbours and sitting in parked cars outside the gate. Old friendships were tested as journalists turned up on their doorsteps, and offered money for stories on me.

Rowling gave the impression of being psychologically more robust than many victims of press intrusion. The impact on someone who was as fragile as Winehouse – and ashamed of her alcoholism, according to her mother Janis – can scarcely be imagined. By 2009, the constant scrutiny had become so damaging that she went to court and obtained an injunction which banned *paparazzi* photographers from within 100 metres of her home; the order was granted under anti-harassment legislation after her lawyers claimed that press attention was making her life unsafe. 'Every time she got in her car she was chased or jostled, and it has become unsafe not just for her but the people around her,' said

a member of her management team.[5] But the injunction
didn't stop the headlines or the photographs; there were
plenty of opportunities for *paparazzi* to snap Winehouse
emerging from a pub or club, unsteady on her feet, with
smeared make-up and a glazed expression.

Friends and family who observed her in her final months
disagreed about whether she realised how sick she was. 'I
don't think for a second she ever thought she would die
or that alcohol or drugs would kill her,' Janis Winehouse
said after her daughter's death. She described a pattern
familiar to those who work with alcoholics, in which
Winehouse would go for weeks without a drink and then
binge on vodka: 'She could go for weeks without having
a drink, but then she'd fall off the wagon. She was like
a little girl who just couldn't resist putting her finger in
the fan, even though she knew it was dangerous.'[6] The
veteran American singer Tony Bennett, who recorded with
Winehouse just four months before she died, got a very
different impression: 'I think Amy knew that she was very,
very ill. She hadn't told anyone else but I look back now
and I realise she did know she was physically in trouble
and that she wasn't gonna live.'[7] It was probably inevitable
that sections of the tabloid press, which had consistently
misread Winehouse's problems while she was alive, would
overlook her alcoholism and jump to the wrong conclusion
when her death was announced: 'Amy Winehouse dead
after "drink and drugs binge"' (*Daily Mirror*, 2011);
'"Amy Winehouse bought £1,200 of crack and heroin the
night before she died", claims fixer' (*Daily Mail*, 2011).
As her post-mortem would show, hard drugs had nothing
to do with it – Winehouse had given them up three years

earlier and died of alcoholic poisoning – but the tabloid obsession with her drug use is telling. Tabloid editors take a censorious line on the subject but showbiz columns frequently presented Winehouse as a rebel, experimenting with heroin and crack cocaine, rather than a young woman struggling with the mood swings, cravings and sickness associated with alcohol addiction.

Within months of her death, an album of previously unreleased material was rushed out under the title *Lioness: Hidden Treasures*. The cover image was a reprise of *Back to Black*, showing a much healthier Winehouse in another strapless dress with the same little-girl jewellery and a huge bow in her hair. The title endowed her with heroic qualities but the bravado of *Lioness* was nevertheless a myth, a consoling fiction for her family at a time when their feelings of loss were (understandably) intense. Winehouse was a performer, but her powerful voice obscured the fact that what she habitually performed was a combination of self-deception and self-loathing. On *Back to Black* she sang defiantly in 'Rehab' about not needing treatment, but she followed it with songs – 'Back to Black', 'Love is a Losing Game', 'Addicted', 'Wake Up Alone' – which recorded relationships soured by addictions and a crippling absence of self-esteem. The girl-woman on the cover of *Back to Black* hadn't grown up, either because she didn't know how or because success brought sufficient wealth to allow her to pursue a chaotic lifestyle. But she tried to make up for it by forcing herself to go on stage when she was physically and emotionally incapable of performing. Footage of that last performance in Belgrade in June 2011 is painful to watch: Winehouse wanders round the stage as though she doesn't know where she is, seeks fatherly hugs from members of her band and sits down on the floor to remove her shoes. Hauntingly, she cannot remember the lyrics of the song – 'You Know I'm No Good' – that best sums up her pessimism about herself and her life.

The following month, she was dead. Even then, she had no privacy; as the news spread, photographers and film crews gathered outside her white-fronted house in Camden. It was still daylight when Winehouse's body was carried on a stretcher to a waiting mortuary van, the outline of her corpse clearly visible under a red blanket. Within six years, the curvy young woman with the self-conscious grin had become a gaunt shadow of her former self, fulfilling just about every tabloid stereotype of doomed femininity. During her brief career, Amy Winehouse's huge talent had to vie with two of women's most corrosive enemies, shame and self-hatred, until it all became too much and she lost the struggle. On that late summer afternoon, the public circumstances of her departure felt like one final, unscheduled performance.

VAGINA CANTATA

They were slender, brash and noisy, five young women in mini-dresses which might have been made in the 1960s. Their faces hidden by colourful ski masks, they rushed into an almost-empty cathedral in Moscow and launched into a satirical song, calling on the Virgin Mary to rescue Russian from Vladimir Putin. The performance lasted less than a minute but caused astonishment and, supposedly, outrage. The following month, three of the women were arrested and held in prison for five months. They were accused of expressing 'hatred and hostility' towards members of the Russian Orthodox Church but the prosecution struggled to produce credible witnesses, relying on security guards, altar boys and candle-sellers rather than members of the public. A candle-seller called Lyubov Sokologorskaya claimed to have seen 'demonic jerking', using language that recalled medieval witch trials. 'They were throwing their legs up and everything that was below the waist was visible,' Sokologorskaya declared, revealing a rare ability to see through opaque tights.[1] Even so, the three women were tried and convicted of 'hooliganism motivated by religious hatred' and sentenced to two years each in one of Russia's penal colonies. Shortly afterwards, two more members of the band fled Russia as police searched for them. What had begun as 'a small and somewhat absurd act' had 'snowballed into an enormous catastrophe', in the words of Pussy Riot member Maria Alyokhina.[2]

Such was the sequence of events after the feminist punk collective Pussy Riot – they write their name in Roman letters – staged a guerrilla performance in the cathedral of Christ the Saviour in Moscow in February 2012. Alyokhina, Yekaterina Samutsevich and Nadezhda Tolokonnikova used their closing statements to deny any hostility to the Orthodox Church, insisting that their performance was political. They criticised the close relationship between Putin and the head of the Church, Patriarch Kyrill, who is a confidant of the President and presented him with a valuable (though clearly ineffective) icon of Our Lady of Tenderness. The timing is suggestive: Alyokhina and Tolokonnikova were arrested the day before Putin returned for his third term as President, and Samutsevich twelve days later. The women placed themselves firmly in a tradition of persecuted poets, novelists and artists in the old Soviet Union, including Joseph Brodsky and Aleksandr Solzhenitsyn. Tolokonnikova quoted the poet Alexander Vvedensky, who was purged by Stalin in 1937 and died on his way to a labour camp in 1941. She said:

> Pussy Riot are Vvedensky's students and heirs. His principle of the bad rhyme is dear to us. He wrote, 'Occasionally, I think of two different rhymes, a good one and a bad one, and I always choose the bad one because it is always the right one.'[3]

Pussy Riot's playful grasp of the power of shocking or 'bad' art wrong-footed the Russian authorities. Their

heavy-handed response produced an outpouring of
international support for the band, as well as highlighting
the fear and corruption on which Putin's power rested.
Madonna performed in Moscow with the band's name
scrawled on her back and pulled on a balaclava in a
demonstration of support, telling cheering fans that 'these
three girls ... have done something courageous.' The 'girls'
were all in their 20s – two of them had young children –
but Madonna was right to emphasise their gender, linking
their shock tactics to her own use of explicitly sexual
imagery. Madonna's sexual politics have sometimes seemed
confused but she instinctively grasped an important point:
Pussy Riot's challenge to Putin's authoritarian rule was all
the more powerful because they were sexually confident
young women.

'Pussy' is a slang term for the vagina. It is less loaded,
and therefore more widely used, than the word 'cunt'. In
American English, 'pussy' is a sort of halfway house, clearly
referencing the vagina but acceptable right across popular
culture. It came into use as a name for cats in the early
17th century, was quickly applied affectionately to women
and to this day retains elements of endearment entirely
missing from 'cunt'. Because of its frequent use as an insult
to denigrate men and women, 'cunt' is problematic even
for feminists who have spent decades trying to reclaim it.
It's worth the struggle: one of the most annoying effects of
using 'cunt' pejoratively is to reduce still further the already
limited choice of non-anatomical words to describe a very
important part of the female body. As long ago as 1966, the
Pop artist Caroline Coon titled one of her first paintings
'My Beautiful Cunt', while a columnist on *The Times*,

Caitlin Moran, championed the word in her autobiography
How To Be A Woman almost half a century later. This
project has been given added impetus by the arrival of
Twitter, where casual use of the world 'cunt' as an insult
has angered many women; at the time of writing, there is a
Twitter account in the name '@cuntoftheday' whose stated
purpose is, ironically, to expose bad behaviour.

Used about a woman, 'cunt' is a nasty example of
metonymy, reducing her to the status of an ambulant sex
organ; about a man, it's a castration fantasy invoking all
the negative connotations of being female. (No one ever
said 'You're a cunt' and meant it as a compliment.) Its use
between rival sportsmen has become so commonplace that
an entire court case involving two highly paid footballers,
the England and Chelsea captain John Terry and the QPR
player Anton Ferdinand, turned on whether one had
described the other as a 'black cunt'. (Terry denied it and
was acquitted on a charge of racially abusing Ferdinand,
but the FA banned him for four matches.) Tellingly, the
controversy focused on Terry's alleged use of the word
'black', as though 'cunt' was a regrettable but familiar form
of discourse between professional players. But confusion
about the word's acceptability was confirmed in rather more
surprising circumstances, an act by the stand-up comedian
Stewart Lee in which he took a *Sun* columnist, Richard
Littlejohn, to task for misogyny. During a sensational
murder case, Littlejohn railed against broadcasters who
used the phrase 'women who work as prostitutes', claiming
it was an example of 'political correctness gone mad'. Lee
rightly responded that the word 'prostitute' used on its
own is pejorative – it's not just another job description like

'dentist' – and likely to distress relatives of the murdered women. But Lee's own sensitivity to sexist language failed him in the finale of the sketch, when he tried to conjure the worst insult he could think of to describe Littlejohn. With depressing inevitability, the comedian called the columnist a 'cunt'.

It's profoundly shocking that the most taboo word in the English language, the worst thing one human being can call another, is a synonym for one of the principal female sex organs. (It is worth noting that the clitoris, which is more significant for many women, barely registers in this sinister discourse.) The persistent use of 'cunt' as an insult is a reminder of the fear and anxiety which exist in relation to the female genitalia. Freud was well aware of the phenomenon and attributed it to the boy's misunderstanding of the vulva, thinking that a male child would interpret it as the site of a castrated penis: 'Probably no male human being is spared the fright of castration at the sight of a female genital,' he wrote in 1927 in his essay on fetishism.[4] Freud was right about the anxiety engendered by the vagina but there are more obvious and convincing explanations of its origins. The ubiquity of phallic imagery says a great deal about the importance to men of the erect penis, yet it is a simple fact that the male organ enters the vagina in a state of rigidity and emerges flaccid. Hence the vagina is endowed with an almost mythic capacity of reduction, but I suspect that the anxiety produced by the temporary disappearance of the penis inside a woman's body stirs up an even more profound fear that *she might not give it back*. This was supposedly one of the most deadly tricks played by medieval 'witches' who were believed to have the power to cast spells which would make the penis invisible; in *Misogynies*, I pointed out that an entire chapter of the 15th-century witch-hunters' manual, the *Malleus Maleficarum* or *Hammer of Witches*, is devoted to describing 'How, as it were, they Deprive Man of his Virile Member'. Fear of losing the penis is also evident in the paranoid notion that the female organ is equipped with hidden teeth, encapsulated in the sinister phrase *vagina dentata*. This is very obviously a castration fantasy in which an equivalence is made between the vagina and the mouth, endowing the female organ with the power to sever the penis altogether. It is such a recurring motif that it seems likely that it expresses a deep-seated anxiety about the danger posed to men by intercourse with a woman.

Now we begin to see why some men are so disparaging about the vagina, to the point where we can reasonably identify the phenomenon as vagina-phobia. If the female sex organ poses such an ever-present threat, it follows that it needs to be diminished, controlled and even excluded from public discourse. In the US, where the religious right has made repeated assaults on women's sexual freedom, the battleground has been (and remains) access to contraception and abortion. Restricting either is a very effective way of controlling the vagina because it increases the risks associated with sexual activity, and it has thus been on the Republican agenda for decades. Republican presidents have consistently supported the notorious 'global gag rule', which has been described as a back-door way of restricting access to contraceptives for women in developing countries; the rule threatens the *total* withdrawal of American aid from any foreign NGO which provides or advocates legal abortion, even if it uses funds from other sources for that part of its work. The frankly ideological nature of the rule is confirmed by its history: it was introduced by Ronald Reagan in 1984, rescinded by Bill Clinton in 1993, reinstated by George W. Bush in 2001 and rescinded by Barack Obama in 2009. In the domestic sphere, no fewer than 67 bills have been introduced in Congress since 1989 in an attempt to introduce a Constitutional amendment protecting the foetus, and the Republican party's *liberal* position on abortion is to allow it in cases of rape and incest.

So fanatical are some Republican anti-abortionists that they've invented a pseudo-science, dating back to the 1980s, in which abortion is unnecessary even in the event of rape because it supposedly cannot result in pregnancy. In 2012, a Republican Congressman and Senate candidate from Missouri, Todd Akin, claimed to have identified a mechanism in the female body which prevents conception arising from rape, thus obviating the need for abortion. 'If it's a legitimate rape, the female body has ways to try to shut that whole thing down,' he explained.[5] Astonished opponents questioned both the existence of the mechanism and the body's ability to distinguish between 'legitimate' and other forms of rape. But Akin was merely repeating a claim made in 1988 by a Republican Congressman from Pennsylvania, Stephen Friend, who announced that the shock of being raped causes women to 'secrete a certain secretion' which happily turns out to be spermicidal.[6] Another Republican, Henry Aldridge from North Carolina, elaborated on the theory in 1995, explaining: 'The facts show that people who are raped – who are truly raped – the juices don't flow, the body functions don't work, and they don't get pregnant. Medical authorities agree that this is a rarity, if ever.'[7] But another 2012 Republican Senate candidate, Richard Mourdock from Indiana, broke ranks with his colleagues and suggested helpfully that these non-existent pregnancies were 'something that God intended to happen'.[8]

In fact, thousands of rape victims become pregnant with their attackers' child. A study published in the *American Journal of Obstetrics and Gynecology* in 1996 suggested that that 5 per cent of rape victims of reproductive age are likely to get pregnant, resulting in slightly more than 32,000 pregnancies in the US each year.[9] President Obama's joke that Akin had 'somehow missed science class' reinforced the Republican party's image as scientific illiterates, flat-earthers in the debate about sex and reproductive rights. Under pressure from his own side, Akin issued a mealy-mouthed correction, saying he had meant to use the word 'forcible' rather 'legitimate', but insisted that all he'd done was 'mis-spoke one word'. He received the backing of a Republican congressman from Iowa, Steve King, who has opposed public funding for abortions even in cases of statutory rape and incest. King praised Akin as a 'strong Christian man' and said he'd never heard of a child victim of rape becoming pregnant. 'I just haven't heard of that being a circumstance that's been brought to me in any personal way,' he declared.[10] Sensing electoral disaster in a close-fought presidential year, the Republican candidate Mitt Romney intervened and called on Akin to step down from the Senate race. But the row merely served to highlight his own reactionary views on contraception and abortion: in 2005, when he was Governor of Massachusetts, Romney tried to veto a bill designed to offer rape victims access to emergency contraception. His vice-presidential running mate, Congressman Paul Ryan from Wisconsin, has opposed abortion even in cases of rape and incest. Two would-be Republican presidential candidates, Rick Santorum and Mike Huckabee, have also supported a ban on abortions for rape victims. President Obama went to the heart of the issue when he observed that Akin's comments underscored 'why we shouldn't have a bunch of politicians, a majority of whom are men, making health care decisions on behalf of women'. A majority of voters agreed: Romney and Ryan were defeated in the 2012 presidential election, while Akin and Mourdock failed to win Senate seats.

It's clear that, for many on the religious right, unmarried women who seek to control their own vaginas are equivalent to prostitutes. The talk show host Rush Limbaugh said as much during a misogynist tirade in 2012 when he targeted Sandra Fluke, a law student at Georgetown University. Fluke had been invited to address a Congressional committee in support of an Obama law requiring insurers to offer birth control to workers who have health insurance in their employment contracts. In the event, Fluke was not allowed to speak, but that didn't bother Limbaugh. He said:

What does it say about the college co-ed Susan [sic] Fluke, who goes before a congressional committee and essentially says that she must be paid to have sex. What does that make her? It makes her a slut, right? It makes her a prostitute. She wants to be paid to have sex. She's having so much sex she can't afford the contraception.[11]

After several advertisers withdrew from his show, Limbaugh claimed that his remarks were intended to be 'humorous' and apologised. But his conflation of safe sex and prostitution spoke volumes about the right's contempt for sexually active women. A few months later, in a sequence of events which revealed how widely vagina-phobia had penetrated conservative thinking in the US, Republican politicians tried to ban the word from political discourse. A Democrat, Lisa Brown, used the word in the Michigan House of Representatives during a debate on yet another bill to restrict abortion. Brown ended her speech with a sarcastic swipe: 'Finally, Mr Speaker, I'm flattered that you're all so interested in my vagina but no means no.' A Republican, Mike Callton, responded that Brown's use of the word 'vagina' was 'so offensive I don't even want to say it in front of women. I would not say that in mixed company.'[12] The next day, Brown was banned from speaking in an unrelated debate by the Speaker, James Bolger, who claimed she had 'failed to maintain the decorum of the House of Representatives'. Brown hit back, declaring:

> I used that word because we were debating a women's health issue. Vagina, by the way, is the correct, medical name of a part of women's anatomy these lawmakers are trying to regulate.[13]

British lawmakers are less squeamish: at a meeting in support of Pussy Riot in the Grand Committee room at Westminster in November 2012, I used the words 'vagina' and 'cunt' without anyone raising an eyebrow. But it isn't surprising, given how troublesome vaginas seem to have become, that medical help is at hand. The cosmetic surgery industry has never been slow to spot an opportunity and procedures which fall under the heading 'vaginal rejuvenation' are on the rise. They're more popular in the US than the UK but clinics offering 'cosmetic gynaecology' now advertise widely in both countries. (Bizarrely, some websites carry warnings that prospective patients might be exposed to photographs of female genitalia.) Clinics acknowledge that some women find this area of their body 'embarrassing' and offer reassurance that procedures to improve the look and feel of the vagina and labia are increasingly popular. This is what one London clinic tells women:

> There is no longer a taboo about this surgery and more women than ever are realising that they can change the way their labia and surrounding vaginal tissue look with the help of vaginoplasty. If you are unhappy with the appearance of your genitalia, or it is causing you embarrassment or discomfort, book in for a consultation ...[14]

Vaginoplasty is a cosmetic procedure in which the female sexual organ is reshaped and tightened to produce a 'more toned and tight' vagina. Other options are labioplasty or vulvoplasty, in which those annoying vaginal lips can be reduced in size and reshaped. The language of the adverts is strikingly similar to that used by the slimming industry, as another website reveals:

> [Vulvoplasty] is cosmetic surgery performed on the outside genital structures include [sic] removal of *unwanted fat*

from different parts of the vulva, such as in the pubic area, around the outer lips [my italics].[15]

Why any woman would entrust herself to a clinic which can't even construct a grammatical sentence isn't clear. But the promises made by the clinics speak volumes about the worries a growing number of women are starting to have about their vaginas: too slack, too weak and encumbered by 'oversized, elongated or asymmetrical' lips. The effect of surgery is often described as 'giving a woman back the vagina she had before she had children', restoring her pleasure and that of her male partner. Some clinics go further, offering a procedure called 'hymenoplasty' in which a torn hymen is repaired or rebuilt to give the impression that the woman is still a virgin. It's an operation which has been carried out for years in Middle Eastern countries where men are obsessed with female sexual purity, but it's increasingly being offered to women from ethnic minorities in some Western countries. One website which offers advice on hymenoplasty explains that the purpose of the procedure is 'to imply the virginal state of a woman' and promises 'the utmost discretion'.[16]

The most extreme manifestation of vagina-phobia is infibulation. It's a drastic form of female genital mutilation (FGM), in which the external sex organs are totally excised and the entrance to the vagina is sewn up to make the aperture as small as possible. It's sometimes known euphemistically as 'Pharaonic circumcision' but the term hardly begins to acknowledge the pain and mutilation endured by girls and women on whom it is performed. Men who marry women who have undergone infibulation are not always able to penetrate them, leading to horrific 'procedures' to widen the aperture; some women are repeatedly cut to allow coitus and childbirth and then sewn up again. In some cases, this dreadful practice even causes death; according to one study, scar tissue obstructs birth, while tears and haemorrhaging are 'likely contributors to the very high rates of maternal mortality' in some countries. There is no medical reason for the procedure, which is carried out solely to reduce sexual pleasure. According to the World Health Organisation (WHO):

FGM is in many communities believed to reduce a woman's libido and therefore believed to help her resist 'illicit' sexual acts. When a vaginal opening is covered or narrowed, the fear of the pain of opening it, and the fear that this will be found out, is expected to further discourage 'illicit' sexual intercourse ...[17]

The WHO estimates that about 140m girls and women worldwide are living with the consequences of FGM. It is practised in 28 African countries and a few in Asia and the Middle East; it's not widely realised that almost two-fifths of the female population of Yemen have been subjected to it. Somalia has one of the highest rates of FGM in the world, affecting 97.9 per cent of women aged between 15 and 49; other countries where most women are affected include Egypt (91.1 per cent), Eritrea (88.7 per cent), Guinea (95.6 per cent), Mali (85.2 per cent) and Sierra Leone (94 per cent).[18] There is also evidence that it is being carried out among ethnic minority communities in Western countries, either secretly at home or when girls are taken back to their parents' country of origin. Little research has been done on how widely it is practised in the UK but a ground-breaking study published in 2011 by Imkaan, the national black, minority ethnic and refugee charity, offered a startling insight into its prevalence in London. Imkaan estimated that 7,000 women who've undergone FGM give birth each year in the capital alone, and pointed out that the female children of those women are at risk of being mutilated in turn.[19]

FGM was banned in Egypt in 2008 following the death of a 12-year-old girl, Budour Ahmad Shakar, in a private clinic in Minya province in Upper Egypt a year earlier. But the new law didn't prevent the death of another girl, aged 13 this time, in Menoufiya province in 2010. In her book *Khul-Khaal*, the Egyptian writer and artist Nayra Atiya spells out what the practice involves in an interview with Alice, a Coptic Christian woman from Minya, who underwent FGM when she was eight years old. In Alice's case, it was performed by a midwife who arrived at five o'clock in the morning:

> I was to be the first because I was the eldest. They did the operation and then pounded an onion and salt mixture to put on the wound to cauterize it. When it was all over, they carried me and put me to bed. They told me to keep my legs straight in front of me and my thighs apart to keep the wound from healing over.[20]

After a week of immobility, Alice was allowed to get up but the ritual was not over. All the girls who'd undergone FGM were given new dresses and told to tie their severed clitorises in the hems. She continued:

The family then paraded us through the streets like brides and took us for a picnic by the river. We were told to throw our clitorises in the Nile. This would bring us happiness. Words!

... This operation makes it harder for a girl to enjoy sex, and as sex is all important to men, then where is the happiness this custom brings?[21]

Following the Arab Spring, FGM began to be discussed more openly in Egypt and organisations supporting women's rights spoke out against the practice. The Egyptian-American journalist Mona Eltahawy wrote a controversial article for *Foreign Policy* magazine in which she revealed that her mother and all but one of her six aunts 'have had their genitals cut in the name of modesty'. But an Islamist MP, one of a handful of women elected to represent the Freedom and Justice party, the political wing of the Muslim Brotherhood, called for the law banning FGM to be repealed. Azza El-Garf described the practice as 'beautification plastic surgery' and said it should be up to individual women to decide whether to have it.[22] El-Garf's support for the banned practice caused outrage and Egypt's feminist New Women Foundation threatened to take her to court.

In Sierra Leone, which was ravaged by a brutal civil war in the 1990s, the practice is still not illegal. Astonishingly, some young women who missed undergoing FGM during the war later volunteered to have it done as adults, fearing they would not otherwise be acceptable to prospective husbands. The story of one of them, Fatmata, is told by Mariatu Kamara in her harrowing book *Bite of the Mango*.

Mariatu's own history is tragic: she comes from a village in the east of the country where she underwent FGM on the dirt floor of a hut at the age of nine. In her book, she recalls the 'excruciating' pain as her skirt was lifted and a knife cut into her genitals; she screamed and bit one of the women who was holding her down. Mariatu recalls:

> When the Bondo, or cutting, was done, I had to sit in a chair with strips of cotton between my legs to stop the bleeding. I watched as [her cousin] and the other girls from my village went through the same ordeal. We were all in pain for days afterwards, but at least sharing the experience let us laugh about how awful we felt.[23]

Two years later, when the civil war started, Mariatu's hands were chopped off by 'rebels' who were trying to overthrow the government of Sierra Leone. She managed to get to Freetown, where she lived for a time in an amputee camp at Aberdeen. Her friend Fatmata was undamaged and she became a second mother to Mariatu. One day Fatmata announced that she was getting married but was anxious because she hadn't been 'initiated' when she was a girl. 'Well, you can't marry until you are. We will do it immediately, here at the camp,' Mariatu's aunt exclaimed.[24] It is a horrifying anecdote: a young woman voluntarily undergoing mutilation of her sexual organs at a camp for men, women and children who had themselves been mutilated in a savage conflict. Until very recently, Sierra Leone had one of the highest rates of maternal mortality in the world; because of poor health care and FGM, the risk of a Sierra Leonean woman dying in childbirth was one in eight.

As we have seen, vagina-phobia is a worldwide phenomenon. Throughout history, women's sexual organs have been denigrated, mutilated and treated as a cause of shame; they have been endowed with fantastic powers, symbolic functions and even teeth. The Russian feminists who founded Pussy Riot knew this history and chose the name of their band deliberately; there is a direct line of descent from the British punk band The Slits through the American Riot Grrrl movement. From the start, gender politics and opposition to authoritarianism were entwined: the collective was founded in September 2011, when Putin announced he intended to stand again for president. Band members use pseudonyms and 'Serafima' explained their thinking in an interview before the arrests:

> ... at that point we realized that this country needs a militant, punk-feminist, street band that will rip through Moscow's streets and squares, mobilize public energy against the evil crooks of the Putinist junta and enrich the Russian cultural and political opposition with themes that are important to us: gender and LGBT rights, problems of masculine conformity, absence of a daring political message on the musical and art scenes, and the domination of males in all areas of public discourse.[25]

Since he emerged as Russia's most powerful politician, Putin has been photographed in a series of Action Man poses: stripped to the waist to go riding, diving to 'find' ancient amphorae on the sea bed and posing with endangered species. These staged events suggest an unstable combination of narcissism and insecurity, not to mention an individual unlikely to see the funny side of being challenged by a bunch of young women named after their vaginas. Putin is used to dealing with male oligarchs whom he could bribe or threaten, while critics of his regime who used conventional tactics faced enormous risks; the journalist Anna Politkovskaya, who attacked him relentlessly in books and articles, was first poisoned as she tried to get to the Beslan siege in 2004 and then assassinated in her apartment block in Moscow in 2006. (Politkovskaya was shot dead on Putin's birthday. He deplored the murder of 'a woman and a mother' but said she did not have 'a serious impact on the political mood in our country'.)

It soon became clear, however, that Putin was personally infuriated by Pussy Riot. In a documentary aired on his 60th birthday, two days before the women's appeal was due to be heard in Moscow, he denied having anything to do with the verdict but sneered: 'They got what they wanted.' At the appeal, Samutsevich had her sentence suspended but the two-year prison terms on Alyokhina and Tolonnikova were upheld. But it wasn't just Putin who was bewildered when the band exploded on the scene. 'What the hell do these English letters on your banner stand for?' FSB agents and cops demanded when the women staged their first interventions in Moscow. The answer came in an interview when 'Garadzha' explained that Pussy Riot's project went beyond the specific circumstances of Putin's Russia. She said:

A female sex organ, which is supposed to be receiving and shapeless, suddenly starts a radical rebellion against the cultural order, which tries to constantly define it and show its appropriate place.[26]

Pussy Riot's aim is nothing less than to transform the vagina from a passive space without firm boundaries into a site of rebellion. Their credo is a rallying cry, reclaiming the female sex organ and rejecting attempts to ban it from public discourse. These young women in their bright balaclavas have given us a potent symbol of defiance, challenging the *vagina dentata* and all the other slanders imposed on our bodies. This is pussy politics in its most vivid form: thanks to Pussy Riot, we're living in the age of the *vagina cantata*.

CONFORMITY

QUEEN WAG

Nineteen eighty-two was a year of contrasting images of women. In April, the UK's first woman prime minister, Margaret Thatcher, took the country to war against Argentina over the Falkland Islands, revealing a steely side to her character which would lead to her being nicknamed the Iron Lady. In July, the Princess of Wales, who had married into the royal family with great fanfare just a year earlier, fulfilled expectations by producing a son who immediately became second in line to the throne. In December, thousands of women gathered at Greenham Common, an American air base in Berkshire, and formed a human chain around the six-mile perimeter fence; some of them joined the peace camp set up outside the base a year earlier to protest against the presence of American cruise missiles in the UK, living in polythene 'benders' and signalling the arrival of a new and overtly feminist form of direct action. Also in 1982, an unknown singer called Madonna Ciccone released her first single, going on to achieve worldwide fame and blazing a trail for performers like Lady Gaga. And it was the year a baby was born, unremarked outside her family, who would one day grow up to become the most photographed woman in the country. Despite the increasing role of women in public life – even in 1982, almost 60 per cent worked outside the home, including her own mother – she would become famous not for her achievements but her willingness to play the most traditional feminine role of all: waiting for a husband, getting married and not long afterwards becoming pregnant.

Kate Middleton is solidly middle-class. She was born in Berkshire on 9 January 1982, five months before Prince William, whom she would one day wed in front of prime ministers, monarchs and sundry dictators at Westminster Abbey. Middleton's parents, Carole and Michael, both worked as flight attendants for an airline but later set up a mail-order business in the Berkshire village of Bucklebury, where the family owned a detached house with five bedrooms. At the time of her elder daughter's engagement, much was made of the fact that Carole Middleton came from a working-class family but her children grew up in very different circumstances. The Middletons became self-made millionaires, running a business with an estimated value of £30m, and were able to send their children to prep school and Marlborough College, a middle-ranking public school in Wiltshire. Middleton did better at school than her would-have-been mother-in-law, Princess Diana; she got A-levels and went to the University of St Andrews in Scotland, where she took a degree in History of Art. It was also where she met Prince William, catching his attention in one of the few unexpected episodes in her biography, when she wore a transparent dress over black underwear at a charity fashion show in 2002. (The 'dress', actually intended to be worn as a skirt, sold for £78,000 at an auction in London just before her wedding.) After graduating in 2003, Middleton might have been expected to look for a job where she could use her degree, but it was the beginning of a period when her life deviated rapidly from that of other women of her age and class. Middleton's relationship with William was public knowledge by 2004, when they went on a skiing holiday together, but she had to wait six more years before the announcement of their engagement in 2010. In the period between leaving university and her marriage, her CV was unimpressive: in November 2006 she became an accessory buyer for the fashion chain Jigsaw but the job lasted barely a year, after which she worked part-time for the family business, Party Pieces. (Among other themes, its website offers 'Princess Parties' which will help clients 'transform [their] house or party room into a magical wonderland, put on the perfect princess tea party and entertain the court with party games and activities'.) The media started calling her 'Waity Katie', a nickname which would have seemed cruel had Middleton's lack of interest in a career not suggested its accuracy. By 2008, the question of what she actually did with her time, apart from waiting to get engaged, was reported to be causing anxiety 'at the very highest level', with the Queen said to be 'increasingly concerned' that Middleton still didn't have a job. The solution, according to royal aides, was to suggest that she should take on a little light charity work 'to counter the potentially damaging public perception that she is workshy'.[1] The Palace was caught in a trap of its own making, for the monarchy has always kept well away from women with demanding careers – it was hard to imagine William or his brother Harry dating a businesswoman or indeed a social worker – but even the royal family was disturbed by Middleton's ease with her role as literally a lady-in-waiting.

Two years later, when the engagement was finally announced, she was 28 and had still done nothing noteworthy. But she embraced her new status wholeheartedly, adopting the uniform of an older generation and picking out clothes more suited to a middle-aged woman with conservative tastes: the knee-length dress, the plain court shoes, the lady-like clutch bag. Instead of avoiding comparisons with her fiancé's mother, Middleton actually seemed to seek them out; the blue dress she wore for a TV interview with William was an eerie visual echo of the frumpy blue suit Lady Diana Spencer wore for her own engagement picture in 1980. While other women of her age and class progressed up the career ladder, Middleton embarked on the apparently gruelling process of becoming a royal bride, amid breathless speculation about her wedding dress. The popular press abandoned its 'Waity Katie' scepticism, plunging into an orgy of admiration for her meagre accomplishments: the ability to walk beside her fiancé, wear clothes and say as little as possible. Royal correspondents plumbed new depths of fawning, even providing extensive coverage of a royal visit to Belfast when Middleton ... tossed a pancake. When she asked her favourite designers to amend their designs, lengthening hems and sleeves, fashion writers swooned. As her taste in clothes became even duller – after the wedding, she began turning up at parties in ankle-length dresses with high necks – they urged other women to follow suit. The *Daily Mail*, which had previously expressed incredulity about Middleton's failure to find a job, promoted her as a leader of fashion, gushing to its readers that it was now 'fashionable to cover up'. It was not an entirely convincing message at a moment when the biggest star in the world was Lady Gaga, a woman who once stepped off a plane after a transatlantic flight wearing just a body stocking and heel-less boots.

The Middleton phenomenon was a puzzle: at a time when almost three-quarters of adult women worked outside the home, the royal family had once again managed to find a royal bride who seemed to believe that engagement and marriage constituted a full-time job. One website described even Middleton's post-wedding occupation, apparently without irony, as 'duchess' (I'd love to see the job description). The woman who had been hailed as a 'breath of fresh air', proof that the royal family was breaking free from old class stereotypes, looked more and more like a throwback to an earlier age; there was still no question of her going out to work, even when Prince William's job as an RAF search-and-rescue pilot took him to the Falkland Islands and she was left alone, apart from a security detail, in the house they shared on Anglesey. Even that wasn't enough to ward off the unsolicited advice of royal correspondents and celebrity watchers, who told anyone who would listen that it was vital the new Duchess should take care not to outshine her husband. It was a glimpse of the anxiety still widely felt by royal watchers about Princess Diana's impact on the family, and an acknowledgement of how much Middleton's role was being shaped by the woman whose engagement ring she wore.

The marriage of the Prince and Princess of Wales had been a disaster for the royal family and very nearly for the monarchy, which experienced the unrestrained fury of Diana's fans after her sudden death in a car crash in Paris

in 1997. It was far from being a republican moment, as
some excitable commentators characterised it at the time,
but it was clear that the bruised royals would have to
think about how best in future to avoid the unpopularity
Diana's divorce and death had caused them. The answer to
their prayers, it seemed, was a nicely brought-up girl who
had shown herself to possess an abundance of discretion:
Middleton was considered acceptable as a royal bride
not just because William wanted her, although that was a
consideration, but because she had so thoroughly absorbed
the not-being-Diana part of her script. She might dress like
the Princess at the beginning of her royal adventure, when
the young Diana Spencer was still feeling her way, but
Middleton was personable without being charismatic. The
circumstances of the two women appeared very different:
Middleton was 10 years older at the time of her marriage
and had had a decent education, whereas Spencer had
left school with next to no qualifications. She married
at 19 and was not quite 20 when she became a mother,
posing with her baby and husband for photographs
which embodied the nuclear family at a moment when it
was under attack from all directions. But while she was
widely admired for her hands-on style of parenting, her
public commitment to motherhood was not quite what it
seemed; she sent her sons to boarding school and spent
so little time with them that royal aides discovered after
her death that it had left fewer than expected gaps in the
boys' schedule. And if the royal family had believed that
Diana was biddable, she turned out to be anything but,
railing (reasonably enough) against her husband's coldness
and responding with an array of behaviours, including

self-harm and bulimia, which suggested acute distress if not mental illness. Playing second fiddle to her husband was too much even for a woman as traditional as Diana, leading to her eventual expulsion from the family; divorced and denied the HRH title which meant so much to her, the Princess raged against her fate, hating the role she'd been assigned but unable to articulate what was wrong with it except in the most personal terms. Her critique was apolitical – her most significant achievement was to turn the royals from figureheads into celebrities – and she never wavered in her support for the monarchy as an institution, even if she would have liked the order of succession to skip a generation. But even the Princess of Wales appeared to have learned towards the end of her short life that living for and through a man was not the wisest of moves for a modern woman: 'You know, people think that at the end of the day a man is the only answer,' she observed ruefully in her 1995 *Panorama* interview. 'Actually, a fulfilling job is better for me.' Diana's idea of a job was somewhat different from other women of her generation, but at least she came to recognise that modern women need more than a husband to lead a rounded existence.

In the aftermath of the Princess's death, it became clear that millions of women identified with at least one aspect of her experience: romantic disappointment. They overlooked differences in wealth and status, seeing a woman who'd been disappointed in love and was, by virtue of that fact alone, 'just like us'. In the modern world, this aspect of the Diana debacle wasn't too difficult for the monarchy to fix. Dynastic marriages were going out of fashion as European royals married TV presenters and personal trainers, and it was always clear that Diana's elder son would have more latitude when it came to choosing someone to marry; in addition, the candidate would not have to submit to the humiliating speculation about her 'past' which William's mother had experienced when an uncle publicly (and tastelessly) confirmed her virginity. There was another significant difference as well, for Prince William did not follow his father's example by embarking on a series of widely publicised affairs in his 20s. By the time William reached the age at which he was expected to marry, he was in a long-term relationship with Middleton and had even lived with her in the Anglesey cottage. The couple had been together for eight years when they married on 29 April 2011, and the longevity of the 'courtship' suggested that William's family wanted to be as certain as they could that his bride would not spring a series of unwelcome surprises of the kind they had endured from his late mother. Because of her unhappy marriage, the Princess of Wales blew her chances of becoming Queen consort, but she made up for it with a successful bid for the affection of millions of ordinary people. She became a blank screen for people's fantasies, shedding her matronly style and becoming a by-word for the glamorous single life. Middleton's marriage, by contrast, was universally assumed to be happy, a notion she encouraged with occasional remarks about her husband 'spoiling' her.

Nevertheless, some parallels with the late Princess remained impossible to ignore, and the most obvious was the question of weight. Diana was a chubby teenager when she got engaged to Prince Charles but lost weight dramatically before her wedding, getting through the day in a giant puffball dress which could have come from a little girl's dressing-up box. Middleton's weight loss after her engagement was equally striking, accentuated on the day of her wedding by a tight-fitting dress which looked as if it had been designed to be worn by an altogether curvier woman. After her wedding, Diana tried to conceal her weight problem in dresses which were ruched and padded like body armour, but Middleton stuck to a silhouette which emphasised how painfully thin she had become. By the time she appeared at the Queen's Diamond Jubilee pageant in 2012, her slender figure caused intakes of breath; comparisons between photographs from the weekend's events and a couple of years earlier showed a woman whose body shape had changed out of all recognition. It was a striking visual metaphor: once again, the Windsors had been struck by shrinking royal bride syndrome, emphasising the continuing inability of the British monarchy to imagine a modern role for its female members.

Indeed, 20 years after Diana Spencer was its first victim, Middleton's appearance highlighted the unresolved contradiction at the heart of the monarchy: with the exception of the Queen, women remained second-class citizens in the royal family. This fact was underlined in June 2012 when the *Daily Telegraph* reported that the Queen had updated the Order of Precedence in the royal household to take account of the family's newest member. According to the paper, the key condition was that Middleton would have to curtsy to the 'blood princesses', including Princess Anne, Princess Alexandra, and the daughters of the Duke of York, except on occasions when her husband was with her.[2] Buckingham Palace declined to comment but the royal family had finally come round to abandoning the principle of male primogeniture only a year earlier, despite the mixed (to say the least) record of the kings it produced in the 20th century; Edward VII was a playboy who opposed votes for women, while Edward VIII's sympathy with Hitler was well known. Even in 2011, the change in the rules of succession was not scheduled to come into effect until after the birth of the first child of the Duke and Duchess of Cambridge, always assuming that the infant happened to be a girl. Nor was it reflected in the public roles of individual members of the royal family: the Windsor men continued to serve in the armed forces, allowing them to cut a dash on active service and wear uniforms of almost Ruritanian splendour on official occasions. But Middleton stuck to the most traditional of female roles, visiting projects to do with children: 'Duchess of Cambridge paints and plays music with hospice children' (*Daily Telegraph*, March 2012); 'Duchess of Cambridge joins city children in the countryside' (*Daily Telegraph*, June 2012); 'Duchess of Cambridge joins charity children for *The Lion, The Witch and The Wardrobe*' (*Daily Telegraph*, June 2012). Eighteen months after the wedding she duly became pregnant, the announcement being made prematurely when she was admitted to hospital with severe morning sickness.

Middleton's post-wedding schedule confirmed that the Windsor women, with the exception of the elderly Queen and irascible Princess Anne, were silent figures with only two occupations open to them: charity work and sport. The former has been the province of wealthy women for centuries while show jumping, the favoured sport of

Anne and her daughter Zara Phillips, is so expensive that it isn't open to people on ordinary incomes. Even when gender roles widened for women in the general population, the royal family continued to maintain a degree of sex differentiation more appropriate to the 1950s than the 21st century. After her marriage, Middleton seemed content with her limited role and two factors shielded her from the criticism she might otherwise have received: her entry into a protective royal bubble and the Windsors' highly efficient PR machine. The country was in the grip of a painful economic crisis and her parents, who bought a much grander house in 2012, were not immune from accusations of cashing in on their royal connections. Neither was her sister Pippa, whose book of party tips became the target of spoof accounts on Twitter. But Middleton herself was untouchable, even though the popular press is renowned for its sexism and fascinated by the phenomenon of Wags. The acronym emerged when the wives and girlfriends of members of the England football team took up residence in a luxury hotel in Baden-Baden during the 2006 World Cup, prompting accusations that they had distracted their partners from the game. Since then it's been applied many times, sometimes quite unfairly, to just about any woman who has a relationship with a famous man. The best-known examples are instantly recognisable – Coleen Rooney, Victoria Beckham, Cheryl Cole – and tend to come from a working-class or lower middle-class background. So it's all the more telling that the prime candidate, the woman who arguably deserved the title more than anyone else, never appeared on lists of the country's leading contenders.

By the age of 30, the new Duchess of Cambridge had

done little since leaving university except play a supporting role to her boyfriend, marry him with great pomp and ceremony and get pregnant for the first time. She had never really enjoyed an independent identity or income – even her clothes were paid for by her father-in-law – and didn't seem to aspire to either. Unambitious, uncontroversial and bland, Kate Middleton was Queen Wag in everything but name.

CALM DOWN, DEAR

The Tories have always had a problem with women. Paradoxically, the party which produced the UK's first female prime minister has a poor record of encouraging women to become MPs and actively opposed much of the legislation designed to protect women in the workforce and education. Pioneering laws including the 1970 Equal Pay Act and the 1975 Sex Discrimination Act were passed by Labour governments, as was the 2010 Equality Act which tried to put right some of the flaws in the earlier legislation. While Labour ministers have often been too timid in their efforts to establish such basics as equal pay, the Tory party has always seemed perplexed if not actually hostile to the idea of gender equality, a fact reflected in its continuing failure to get even a respectable number of women into Parliament. Indeed, Margaret Thatcher's stunning success in the 1979 general election obscured another reality, which was that the result was dire for women generally, producing the lowest number of female MPs for 30 years.

Thatcher was one of only eight women on the Conservative benches in 1979, and she did not consider any of her female colleagues worthy of a seat in her first Cabinet. She herself was only the second Tory woman to achieve Cabinet rank,[1] serving as Secretary of State for Education – and earning the nickname Milk Snatcher for her attempt to axe free school milk – before she became Prime Minister. Her arrival in Downing Street appeared revolutionary but it was anything but as far as other women was concerned; her 13 years as prime minister did nothing to further the cause of women in the Conservative party and actually did them a disservice. Thatcher appointed only one woman, Baroness Young, to her Cabinets and Young served for such a short period that she was quickly forgotten even by members of her own party. Thatcher's Iron Lady nickname challenged traditional ideas about gender while boosting her upper middle-class pretensions but she unsettled male colleagues, many of whom suffered from maternal deprivation after being sent to boarding school. They responded to her flirtatiousness, an aspect of her character which was much commented upon, but were repelled by the way in which she embodied her power. The French president, François Mitterrand, took a more relaxed view:

'Of course it is only power that matters,' he said late one night in 1982. 'You can do nothing without it. That's why I admire Thatcher.'[2]

This conversation was noted and published by Mitterrand's aide, Jacques Attali. He acknowledged that there were tensions between the two leaders but confirmed Thatcher's shrewd use of her femininity with his boss, observing that 'they had a relationship of seduction, the rapport of man-woman'. The former president has often been quoted as comparing Thatcher to Caligula but Attali recalled a different version, insisting that Mitterrand actually said she had 'the eyes of Stalin and the voice of Marilyn Monroe'.[3] The ruthlessness of a dictator and the girlishness of a 1950s movie star: it was a daring but also a risky combination in right-wing politics, isolating Thatcher from men *and* women in her own party. Conservative MPs might admire her but they did not warm to her, while she made the classic mistake of the 'token' woman, enjoying her own success and not bothering to make alliances with women desperately trying to follow in her footsteps. When she had to fight for her political life in the autumn of 1990, she discovered how few friends she had in the House of Commons, appearing genuinely shocked by her failure to get sufficient votes in the first round of the leadership contest. Ousted in a manner that seemed ignominious, she left behind a party which remained overwhelming male; so few Tory women had ministerial experience at any level that her successor, John Major, did not appoint a single woman to his first Cabinet. Edwina Currie, who was a junior health minister during Thatcher's premiership, overlooked Baroness Young's brief stint in Cabinet when she acknowledged Thatcher's negative impact on women:

Margaret Thatcher was definitely not a feminist. She'd have said that she did not campaign for more women to enter Parliament, she simply got on with it. In her early years she admitted that prejudice against women did hold us back. But later, her view was that women should stop blaming other people, or men, or the system, and simply strive to be good enough to make the grade. And this was where many ambitious women would part company with her. For in the 11 years she was in Number 10, Mrs T never promoted any female Cabinet Ministers. And she never appointed any women to the Tory Whips' Office. Those failures seem bizarre, but she ceased to be a feminist icon for many of us.[4]

Currie's own marginalisation is emblematic of the fate of Tory women in this period. Sacked by Thatcher, she waited in vain to make a come-back under John Major who, it later emerged, had considered her more suitable material for a sexual liaison. Their affair lasted for four years in the 1980s and Major discussed making her his parliamentary aide after he became Prime Minister. It came to nothing and Currie revealed the affair when she published her diaries in 2002. The revelation of such intimate matters is unsettling but it did at least expose the reflexive misogyny of leading Tories, who rushed to Major's defence; his former Cabinet colleague David Mellor, who had himself resigned as Heritage Secretary over an extra-marital affair, claimed that Currie had 'sold John Major down the river for cash, like a cheap trollop'.[5] That she and other Tory women had a legitimate grievance about their exclusion from the inner circle didn't seem to enter Mellor's head, yet the leadership's failure to encourage and promote women was self-reinforcing. Inevitably, it limited the pool of women MPs from which prime ministers could select ministers, and exposed the few women who were singled out to the old charge of tokenism. As a consequence, Major's eventual appointment of two women, Virginia Bottomley and Gillian Shepherd, to Cabinet jobs did little to address the party's historic failure. The Tories were heading for a fall and it duly came in the 1997 general election.

In that year, a revitalised Labour party under the leadership of Tony Blair fielded a record number of women candidates. It changed the face of the House of Commons overnight, even if Labour's record intake of 101 female MPs was patronisingly referred to in the press as 'Blair's babes'. While the new Prime Minister flashed his trademark grin surrounded by a new generation of Labour women, there were still only 13 women on the Conservative benches; the Liberal Democrats, whose own problems with gender would have a significant impact on the shape of the government after the 2010 general election, managed only three. Women took five seats in Blair's first Cabinet, eventually securing eight in his final reshuffle before he stepped down as Prime Minister in 2007. Gordon Brown reduced the number to five in his first Cabinet although he made history by appointing Jacqui Smith as the country's first female Home Secretary, one of the three great offices of state after the Prime Minister.

When David Cameron became Prime Minister in a Coalition government in 2010, the woman problem immediately reared its head: the Tories and the Lib Dems had only 56 female MPs between them, compared with Labour's 81. Shamefully, the Lib Dem leader Nick Clegg didn't give any of his party's five Cabinet seats to women, and Cameron found spaces for only four. Overall, the proportion of women ministers fell from 30 per cent before the 2010 election to 17 per cent. (One of the few Conservative women with a high public profile, the backbencher Louise Mensch, resigned her seat in August 2102 after spending just over two years in Parliament. It was an unhappy episode for the Tories, who lost the seat in the subsequent by-election.) But Cameron's premiership was a setback in other ways as well, marking the return to power of a wealthy elite after a period in which the party's prime ministers had middle- or lower middle-class origins. After his election as leader in 2005, Cameron had done his best to present himself as a new breed of Tory: modern, relaxed, in touch with ordinary people and their problems. His background was in TV and PR and he understood the power of images; there were endless pictures of him in casual outfits, holding hands with his wife Samantha, holidaying in Cornwall with his young family, and even parading his green credentials by posing with huskies in Norway's Arctic region. Few people doubted Cameron's devotion to his children, including a disabled son who died suddenly in 2009, but his public performance of modern fatherhood also sent a message that the Tories had finally updated their attitudes to gender roles. Even so, Cameron could not disguise the fact that he was educated at the country's top public school, Eton, and had married the daughter of a baronet, Sir Reginald Sheffield; until the election, when she went part-time, Samantha Cameron earned a substantial salary as creative director of Smythson, an upmarket stationery company. The Prime Minister's closest colleagues and their wives came from equally privileged backgrounds: the Chancellor of the Exchequer, George Osborne, was educated at another top public school, St Paul's, and stood to inherit an Irish baronetcy. Osborne's wife Frances was an author and the daughter of a Tory grandee, Lord Howell, who was a Cabinet minister under Thatcher and returned to office as a junior Foreign Office minister in the Coalition. Even the deputy Prime

Minister, Nick Clegg, was educated at public school and married to a successful Spanish lawyer, Miriam Gonzalez Durantez, whose father had been a senator in Spain's right-wing People's Party. The 2010 Cabinet was also notable for its wealth: at a time when median gross pay for single mothers was less than £200 a week, two-thirds were millionaires. The personal wealth of the Camerons was estimated at £3.8m in 2012, while Osborne was thought to be worth more than £4m, William Hague and Jeremy Hunt almost £5m each, and Philip Hammond more than £8m. One of the new Tory intake, the backbench MP Zac Goldsmith, was said to be worth almost £300m, dwarfing the estimated £2m personal wealth of Nick Clegg.[6]

It's hard to imagine a group of people less able to empathise with the struggles of ordinary people, and in particular the millions of women who worked in the public sector. During Blair's first administration, the Tories had fiercely opposed the introduction of a minimum wage, despite the fact that its chief beneficiaries were likely to be women in poorly paid occupations. In the run-up to the 2010 general election, Cameron supported the notion of tax breaks for married couples, a scheme dreamed up by Iain Duncan Smith's socially conservative Centre for Social Justice; critics pointed out that one of its perverse effects would be to give a financial advantage to abusive husbands, as long as they stayed married, while doing nothing for women who left violent relationships. Cameron and Osborne fought the election with a warning that they would have to cut public spending but the Labour leader Gordon Brown was unpopular and voters wanted a change, even if they were unenthusiastic about a Tory administration. What many people seemed not to realise was that Osborne's proposed cuts would have a devastating and disproportionate effect on gender: starting from a position of systemic disadvantage, women do not have the resources to absorb the impact of swingeing cuts in public spending and services. It is a simple fact that, until the far-off day when gender equality is achieved, women will go on depending more on the state in terms of jobs, benefits and wider support. Few women want this dependence but the female half of the population gets a worse deal than men across a whole range of indicators: almost two-thirds of low-paid workers are women, two-fifths of ethnic minority women live in poverty, and nine out of ten lone parents are female. The failure of even progressive governments to deliver equal pay is a running sore and largely due to a long-standing reluctance to take a necessary step, namely the introduction of an obligation of transparency about pay scales on employers. For decades, women who suspected they were paid less than male colleagues were unable to get access to the information they needed to bring a case under the 1970 Act and its updates. This failing was finally addressed by section 78 of the 2010 Equality Act, which created a power to force employers to publish information showing whether men and women are paid different amounts, but it did not take immediate effect and companies with fewer than 250 employees are exempt. Unequal pay has knock-on effects, limiting women's access to housing and childcare – childcare costs in the UK are among the highest in the world – and the impact on pensions is dramatic. On average, women's personal pensions are only 62 per cent of the average for men,[7] and two-thirds of retired people who live in poverty are women.[8] Some estimates suggest that half of all women are unable to make adequate provision for their old age.[9]

Traditionally, millions of women had sought a means of sheltering themselves and their families from the worst effects of inequality by working in the public sector, where the fact that wages were lower was balanced by better conditions; in 2011, the full-time pay gap was only 13.2 per cent in the public sector, compared to 20.4 per cent in the private sector.[10] When the Coalition came to power, around 40 per cent of working women in the UK were employed in the public sector, and they accounted for almost two-thirds of the public sector workforce overall.[11] Three-quarters of local government workers, 77 per cent of NHS employees, 80 per cent of adult social care workers and 82 per cent of employees in the education sector were female; in some regions, such as the North-East of England, the public sector provided almost half the jobs available to women.[12] What this meant, when the Coalition government began slashing public expenditure in 2010, was that women were peculiarly vulnerable to the cuts. According to the Office for Budget Responsibility, 710,000 jobs were to be lost in the public sector by 2017,[13] and a number of commentators were quick to point out the asymmetrical impact on gender. Labour's shadow work and pensions secretary, Yvette Cooper, argued that women would be hit three times as hard as men, pointing out that £6bn of the Chancellor's £8bn spending cuts would adversely affect women. Because so many children are dependent on their mothers' incomes, Cooper went on to accuse Osborne of 'launching the biggest assault on the family in the entire history of the welfare state'.[14] In an unprecedented move, the Fawcett Society tried to challenge the 2010 budget in court, claiming that ministers had failed in their duty to consider its impact on equality. It lost the action, but won a ruling that 'the preparation and presentation of measures outlined in national budgets are subject to equality law.'[15]

Did Cameron care? In office, a new and unexpected side to his character had begun to emerge, revealing a short temper and a tendency to sneer at his opponents in the House of Commons. On the Labour side, many of them were women and they represented aspects of the modern world – feminism, equality, a non-traditional attitude to gender roles – which he seemed to find alien. Despite having promised to end 'Punch and Judy politics' during the weekly ritual of Prime Minister's Questions, he revealed a laddish taste for innuendo which recalled a long-gone generation of northern comedians. A Tory backbencher, Peter Bone, provided an early opportunity when he began to make a habit of referring to his wife in questions to the Prime Minister. 'I do feel now that a very big part of my life is trying to give pleasure to Mrs Bone,' Cameron smirked, prompting howls of glee among Tory MPs. He added: 'I feel on this occasion I can only go so far.'[16] He got a similar reaction when he replied to another of his backbenchers, Nadine Dorries, who challenged the traditional image of Conservative women with her short skirts and high heels. 'I know that the honourable lady is extremely frustrated,' the Prime Minister began, and flashed a big grin when the rest of his sentence was drowned out by gales of knowing laughter (Dorries walked out[17]). He seemed to reserve particular venom for people unlike himself, such as the ex-miner Dennis Skinner and Labour's Shabana Mahmood, a barrister and one of the first Muslim women to be elected to Parliament. 'Well read,' he sneered when Mahmood asked him an unwelcome question about the disastrous state of the economy.[18] But the most notorious of these episodes involved Angela Eagle, Labour's shadow chief secretary to the Treasury, and one of the few MPs to have come out as a lesbian. When Eagle challenged his claim that a former Labour MP, Dr Howard Stoate, supported the Tories' controversial NHS reforms, Cameron smirked across the chamber at her. 'Calm down, dear, calm down,' he told her. 'Listen to the doctor. Calm down and listen to the doctor.'[19] It was the authentic voice of patriarchy, arrogant and unthinkingly sexist as he put the little woman in her place.

The Labour leader, Ed Miliband, began comparing his rival to Flashman, the misogynist, public-school-educated bully in the novels of George MacDonald Fraser.[20] Within months, it became clear that even No. 10 could no longer ignore the party's (and the Prime Minister's) woman problem. A memo marked 'restricted-policy' was written in the No. 10 policy unit, then headed by Steve Hilton, and circulated to government departments, where it was soon leaked.[21] It began by summarising 'the problem':

> We know from a range of polls that women are significantly more negative about the Government than men. We don't at present have a finer-grained analysis than this, though there is some suggestion that **fear for the next generation** is a major factor for many women. In addition, the group of Cabinet Office and No. 10 women we assembled felt strongly that the general tone and messages of government

communications, particularly around deficit reductions were an issue – with women, especially in the public sector feeling targeted; a general sense that families who had been struggling to get by even in the 'good times' resented being told to tighten their belts; and even a view that the Government's choice of leaders on the economy gave the implication that 'now there's a real job to be done sorting out the mess, it can only be done by men.'

As a belated attempt to address the Tory problem with gender, the memo left much to be desired, and its author hastened to add that all these impressions were 'anecdotal'. But he or she went on to acknowledge that the government had pursued a raft of policies 'which are seen as having hit women, or their interests, disproportionately', including the huge rise in university tuition fees, changes to child tax credits and child benefit, and the rising cost of living. Number one on the list of issues turning women away from the Tories was public sector pay and pensions, and the memo contained a nervous addition in parenthesis: '(particularly as contrasted with – mostly male – bankers, in the popular narrative)'. It is traditional in such circumstances to blame the messenger, and the author complained that many positive things 'had received far less profile and attention'. But he or she could not avoid mentioning a stark reality:

There are also many areas where we have made bold statements or promises but haven't delivered enough – including, for example, our overarching claim that we would be 'the most family friendly Government ever'[.]

Evidence from polls showed a confusing picture. In July 2011, an Ipsos-MORI survey found only 25 per cent of women were satisfied with the way the government was doing its job, a figure replicated in a YouGov survey the following month. An Ipsos-MORI poll published in October found little change overall in women's support for the Conservatives but there were striking differences among socio-economic classes; among C2 women, who are mostly low-skilled, the Tories had lost seven points during 2011 while Labour's support had rocketed by 17 points. Ipsos-MORI reported that 'the government performs worse among women than among men on a number of … measurements of political attitudes'.[22]

This disillusionment was hardly surprising, as dire warnings about the impact on women of the government's policies began to be borne out. In March 2012, the Office for National Statistics duly announced a grim milestone: unemployment among women had reached its highest point for 25 years. It stood at 1.13m, an increase of almost 20 per cent since 2009, while male unemployment had risen by a barely significant 0.32 per cent in the same period. The figure would have been even worse had it not been for the fact that three-quarters of a million women were working part-time because they couldn't find full-time jobs, the highest level since comparable records began in 1992. Job losses in the public sector were dramatic:

◆ Women accounted for 76 per cent of the drop in the number of employees in local authorities in the South-East

- Women accounted for 100 per cent of those losing their jobs across 19 councils in England and Wales

- Black and minority ethnic (BME) women were particularly badly hit by job cuts in local authorities. A trade union, Unison, surveyed 17 out of 27 local authorities in London and found that BME women were disproportionately affected in 12 of them. In one local authority, they made up 5 per cent of the workforce but 23 per cent of redundancies[23]

Even women who still had jobs were disproportionately affected by a two-year pay freeze for all public sector workers earning more than £21,000; almost three-fifths of the employees it affected were women.[24] They also had to cope with a three-year freeze in child benefit until 2014, which might not seem significant for middle-income households but left a low-income family with three children £285 a year worse off.[25] Meanwhile hundreds of thousands of older women were plunged into financial uncertainty by a dramatic acceleration in changes to the state pension age. It was widely accepted that the old disparity in retirement ages – 60 for women, 65 for men – was no longer justified, and Labour had already embarked on a process of equalisation. But the Coalition speeded it up, confronting half a million women in their 50s with the prospect of having to work two more years before they could retire on a state pension. Angry women pointed out that they needed time to revise their finances and the government backed down slightly, saying the rise in women's pension age to 66 would be delayed by six months until October 2020.

With so many areas to choose from, it was hard to identify the biggest gap between the government's 'family-friendly' rhetoric and its actual impact on women's lives. But NGOs and campaigners became increasingly worried about the issue of safety, with the Women's Institute expressing concern in 2012 that job losses in the rail industry would make train travel a 'dangerous and daunting' option for women.[26] There was also alarm about the effect of expenditure cuts on women suffering from domestic violence, as refuges up and down the country were faced with reductions in grants or a complete withdrawal of public funds. The Tories knew how grave the problem was, and had criticised the previous government for its supposed failure to tackle it. In January 2010, for instance, Duncan Smith made a speech claiming that 13 years of Labour government had inflicted 'grave damage' on the family. 'Most shocking of all, the government now admits that 200,000 children live in homes where there is a known high risk of domestic abuse and violence,' he said.[27] Four months later, Duncan Smith became Secretary of State for Work and Pensions and his Cabinet colleague Theresa May, the Home Secretary, found herself in charge of policy on domestic violence. May said all the right things, declaring in 2011:

No level of violence against women and girls is acceptable in modern Britain or anywhere in the world ... As women and as a society we have made great strides but we need to do more to ensure that women and future generations are not held back. My ambition is nothing less than ending violence against women and girls.[28]

It was not easy to square this ambition with what actually happened to organisations tackling the problem of domestic violence in the first two years of the Coalition Government. Faced with substantial cuts in their income from national government, local authorities reduced grants to refuges and projects up and down the country or cut them altogether. The result was stark: on a typical day in 2011, Women's Aid turned away 230 women seeking refuge from a violent husband or partner.[29] One NGO which worked to reform male perpetrators of domestic violence was forced to reduce the number of clients it dealt with while another, which provided services to BME women, had to close two of its six specialist refuges.[30] In a report published in February 2012, Jude Towers and Sylvia Walby observed that:

- Almost a third of funding from local authorities to domestic violence organisations was cut between 2010/11 and 2011/12, from £7.8m to £5.4m

- Eight organisations providing independent domestic violence advisers for almost 14,000 clients faced funding cuts of between 25 and 100 per cent

- Organisations with smaller budgets were the worst hit, with a 70 per cent reduction in funds for NGOs with funding of less than £20,000. Those receiving more than £100,000 suffered an average cut of 29 per cent[31]

The Fawcett Society was one of many organisations which expressed concern about the short-sighted nature of these policies, while Towers and Walby were in no doubt about the grave consequences for women:

> Substantial reductions in national budgets are leading to cuts in local services to prevent and protect against gender-based violence against women and girls. These cuts in service provision are expected to lead to *increases in this violence* [my italics].

If victims of domestic violence were being denied the support they needed because of budget cuts, the outlook for trafficked women was even worse. As well as wanting to strengthen traditional marriage, an influential lobby within the Cabinet wanted to see American-style 'faith-based' welfare imported into the UK. One of the first victims was the widely admired Poppy Project, the acknowledged leader in providing support and accommodation for women who had been trafficked into the country to work as sex slaves. In April 2011, it lost its £1.8m annual Home Office funding to the Salvation Army, an organisation whose stated aim is to 'reach people with the Christian gospel through evangelism'. The government denied that cost was a major consideration but the Salvation Army – well known in the 19th century for its mission to save 'fallen' women – offered to provide services while spending 60 per cent less per victim. Trafficked women come from many backgrounds and some need to have abortions, but the Salvation Army believes that unwanted pregnancies should be carried to term except in cases of 'proven rape or legally defined incest'. Yet the government insisted that the evangelical organisation was better placed to help victims than the secular Poppy Project, which was forced to reduce the number of bed spaces it offered from 54 to 16.

Governments come and go, and some leave a more lasting mark than others. The striking thing about the administration which came to power in 2010 was that it lacked a clear mandate – even under Cameron, the Tories were unable to win a parliamentary majority – but that didn't stop ministers behaving with ideological fervour. Reducing the size of the public sector had long been an aim of the Conservative party, just as Republicans in the US rail against so-called 'big' government, and the economic crisis provided an irresistible opportunity. But the notion that private was always better than public in terms of providing jobs and services mirrored another deeply held conviction. Even among Tories, it was no longer fashionable to repeat Margaret Thatcher's insistence that 'there is no such thing as society', but the party held firm to the notion that the family was more important than the state. Cabinet ministers who lived conventional upper middle-class lives had an instinctive hostility towards the idea of equality – 'It's about quality, not just equality,' Cameron said glibly[32] – and invoked the idea of the 'family' as the remedy for every social ill. (Towards the end of 2012, he ended equality assessments in a drive to get rid of the 'bureaucratic rubbish' which he said was getting in the way of British business.[33] He also used a Cabinet reshuffle that autumn to move the women and equalities ministerial brief from the Home Office to the less powerful Department for Culture, Media and Sport.)

It was a return to 'traditional' values, dressed up as an economic imperative, and the Fawcett Society correctly identified its retrogressive nature:

While we have become used to slow but steady progress towards equality between women and men, we have now hit a tipping-point. Austerity risks turning back time: fewer women working, more women living in poverty, the gap in women's and men's incomes and earnings widening, women's financial autonomy undermined and women's basic rights to safety and justice under threat.[34]

In a very short space of time, the country had become a bleaker place for women. And while the UK's financial difficulties were real, the Tory response was to implement a project of restoring the primacy of private remedies for social and economic problems. With jobs, benefits and services cut or under threat, women had little choice but to turn to relatives – parents, grand-parents, husbands, partners – for help with everything from childcare to paying the mortgage. (Meanwhile ministers appeared to have overlooked the fact that the home was not a safe place for women suffering domestic violence or the threat of practices such as forced marriage and FGM.) It was a dramatic reversal in the struggle for gender equality which had brought women into the public sphere, giving them a measure of independence for the first time. But it also exposed the true face of modern Conservatism: Cameron's rolled-up sleeves and informal style of parenting hid another reality, which was that the Tory party had never abandoned its reactionary view of gender. He often praised Margaret Thatcher, and took care to appear with the now-frail former Prime Minister on carefully staged public occasions. But Thatcher's historic failure to promote women still resonated through the party, leaving it singularly unsuited – and indeed unwilling – to respect the aspirations and needs of 21st-century women. As the population struggled to survive the worst economic crisis to hit the country for decades, what did her successor have to say to women? Just three little words: calm down, dear.

CRYSTAL'S STORY

Crystal (not her real name) was trafficked to the UK from the Caribbean to work in domestic servitude. She was trying to escape from a violent marriage but ended up working 18 hours a day for a middle-class Nigerian family. She had no friends in this country and was not allowed to go out alone during the first months of her captivity. She escaped after 11 months. When I met her in London, she was 41 and had not seen her four children – who were 13, 11, 8 and 5 when she was trafficked – for several years. This is her story.

When I was seven, I went to live with my mum and her new partner. By the time I was nine my step-father had started to sexually molest me. My Mum was heavily into drugs, it led me into a kind of prostitution with my step-father so he would get her drugs. I ran away at 11 but the police took me back to the house. That same night she beat me. The following morning he was raping me. School was my haven. My mum beat me but the scars were hidden by my uniform. When the other children looked forward to holidays, it was like a prison sentence to me. That meant there was no escape, I would be counting the days down. Every day was just surviving.

The abuse went on for nine years, until I was 18; I then found the courage to run away. I got married in my early 20s, I had kids before I got married. My husband was an alcoholic, I had confided in him about my background and he started to abuse me: 'You're a slut. You're a whore.' I just wanted the earth to open and swallow me up. I remember running away many times but within a couple of days or weeks he would find me and take me back. He said he'd kill me if I tried to leave him or he'd kill the kids and commit suicide. This is something that happens very often in my culture. That lit a light in my head, I had to do one of two things, stay and wait for him to kill me or try to leave him.

I had a friend, a God-fearing woman who had been to the UK. I confided to her that I wanted to leave him. She said, 'Listen, I can help you leave but you can't come back. The only way you can leave this man is to leave the Caribbean'. She first spoke about it 18 months before I made the decision. I had no reason not to trust her. She was godmother to one of my kids. I didn't have a clue. I had heard of drug smuggling in my country, it's a hub for drug smugglers, but I never heard anything about trafficking. I had no reason to doubt her. When she said she would help make the arrangements, I didn't expect her to put me in the situation I ended up in.

She told me about a Christian family she'd been in contact with in the UK. She said this person was Christian like myself, and she introduced me to the lady on the phone. One of my interests was to study accountancy and she was an accountant. She said she had experienced domestic violence, she knew what I was going through, and we built up a relationship. I wanted to study and she was telling me, 'When you come here I can help you. I can help you to get the kids over.' I looked at that as a lifeline. Oh my God, is this really happening to me? Is it the end of a life of pain? I felt as though a saviour had come to me. I called her my guardian angel. I was very naïve. The thing with traffickers is they tell you what you want to hear.

The International Labour Organisation (ILO) estimates there are 2.4m people worldwide who have been trafficked into forced labour. According to a report published in 2008, there are 270,000 victims in industrial countries, including the UK.

I remember travelling to the airport. My friend and her husband were on either side of me in the vehicle. I asked myself, 'what are you doing?' My friend was very reassuring and kept telling me I was doing the right thing. It was the first time I'd been in a plane or even left my country, I found the whole experience quite frightening. I was strip-searched at the airport and held for 11 hours when I arrived in London. The Nigerian lady met me at the airport, I ran into that woman's arms even though she was a total stranger. I thought I had built a relationship with her. I cried my eyes out. She took me straight to her home.

It was a big house with four bedrooms. There was another woman in the house, she was from my country. K was three or four years older than me. I remember when I got there I was amazed at the amount of housework K was doing. She showed me a picture of when she came to the UK. There was a drastic change – she'd dropped three dress sizes. It jolted me to think what was happening here but by then it was too late. My husband had realised I'd left him and I couldn't go home. I was between a rock and a hard place.

K had been with the woman for a year; at the beginning she kept saying she was really nice. She was saying, 'She's so lovely, she's really nice to me and she's going to help you.' I felt indebted – I didn't have any inkling of what the woman had in store for me. K said you have to be appreciative, she didn't open up to me but she started giving me some signs. She said, 'Just obey her, don't do anything to upset her, she can be really mean.' Later on I realised that the only way for K to leave was for her to get and train her replacement. That was me. The only way I could leave would be for me in turn to get my replacement.

It is often assumed that people are mainly trafficked for the purpose of commercial sexual exploitation. ILO estimates indicate, however, that 32 per cent of all victims were trafficked into labour exploitation, while 43 per cent were trafficked for sexual exploitation and 25 per cent for a mixture of both. (ILO, 2008)

My day started at 6a.m. By 6.30 I had to be downstairs with K and the work started. They had two little kids, a boy and a girl, and we had to get them up and give them breakfast. We took the boy to the nursery, a three-mile walk there and back, and came back to clean the house from top to bottom. The cleaning involved washing all the dishes, washing the floors, cooking, doing the family laundry, gardening – raking up leaves, sweeping, tidying, pruning the plants – making the beds, taking out the bins, sweeping the stairs and wiping the walls, ironing and looking after any guests. All of this I had to do without fail and within a certain time each day.

The boy was in school for three hours, and then we'd go and get him, another three-mile walk. We'd come back, feed the kids, bathe them and do more cleaning. The lady would run her finger along the wall and say, 'You've got to do it again.' Whenever I left the house K was with me, they didn't allow me to speak to anyone. I could only go in the garden with K in case I spoke to the neighbours. The lady said that she preferred people from the Caribbean because we're hard workers and very obedient.

A major root cause of human trafficking is the lack of decent work, especially in the source countries of trafficked victim. However, at the destination of their journey, the skills of migrant workers are also devalued and employment is largely informal. (ILO, 2008)

I felt like a child, they were monitoring my movements. I remember asking her a question: 'What if I don't want to stay with you?' No one has to give an answer to you. She would say, 'I bought you. When I'm tired of you, I'll say you can leave.' That's when I knew I was in trouble. For years I blamed the authorities, they were turning a blind eye. These people could have killed me and no one would have been the wiser. You just have to pray they don't kill you, that you don't get ill. You just have to pray that some miracle or something will happen so you can escape.

We had a single bed so we took turns to sleep in the bed and on the floor. When the woman had visitors we had to give the bed up. I ate when they had finished eating. Most of the time I would eat late, by the time I finished work I couldn't even eat. This woman knew about my past, the physical and emotional abuse. She didn't physically abuse me, it was mental abuse. She would say, 'You are like filth. The only thing you are good for is cleaning the kitchen and my baby's bum.' This is the woman I had opened up to, I had told her my worst experiences. Words go far deeper than physical wounds.

After three months K left. They took her to the airport. The work was much harder for one person; it was midnight or 1a.m. before I got to bed. There was no part of my body that didn't feel pain. When K left the woman produced a contract for me. It stated I would be paid £400 a month. [*The UK minimum wage at the time was £5.05 per hour, which works out at £202 for a 40-hour, five-day week. Crystal was working much longer hours, seven days a week.*] Winter was coming and I had never experienced an English winter in my life. I had nowhere to go. I signed it. Sometimes she gave me money but if she didn't pay me I couldn't complain. In other words, she really got her money's worth. It was a really disgusting thing for one human being to do to another human being.

In 2005, the ILO calculated that global profits from forced labour were $44.3bn (£27.5bn) each year, of which $31.6bn (almost £20bn) came from victims of trafficking. The largest profits – $15bn or £9.3bn – were made from people trafficked and forced to work in industrialised countries.

I just stashed away my money. By then they were giving me a certain measure of freedom and I made friends with a shopkeeper. I parcelled up some of my things in a carrier bag and hid them in the boy's pushchair, then I gave them to the shopkeeper. That was how I got some of my stuff out of the house. My opportunity came when the lady had to travel. She had to go to the Midlands, she was taking the kids with her. She left her husband in the house; he was careless and left the door open. I left most of my things in my room, it was a case of taking the chance when it came. My heart was pounding.

When I escaped I had a choice. How was I going to cover myself with food and shelter in winter? Either I had to go back into domestic servitude or turn to prostitution. I had had enough rape in my life so I went back into servitude. I had to work in order to keep sending money home to the people who were looking after my kids. I did three-and-a-half years of domestic work in all but this time I started collecting evidence of perpetrators who had trafficked women from my country. Because K had left me her phone, I had contacts with other women from my country. I convinced some of them to give me evidence. I became an informant.

I'm 41 years old and 28 or 29 years of my life has been abuse. I haven't been back to my country; I haven't seen my kids for eight years. It's one of the torments I have to live with, on top of the abuse. Nothing beats that. I tried to commit suicide in 2009. There is this saying that you have to reach rock bottom then you have nothing to lose. That's when your life can start to turn around.

My initial reason for coming to this country was for sanctuary and to study. In the last two and a half years I've worked my way up through my studies; now I'm hoping to embark on completing a qualification in management and leadership. Studying helps distract me from thinking about my past and my asylum situation. When I sat down in a classroom for the first time, I felt so intimidated. I was scared but also excited. I had a chance. People wouldn't be looking at me and judging me. I do a lot of mentoring and coaching with asylum seekers and refugees, and survivors of rape, incest and domestic violence. I'm just hoping to keep my sanity so I can be a good Mum to my kids.

In its 2012 report on Human Trafficking, the US State Department listed several Caribbean countries from which individuals have been trafficked for domestic servitude in the US, the UK and Canada. The Nigerian couple who kept Crystal a virtual prisoner when she first came to the UK were questioned by the British police but released without charge.

KEEPER OF THE FLAME

British journalism is not a particularly welcoming place for women. Three-quarters of news journalists on national newspapers are men, and women make up only a third of journalists covering politics and business.[1] They're also less likely to be appointed to senior editorial positions where crucial decisions about policy and personnel are made. That situation was vividly illustrated when the Leveson Inquiry into the culture, practice and ethics of the press held preliminary seminars in Westminster in the autumn of 2011. The guest list was a *Who's Who* of powerful people in journalism and it was overwhelmingly male. I contacted the secretariat and invited myself, which I was able to do as both a victim of phone hacking and a 'core participant'[2] in the inquiry, but what I saw at the Queen Elizabeth II conference centre was a vivid illustration of the gender divide at the heart of the national press. Most of the invited speakers were men, including the *Daily Mail* editor Paul Dacre, *Guardian* editor Alan Rusbridger, the former *News of the World* editor Phil Hall, the former *New Statesman* editor John Kampfner and the former *Sun* political editor Trevor Kavanagh. An ex-editor of the *Sun*, Kelvin MacKenzie, was also invited to make a presentation and his performance was symptomatic of a newsroom culture which is crude and arrogant. MacKenzie has long been a hate figure on Merseyside after he published an untrue front-page headline in the *Sun* about the behaviour of Liverpool fans during the Hillsborough disaster in 1989, but at the seminar he bragged about how rarely he checked sources. He also made a point of insulting the inquiry's chair, Lord Justice Leveson, claiming that the judge couldn't even win his case when he prosecuted the comedian Ken Dodd for tax evasion early in his career. MacKenzie later apologised in his *Mail* column but at the time his remarks were greeted with shock, followed by nervous laughter. When he finished speaking, I couldn't resist getting up and responding with an old Greenham Common slogan: 'Take the toys from the boys.' I don't know what proportion of the audience got the reference but MacKenzie had mentioned only one woman in his speech: 'Rebekah'. The former editor of the *Sun* and the *NoW* was so well known that he didn't need to use her surname, confirming the extraordinary position she had come to occupy in the British media.

During her heyday, Rebekah Brooks was the archetypal woman in the man's world of tabloid journalism. (In this chapter I refer to her by her original surname, Wade, until her marriage to the racehorse trainer Charlie Brooks in 2009 when she took his surname. On occasion, such as her evidence to the Leveson Inquiry, she appeared in the guise of 'Mrs Brooks' but talked about the period in her life when she was still Rebekah Wade.) It is an anomaly of the British press that the tabloids have produced more women editors than their upmarket rivals: women have edited the *Sunday Mirror*, the *People*, the daily and Sunday editions of the *Express*, the *Sun* and the defunct

NoW. Their presence hasn't done much to help other women rise through the power structure and it certainly hasn't challenged the tabloids' view of women, who feature in their pages as footballers' wives, topless models and sources of kiss-and-tell stories. So how was it that Rebekah Wade/Brooks was able to flourish in the brash culture of tabloid newsrooms? She occupied a masculine world without, apparently, losing her femininity, and her flaming red hair marked her out at social gatherings. She partied with prime ministers, pop stars and TV presenters, and socialised with top cops; she was even loaned a retired police horse, Raisa, by the Metropolitan Police, which an embarrassed David Cameron eventually had to admit he had ridden. She wielded extraordinary influence on British life, running populist campaigns and successfully demanding changes in government policy. During the 2010 general election campaign, when Cameron was leader of the opposition, he texted her twice a week and signed his messages 'LOL' under the mistaken impression that the abbreviation stood for 'lots of love'.[3] Until her resignation in the wake of the phone-hacking scandal, she displayed an apparently faultless grasp of how to negotiate male-dominated power structures. And for someone who made a career out of exposing the private lives of celebrities and politicians, she managed to guard her own privacy closely. Even at the height of her power, she rarely gave interviews, delegating the task of defending controversial campaigns to older, more experienced and usually male executives at the *Sun* and the *NoW*. But enough is known to piece together a picture of a woman who started as a secretary and became CEO of the country's most powerful news organisation, News International, in not much more than a decade.

Rebekah Mary Wade was born in a village near Warrington, a town between Manchester and Liverpool, in 1968. Her father was a tug-hand on a boat on the Manchester Ship Canal and her mother worked as a secretary in a local accounting firm. John Wade later started a successful gardening business but her parents eventually separated, on account of her father's drinking according to some accounts. According to a profile in *Vanity Fair*, colleagues at the *NoW* in the early days speculated about Wade's background but knew few facts. One recalled:

In the early days she used this accent, a girls' school accent, meaning she'd been poshly educated, but every now and then the accent would slip and you'd realise: 'Oh, yeah.' There were rumours of a father who 'was absent or who left', of some kind of abandonment or 'betrayal' that was felt deeply by her mother in particular, with whom Wade was, and still is, extremely close.[4]

Wade wasn't privately educated and she couldn't be accused of getting into journalism through family connections. She was an only child and went to a state school, Appleton Hall County Grammar, where she decided at the age of 14 that she wanted to be a journalist; she once said she spent her weekends and school holidays at the local paper, 'making tea and helping out'. When she left school, she spent some time in Paris where she attended a class – once again, the details are vague – at the Sorbonne. She also attended the London College of Printing, where she returned to give the prestigious Cudlipp lecture in 2009, but her career in newspapers began in her home town. Warrington housed a print-works owned by Eddie Shah, a local-newspaper proprietor who challenged the print unions and started his own national title, *Today*, in 1986. Shah owned a tabloid called *The Post*, also based in Warrington, and Wade found an opening there in 1988 as 'Eddie Shah's tea girl'.[5] She swept into the office with characteristic bravado, as the *Post*'s features editor, Graham Ball, recalled:

> She came up to me and said, 'I am going to come and work with you on the features desk as the features secretary or administrator.' I said, 'I'm afraid that's not going to be possible because next week I'm going to London,' and I thought nothing more of it. The following Monday, I got to our new office in London and there she was. She did everything with great finesse, she was very clever.[6]

The *Post* soon closed and Wade got a job, variously described as a secretary or personal assistant, at the *NoW*. Little is known about this period in her career but Roy Greenslade, later to become editor of the *Daily Mirror*, met her not long after she made her move into journalism. She was young, eager and still learning the ropes, as he recalled:

> She encourages you to feel that you're on her team, you're on her side. She'd say, 'What should I do about this? How would I handle that?' And of course once you've given that kind of advice, you are much less likely to be critical.[7]

Wade was already establishing the *modus operandi* she would use in her ascent to the editorships of two national newspapers, flattering male colleagues and learning how to network. Her second statement to the Leveson Inquiry is factual to the point of dullness about her startling trajectory:

> In 1994 I became Features Editor. In 1995, although continuing to look after features, I became Senior Associate Editor of the *News of the World* and, shortly afterwards, Deputy Editor. The Deputy Editor was responsible for editing when the Editor (at that time Phil Hall) was on holiday, and so, in 1996, at the age of 27, I edited my first edition of the *News of the World*.
>
> In 1998 I was appointed as Deputy Editor of *The Sun*. I remained there for two years before returning to the *News of the World* in 2000 as Editor …
>
> At the beginning of January 2003, I became Editor of *The Sun* where I remained until I became CEO of News International in September 2009.

Wade gives very little away here, apart from a fleeting admission of her pride when she edited the *NoW* for the first time. But it's clear that by 1994 her career had moved up several notches and the paper's then editor, Piers Morgan, described her as a 'real rising star' when she got the footballer Paul Gascoigne to admit that he had beaten up his fiancée Sheryl Kyle. Like the true tabloid journalist she aspired to be, Wade was already homing in on the personal lives of celebrities, extracting sensational details about quarrels and break-ups. Morgan and Wade were ambitious, close in age and ready to take risks to get stories, and in his diary Morgan sounds almost in awe of Wade's willingness to get involved in cloak-and-dagger escapades. In the middle of the 1990s, there was intense interest in the disintegrating marriage of the Prince and Princess of Wales, who were not yet divorced, and an army officer called James Hewitt had recently entered the picture. Morgan took on a *Sunday People* reporter who had gone out of his way to cultivate Hewitt, who was reputed to be Diana's lover, and in July 1994 Hewitt agreed to meet a team from the *NoW*. The rendezvous was to take place at the Carlton Towers Hotel in Knightsbridge and Wade set about preparing the venue. Morgan wrote in his diary:

> Rebekah booked a suite and sent over a little 'recce' team in the morning to kit it out with secret tape devices in various flowerpots and cupboards. If all else fails we can always expose him later for even thinking of ratting on Di.[8]

The tabloid fascination with Diana did not abate and a few months later Morgan learned that the *Sunday Times* was about to serialise Jonathan Dimbleby's biography of Prince Charles. The two papers had the same proprietor but that did not diminish the rivalry between them: Morgan sent Wade, disguised as a cleaner, to the room where the *Sunday Times* collated different sections of the paper. She hid in a lavatory for two hours, waiting for the presses to start, burst out of her hiding-place and grabbed one of the first copies. The stunt allowed the *NoW* to run a spoiler in its second edition claiming that Charles had never loved Diana, based on the purloined *Sunday Times* splash.

Despite her dazzling ascent, Wade was not immune from the ingrained sexism of the newspaper industry, as she recalled in her Cudlipp lecture:

When, at the age of 27, I was made deputy editor of the *News of the World*, some struggled with the concept. At the corporate golf day, a senior male executive lost the buttons off his shirt. The editor and I were busy meeting and greeting our high-profile guests when suddenly a golf shirt and some buttons were thrust into my hand.

'When you've got a minute, darlin' – sew 'em back on for me, I'm teeing off in twenty minutes.' Despite needlework not being my strong point, I did have the shirt ready in time.

And we were all sorry to hear what happened to him.

It is a carefully crafted anecdote with a sting in the tail. It also gives a flavour of how Wade operated: not complaining, as many women would have done in such circumstances, but biding her time. Her ruthlessness would emerge on many occasions, not least her handling of a sensitive story in the *Sun* about the health of the younger son of Gordon and Sarah Brown, but it was leavened by a taste for laddish stunts; it might not have endeared her to colleagues but it certainly eased her path through the macho world of tabloid newsrooms. Wade never lost her taste for dressing up but when she became editor she delegated it to subordinates, as a former *NoW* reporter, Graham Johnson, recalled in his book *Hack*:

Rebekah piped up again with another stroke of genius: 'I want you to get dressed up as Sherlock Holmes and

I want you to investigate these unexplained mysteries. I want you to go to the Himalayas and find out about the Yeti. Has the trail gone cold on Lord Lucan? Is he still alive? I don't know. I want to know. Is there a monster in Loch Ness? I want you to go there and see.'[9]

Johnson was so anxious to please Brooks that he eventually went in pursuit of the 'beast of Bodmin', one of the mythical 'big cats' which supposedly roam the British countryside. Johnson and a *NoW* photographer hired costumes before leaving London and set out across Dartmoor dressed as Dr Watson and Sherlock Holmes. When the beast predictably failed to materialise, they faked the pictures using a puma from a local wildlife park. Returning to London, Johnson discovered to his dismay that Wade had booked TV advertising on ITV and Sky to announce the *NoW*'s amazing 'discovery'. The deception came out, and he and the photographer were promptly sacked.

A terror of being seen to take things seriously is a hallmark of newsroom culture, producing lurches in tone between levity and censoriousness. It's an uneasy coexistence, perfectly illustrated by what happened to another of Wade's reporters, Charles Begley, on the day of the 9/11 terrorist attacks on the East Coast of the US. Wade had decided that Begley had a passing resemblance to the main character in J. K. Rowling's novels and she ordered him to become the *NoW*'s Harry Potter correspondent. This involved turning up at the office in costume, an instruction which was not relaxed even when hijacked planes ploughed into the World Trade Center and the Pentagon. Begley was 'dumbstruck' and didn't turn up for work the following day, telling the assistant news editor, Greg Miskiw, that he couldn't bring himself 'to prance about as Harry Potter' when so many people had died. Miskiw was sympathetic to begin with but later rang Begley to ask what he intended to do, making one of the most famous statements about the nature of tabloid journalism: 'Charles, this is what we do – we go out and destroy other people's lives.'[10]

Miskiw's assertion had very nearly come true a year earlier when Wade embarked on her notorious campaign to 'name and shame' convicted sex offenders in the *NoW*. The newspaper's campaign led to mob violence, cars being set on fire and innocent people being targeted by vigilantes, but Wade was unrepentant. She recalled how the campaign started in her Cudlipp lecture:

The entire nation grieved over the abduction and murder of eight-year-old Sarah Payne and like everyone else I was deeply moved by this terrible tragedy.

I had just joined the *News of the World* as editor and after the daily pace of *The Sun*, I was frustrated by the waiting room atmosphere of a Sunday paper newsroom on a Tuesday.

So I took a chance and drove down to see Mike and Sara Payne who were still staying with Sarah's grandparents. The press pack who were outside waiting for the next police press conference, were more than a little surprised when I turned up on the doorstep.

I introduced myself to the Family Liaison officer and I told him I was the editor of the *News of the World* and I would like to offer my help and support to the Payne family.

Inexplicably Mike and Sara agreed to see me and repercussions of that meeting started the campaign you know as Sarah's Law.

Sarah's Law was a campaign to give parents the right to know if a convicted sex offender moved into their area. It raised all sorts of problems, not least the danger of vigilante attacks, but Wade brushed aside every objection. She announced that the *NoW* would publish the names, addresses and photographs of every convicted paedophile in the country until she got what she wanted, and in the first two weeks of the campaign alone the paper identified 83 men. The result was predictable: on the Paulsgrove estate in Portsmouth, an angry mob attacked the flat where a convicted paedophile, Victor Burnett, had been housed after his release from prison. According to the police, five families – none of them with links to paedophiles – had to be moved from the estate for their own safety.

Facing ferocious criticism, the *NoW* suspended the campaign. In the light of the Jimmy Savile allegations, it's clear that Wade was going after 'soft' targets, men who'd already been convicted, rather than powerful paedophiles like the DJ and his cronies; the *NoW* campaign could reasonably be accused of encouraging the myth that men who molest children are, almost without exception, to be found on council estates, not having the run of hospitals and popping in to see Prince Charles. But Wade used her Cudlipp lecture to round on her critics, appealing not for the first time to popular opinion: 'Parts of the media went on the attack with a blatant disregard for the facts of the campaign or more importantly their readers' opinions on the matter,' she said bitterly. In her second Leveson statement, she adopted a less bullish tone, excusing mistakes on the curious ground of urgency:

> I accept this could have been done better with more time but I balanced that with a need to highlight this issue while the readers were aware of the story. Some people were included in the list that should not have been grouped with serious paedophiles. There were risks of vigilantism ...

In the same statement, she defended her campaign for the sacking of Sharon Shoesmith, director of children's services in Haringey, North London, at the time of the dreadful 'Baby P' case. A 17-month-old boy, Peter Connelly, died in August 2007 after suffering horrific injuries over a period of eight months. The child's mother, her boyfriend and his brother were sent to prison in connection with his death, and it later emerged that the mother had concealed the fact that she had a new relationship from social workers. Even so, the boy's injuries had been missed by a long list of people, including doctors and social workers, and the *NoW* delivered a petition to Downing Street demanding that heads should roll. Shoesmith went to court, where her lawyers successfully argued that she was the victim of 'a flagrant breach of natural justice' and had been driven from her job by a media witch hunt.[11] The Appeal Court ruled she had been wrongfully dismissed, but Wade once again appealed to the court of public opinion, telling Leveson:

> With the campaign concerning Haringey Council I am sure that we tapped into and reflected the public mood,

but we were criticized for being tough and harsh and some will say that we should have acted with more restraint. *The biggest risk* is to launch a campaign that the newspaper's readers have no interest in, because this means you have misjudged them [my italics].

It's clear from her witness statements and evidence that Wade made no distinction between morality and populism, repeatedly citing the views of *NoW* and *Sun* readers as sufficient justification for controversial campaigns. 'I accept that there is an associated risk that campaigns can be seen, wrongly, as media witch hunts,' she told Leveson in a dismissive aside.

In fact, despite the violence and criticism that followed the original Sarah's Law campaign, Wade periodically revived her 'naming and shaming' policy towards sex offenders. Mistakes continued: in March 2003, shortly after she became editor of the *Sun*, the paper used a photograph of an entirely innocent man in place of a convicted sex offender. When the error was pointed out, the paper merely apologised for the 'hurt and embarrassment caused by our report', but the man asked for police protection and later received damages. Wade's friendship with Sarah Payne's mother, whom she described as 'an incredible woman', endured for many years but it was to have a curious coda. In July 2011, Sara Payne wrote an article for the final edition of the *NoW*, praising its journalists as 'good and trusted friends'. A couple of weeks later, the police revealed that a mobile phone given to her by the paper during its Sarah's Law campaign might have been hacked. Friends said that Payne, who had been partially paralysed by a stroke two years earlier, was 'absolutely devastated' by the revelation. Brooks (as she had now become) described the allegation as 'abhorrent' and called for a full investigation.

Her women friends included another Sarah, who was married to Gordon Brown; the barrister Cherie Booth, who was Tony Blair's wife; and much later Samantha Cameron. Brooks told Leveson:

In the earlier years I became close friends with [Tony's] wife Cherie Blair – who was a great advocate of women's equality – and also with the Blairs' closest advisors including Alastair Campbell and his partner Fiona Millar.

Wade acknowledged that her friendship with Cherie Booth was tested when the paper published stories which were 'difficult and embarrassing for the Blairs' but her relationship with Sarah Brown was more enduring. Indeed, she provided a fascinating insight into the nexus of power into which she had managed to insert herself in 2008, when Brown had been Prime Minister for a year:

The year I turned 40, Sarah [Brown] was concerned that I had not planned any birthday celebrations. The same year, both Elisabeth Murdoch [Rupert Murdoch's daughter] and Wendi Murdoch [Rupert's wife] also celebrated their 40th birthdays and so Sarah invited all three of us with some mutual friends to have dinner at Chequers [the Prime Minister's country residence] and, due to logistics, to stay over that night and leave after breakfast … Gordon Brown was not present at the dinner but he may have been there the next morning before we all left.

It's a laconic announcement, giving the impression that she saw the Prime Minister so frequently, or was so unimpressed by his presence, that she barely registered whether or not he was there. In retrospect, it's surprising that Wade and Sarah Brown remained friends at all after Wade's decision in 2006 to reveal on the front page of the *Sun* that the Browns' second son was suffering from cystic fibrosis, a debilitating condition which the family understandably wished to keep private. She told the Leveson Inquiry she wouldn't have run the cystic fibrosis story if the Browns had asked her to withhold it but Brown challenged her account, categorically denying that his wife had given her consent to the story appearing in the paper. Brown said that he and his wife were presented with a *fait accompli* and had no choice over the publication, which distressed them enormously. Asked by Robert Jay QC, counsel to the inquiry, why Sarah Brown did not end her friendship with Wade at this point, the former Prime Minister described his wife as 'one of the most forgiving people' who 'finds good in everyone'.

In the event, it was Brooks's decision to switch allegiance to Cameron's Tories that sounded the death knell. Brooks said her in statement:

In the end, the events of Autumn 2009, in particular *The Sun*'s coverage of Afghanistan and support for David Cameron, made it difficult for Sarah and I to be as close as we had been. Indeed, since the election in 2010, I believe we have only seen each other once at a mutual friend's party.

A cynic might observe that the Browns were no longer significant political players after they left Downing Street in 2010. Indeed, Brooks had begun courting Samantha Cameron seven months earlier, sending a gushing text to her husband on the eve of his conference speech in October 2009: 'But as always Sam was wonderful (and I thought it was OEs that were charm personified!).'[12]

It's clear from these and other anecdotes that Wade/Brooks prompted extreme reactions, and certainly not just from admirers. One of the problems with these accounts is that some of them come from not-entirely-reliable sources, and it's not hard to detect a vein of sexism. The former *NoW* features editor, Paul McMullan, met Wade early in her career and eventually became one of her most candid critics. McMullan, who left journalism and became a pub landlord, famously became the target of a sting by the actor Hugh Grant who secretly recorded a conversation in which McMullan boasted about bad tabloid behaviour; he would later transfix the Leveson Inquiry in November 2011 with his claim that 'privacy is for paedos'. McMullan's recollection of a young and ambitious Rebekah Wade was unflattering:

> She was sweet but out of her depth. Most of her ideas seemed to come from old copies of *Cosmopolitan* magazine she'd seen at a doctor's surgery. She used to congratulate journalists for doing the simplest things.[13]

There is no doubt that McMullan blamed Brooks for closing the *NoW* and putting almost 300 of his former colleagues out of a job. Even his attempt at balance was waspish: 'She was so hopeless, she made you want to protect her.' Wade also features prominently in *Hack*, where Johnson offers a highly coloured description of his former editor:

> On paper, Rebekah Wade should have been sexy. Tall and slim, an English rose with a killer streak, deadly as nightshade. But in the flesh she was strangely sexless, her femininity scraped barren by a corporate zealotry incongruous with her alabaster skin and floral prints.[14]

Johnson's description of Wade as an 'English rose' may reflect a conscious strategy on Wade's part, designed to dissociate her from the semi-naked women who regularly appear in the pages of the *Sun* and the *NoW*. (The dark dress she wore for her appearance at the Leveson Inquiry, with its Peter Pan collar and cuffs, certainly looked as though it had been chosen to suggest innocence and purity; the subliminal message was that she was the victim of a witch hunt.) Tabloid journalists are so obsessed by sex and genitalia that they could be living examples of Freud's theory of the 'primal scene', which he described thus in 1925:

> Finally, analysis shows us in a shadowy way how the fact of a child at a very early age listening to his parents copulating may set up his [*sic*] first sexual excitation, and how that event may, owing to its after-effects, act as a starting-point for the child's whole sexual development.[15]

Sex stories often feel as if they've been written by reporters who are still, at heart, little boys peering guiltily round the door into their parents' bedrooms – a point I made when

I gave evidence at the Leveson Inquiry. The fact of sex constantly seems to surprise them and their vocabulary – boobs, bonking, shagging – is correspondingly infantile. The impact of this obsession on our understanding of gender is obvious, not least in the way it reinforces traditional sex roles. So what was Wade's impact when she became editor of the country's two top-selling tabloids? If it offered her an opportunity to change things, it's one she chose not to grasp even though she was one of the founder members (and later chair) of the pressure group Women In Journalism. Wade ran a campaign against domestic violence in the *Sun* in 2005 but it came to grief when she herself was arrested at 4a.m. on suspicion of assaulting her then husband, the actor Ross Kemp. She spent eight hours in police custody in south London before being released without charge, saying only that a row had 'got out of hand'.[16] At the Leveson Inquiry, she denied a rumour that Rupert Murdoch sent a suit to the police station where she was being held so she could face the world looking smart and uncrumpled. The denial was coupled with a complaint that Robert Jay QC was expecting her to respond to 'gossipy items' and she went on to accuse the inquiry and the media of sexism. She claimed that a lot of the coverage of her was 'gender-based – if I was a grumpy old man of Fleet Street no one would write a first thing about it'. It was a breath-taking piece of cheek, especially among commentators who recalled Wade's treatment of the former Labour Cabinet minister Clare Short.

Before she became editor of the *Sun*, it was widely believed that Wade disliked Page 3 and she was even said to have lobbied a previous editor, David Yelland, to abolish it. If so, she underwent a swift change of heart, publishing a photograph of 'Rebekah from Wapping' on Page 3 of her first edition. Four years later, she sanctioned vicious personal attacks on Short when the MP revived an earlier campaign to get rid of topless pictures. The paper described Short as a 'killjoy' and gave space to some of its 'top glamour girls', encouraging them to jeer at Short's appearance. One branded her 'jealous', while another declared 'just because she's fat and ugly doesn't mean to say we all have to cover up.'[17] This kind of bullying of women about their appearance is not unusual in tabloid newspapers and it didn't damage Wade's position in the NI hierarchy, where she succeeded in enlisting a series of powerful male mentors. Among them was one of Rupert Murdoch's closest confidants, Les Hinton, who had worked for Murdoch for almost half a century by the time the phone hacking scandal ended his career in 2011. Crucially for Wade, Hinton became executive chairman of NI in 1995 and she impressed him so much that he threw a 30th birthday party for her at the Belvedere restaurant in Holland Park. According to Wade, Hinton played a key role in her promotions between 1995 and 2000, speaking to her daily and steering her towards a role at the very top. Her growing importance in the company brought her into contact with Murdoch, whose first direct involvement in her career came, as she told the Leveson Inquiry, when she was appointed editor of the *Sun*: 'Thereafter we were in regular contact, although I still continued to report to Les Hinton on a daily basis.'

But the growing warmth between editor and proprietor had been noted as early as 1998, later prompting rumours – which Wade denied – about them swimming together when the tycoon visited London. People who watched the friendship grow told *Vanity Fair* that Murdoch was 'devoted' to Wade or even 'besotted' with her, although there has never been any suggestion that their relationship was sexual. Indeed, a profile in the *Daily Mail* described Wade as 'part nurse, part protector', citing an occasion when she was overheard asking Murdoch if he had taken his pills. The paper quoted one of Murdoch's friends, who said:

> She watches over him and makes sure he is comfortable with whoever he's talking to; making sure his glass is filled. Rupert's not young any more, and it was clear that the older he got, the more he relied on her. She made herself indispensable.[18]

Wade eventually began to be talked about as Murdoch's 'fifth daughter', in addition to the four biological daughters he had with his three wives. Whether the relationship caused friction in the family is hard to know, and Elisabeth Murdoch firmly denied reports that she once railed that Wade and her brother James had 'fucked the company'. But it was evidently a symbiotic relationship: Murdoch needed Wade and vice versa, with the tycoon arguably playing as significant a role in her life as her husbands.

Wade has married twice, each time choosing a husband who reflected the social and political milieu she wanted to inhabit at the time. Early on, as the Murdoch papers switched support from the Tories to New Labour before the 1997 general election, Wade got engaged to Kemp. He was four years older and his background – he was born in Barking to a hairdresser and a police inspector – was similar to her own. Kemp's best-known role at the time was

Grant Mitchell in the long-running soap *EastEnders* but he was also (and still is) a well-known Labour supporter. The engagement was reported in the *Warrington Guardian* in July 1996, less than a year before Tony Blair became Prime Minister, and the paper revealed that Wade's father hadn't heard of his prospective son-in-law until she called to say she was getting married.[19] John Wade died suddenly six weeks later, aged 50, and the couple seemed in no hurry to marry. The wedding eventually took place in Las Vegas in 2002 and Wade didn't change her name, possibly because it wasn't done in the liberal circles in which she then moved. Gordon Brown, David Blunkett and Cherie Booth attended the 40th birthday party Wade hosted for Kemp in 2004; her arrest for splitting his lip the following year came after an evening commiserating with Blunkett, who had just resigned from Cabinet for the second time in a year. There were other claims of disharmony, notably from the Labour MP Chris Bryant, who annoyed Wade during a hearing by the Culture, Media and Sport Select Committee in 2003 when he asked her whether the *Sun* ever paid the police for stories. Bryant is gay and he claimed that Wade subsequently approached him at a Labour party conference, exclaiming: 'Oh, Mr Bryant, it's after dark – shouldn't you be on Clapham Common?' Bryant says Kemp turned on his wife and snapped, 'Shut up, you homophobic cow.'[20] Wade and Kemp separated in 2007, almost unremarked by the media. Once again, it seems, one of her mentors came to the rescue; the satirical magazine *Private Eye* claimed that Hinton phoned newspaper editors, pleading with them not to publish stories about the breakdown of Wade's marriage. Wade and Kemp divorced in 2009.

Wade's second marriage was very different. She first met Brooks – Old Etonian, amateur jockey, former owner of a mail order sex-toy business, racehorse trainer and latterly a novelist – at the Oxfordshire home of the *Top Gear* presenter Jeremy Clarkson. Wade was married to Kemp at the time but she met Brooks again after the marriage ended and she rented a cottage on the Blenheim estate, which is owned by the Duke of Marlborough. Brooks was a school contemporary of David Cameron's brother and Wade's relationship with him cemented her role in what became known as the Chipping Norton set. Through Brooks, she mixed with a heady combination of politicians, business people and leading figures in popular culture: the Camerons, Elisabeth Murdoch and her husband Matthew Freud, Blur guitarist Alex James and Carphone Warehouse founder Charles Dunstone. Her promotion to CEO of NI was announced in June 2009, the month she married Brooks, with effect from September that year. Shortly before the wedding, *Tatler* published a profile of the glamorous couple. It began:

> When Charlie Brooks wakes up in the mornings at his barn in Oxfordshire, he likes nothing better than to fly to Venice from Oxford airport with his soon-to-be-wife Rebekah Wade, the dazzling redhead editor of *The Sun*, for lunch at Harry's Bar.
>
> Later in the day, after shopping and sightseeing, the couple fly back to London for dinner at Wiltons in Jermyn Street.[21]

There was a great deal more in this vein, dropping names which would be familiar to *Tatler* readers but probably not the general public. The wedding in London was followed by a lavish party next to a lake in the grounds of Sarsden, Charlie Brooks's country home. The guests included Sarah and Gordon Brown – still Prime Minister but visibly losing support – David and Samantha Cameron, Rupert Murdoch and the Freuds. Brown's attendance, dutiful or otherwise, did not stop the *Sun* endorsing Cameron a few weeks later, on the day of the Prime Minister's speech to the Labour party conference. But the full extent of Brooks's rumoured closeness to Cameron was confirmed only at the Leveson Inquiry, where she was forced to reveal those 'LOL' texts. Most embarrassing of all was that text on the eve of Cameron's speech at the Tory party conference in 2009 when she wrote:

I am so rooting for you tomorrow not just as a proud friend but because professionally we're definitely in this together! Speech of your life! Yes he Cam!'

The final three words appeared in the *Sun* just two days later, above a leader warmly praising the leader of the opposition.

By the age of 41, the scale of Brooks's triumph was evident. The ambitious girl from Warrington had risen to the top job in British journalism. She had married a neighbour of the next Prime Minister, boasted a warm friendship with Cameron and his wife, and was regarded as a surrogate daughter by one of the world's most powerful media magnates. It was a stunning achievement, underlined when Murdoch flew to London in July 2011 to deal with the media storm created by the *Guardian*'s revelation about the hacking of Milly Dowler's phone. Asked by a reporter about his immediate priorities, Murdoch's response was surprising: 'This one,' he said, nodding at Brooks. But even Murdoch could not save her job and Brooks resigned as CEO five days later.[22] Her close friend and neighbour, David Cameron, left it to an official spokesman to observe tersely that she had made 'the right decision'. It was a sudden end to a spectacular career, but not entirely without precedent. Throughout history, ambitious women have sought out powerful male mentors, often at the cost of their independence and friendships with other women. Rebekah Wade tried to preserve her femininity but she couldn't avoid becoming de-sexed in one crucial respect, identifying so closely with the misogynist culture of the newsroom that she became one of its guardians. By the time she turned into Mrs Brooks, she had transformed herself into one of the principal keepers of the patriarchal flame. Her rise and fall are a modern morality tale – and a warning to other women.

VEILED MESSAGES

One of the most arresting – and horrifying – images of the Arab Spring was the beating of a young woman by soldiers in Tahrir Square in Cairo on 17 December 2011. The incident was filmed as men in riot gear surrounded the woman during a demonstration, handling her so roughly that her black cloak (*abaya*) was pulled up and her blue bra exposed. Unmoved by her vulnerability, one of the men even went so far as to stamp on her exposed chest. Video footage of the incident was viewed around the world and the woman acquired a queasy nickname, 'blue bra girl', which became shorthand for the brutal treatment of female protesters by the security police and army. Among many such episodes, one had already become notorious: nine months earlier, on 9 March 2011, a number of women were arrested in Tahrir Square and several of them were subjected to so-called 'virginity tests'. One of them, 25-year-old Samira Ibrahim, later filed a case against the military for sexual assault. The military's initial response was to deny that the 'tests' had taken place but then the story changed: they had been necessary to protect the army from accusations of sexual assault or rape. Interviewed on American TV, an Egyptian general said:

The girls who were detained were not like your daughter or mine. These were girls who had camped out in tents with male protesters in Tahrir Square ... We didn't want them to say we had sexually assaulted or raped them, so we wanted to prove that they weren't virgins in the first place. None of them were [virgins].[1]

The implication – that only women who have never had sex can be raped – spoke volumes about attitudes to women among Egypt's ruling elite, but Ibrahim was not intimidated. This young woman, a marketing manager who wears the headscarf (*hijab*), comes from a family of dissidents and was first detained by the regime of President Hosni Mubarak when she was 16. In 2011, she chose to speak publicly about what happened to her in a military prison after around 20 female protesters were arrested, losing her job as a result. She described how two officers entered the cell where all the women were being held and asked which of them were married. Seven single women were then separated from the rest and told they would be subjected to the 'tests'. Ibrahim was taken to a bed in a corridor which was full of soldiers. She asked if they could move away but was 'examined' in full view by an army officer. She said:

He had his hand stuck in me for about five minutes. He made me lose my virginity. Every time I think of this, I don't know what to tell you, I feel awful. I know that to violate a woman in that way is considered rape. I felt like I had been raped.[2]

It took extraordinary courage for Ibrahim to talk openly about such matters. Nine months later, a court in Cairo ruled that the 'virginity tests' were illegal and ordered an end to the practice. Ibrahim welcomed the decision but three months later a military court cleared Ahmed Adel El-Mogy, an army doctor who had been accused of assaulting the women, of public indecency.

These incidents stoked loathing of the Supreme Council of the Armed Forces, which effectively ran Egypt for a time after the deposing of Mubarak early in 2011. But attacks on female demonstrators were by no means confined to the police and military. Women who stood beside male protesters during January 2011, risking their lives as they called for an end to the Mubarak regime, discovered that they were just as likely to be attacked by men who had nothing to do with the security forces. The situation became so bad that an Egyptian NGO, Nazra for Feminist Studies, began collecting testimony from women who'd been targeted in Tahrir Square. One of them, who went to the square with a group of male and female friends, described how she was attacked by a mob whose members grabbed her breasts, buttocks and crotch. She said:

> I cannot express how horrible the experience was. I was completely sexually assaulted by groups of men, pulling on me, grabbing every inch of my body. I remember looking at some of them, yelling at them. They all had the same smirk on their faces, they were enjoying attacking me, they were all enjoying it. It was a crazy face, like they had lost all their senses: they were acting like complete animals. Animals, that is the best way I can describe their behaviour.[3]

This young woman was rescued by a group of older men, who took her to a part of the square where they were protecting six other women. Her friend, who isn't Egyptian but had been to the square on several previous occasions to watch demonstrations, was thrown up against a wall where a motorcycle was parked. She said:

> I was standing on top of the bike while my friend and a few other men tried to make a half circle to protect me. But there were more men trying to hurt than protect me and I was grabbed all over and my pants and shirt were ripped. In that moment it was as if the men got even more crazy. My pant [sic] was pulled down by the many men and they raped me with their dirty fingers.[4]

This young woman said she didn't know who was trying to help her and who was merely pretending in order to get closer and join in the assault. She was dragged through a door into a hallway where around 20 men were waiting for her. She said:

> Again I was surrounded, this time from all sides in the middle of the floor. There was even a man lying on the floor being stepped on by the others, forcing his fingers between my legs. That happened from all sides and more fingers at the same time. I was sure that they wouldn't stop until I was lying dead in that hallway. I really tried to fight and protect my body but it was impossible.[5]

She compared these men to 'lions around a dead piece of meat'. She was eventually rescued by several other men, including an older man who laid about her assailants with a stick. A third victim who supplied testimony to the NGO was groped and had her *hijab* torn off. She asked:

> Who should I blame for this? Mubarak for destroying my country's education system so those men have no respect for women and have become just animals? Our useless police who are incapable of defending us? Our religious leaders who claim that they want what's best but they don't go to these young men and teach them what's right? Our educators who turned into business men? ... Our politicians who just want power? Who???!!!![6]

Unsurprisingly, this young woman felt conflicted, passionate about the revolution but furious about the way she and her friends were assaulted. She said:

> I know that many will not like that I wrote this about Tahrir Square, thinking I am trying to vandalise the image of the Egyptian revolution ... but this is not my intention. I have participated in almost all the battles and marches since Jan 28 2011 but sexual harassment in Egypt is growing and growing and we need to address it. We ignored it for too long and it is becoming a monster that is eating us all ... I feel hate towards those men who molested us ... I can't smile in the face of anyone that I don't know any more ... Hell, I can't smile the way I used to.[7]

Egyptian and foreign journalists were targeted as well. An American TV correspondent, Lara Logan, was surrounded in Tahrir Square, stripped and sexually assaulted; so was a

British journalism student, Natasha Smith, who described how men grabbed her breasts and forced their fingers inside her body. Other attacks received less attention, but some emerged in video footage posted on the internet, including a short film showing a mob attacking a screaming woman in Alexandria.

In fact, what's striking about the phenomenon of sexual harassment in Egypt is that it has been happening for years to women of all ages and backgrounds. Long before the revolution, some brave women had begun to campaign for the right to walk along streets and use public transport without being jeered and groped. Similar campaigns have been set up in other Middle Eastern countries, although they've tended to receive less publicity; feminist organisations have documented high levels of sexual harassment in Tunisia, even though it is widely regarded as having one of the best records in the region on women's rights. A business studies student said that harassment was part of everyday life in Tunis:

> You cannot avoid it. Men are in the street with you, and you have to go to school, you have to go to work. Because it is in our daily life, because it is our everyday experience, we end up accepting it. You leave your house mentally prepared. You just deal with it.[8]

But it is in Egypt that the phenomenon has been documented in greatest detail. In 2008, the Egyptian Centre for Women's Studies published its own research, based on interviews with men and women, on the prevalence of sexual harassment. The report, *Clouds in Egypt's Sky, Sexual Harassment: from*

Verbal Harassment to Rape,[9] offers a shocking picture of what girls and women routinely have to deal with: 83 per cent of Egyptian women in the survey reported that they had suffered sexual harassment, and 98 per cent of foreign women. Almost 47 per cent of Egyptian women said they had been harassed *on a daily basis*, and 52.3 per cent of foreign women said the same. But it was the interviews with men which produced the most startling insights:

- 62.4 per cent said they had harassed women. The harassment ranged from ogling women's bodies (49.8 per cent) and shouting sexually explicit comments (15.9 per cent) to unwanted touching (13.4 per cent), following and stalking (12.2 per cent) and exposing the penis (4.3 per cent)

- 69 per cent of these incidents took place in the street, 49.1 per cent on public transport, 42.4 per cent in parks and coffee shops, 29 per cent in educational institutions, 19.8 per cent on beaches and 6.2 per cent in the workplace

- The vast majority of respondents said they harassed women approximately *once a day* [my italics]

- 41.8 per cent 'believe that harassing behaviour works to satisfy their repressed sexual desires'

- 23.1 per cent said that 'harassing women made them feel more masculine, more confident, stronger in relation to women'

- 19.3 per cent said they experienced 'no positive or negative feelings when they harassed women because they are accustomed to doing it since they were young'

- More than half (53.8 per cent) blamed sexual harassment on women for 'dressing indecently (unveiled)'. Two-fifths blamed the woman's 'beauty'. Other said they harassed women 'because women enjoy it'

In the midst of these confused and self-exculpatory responses, one thing stands out: more than half of men who sexually harass women blame the victims' appearance, even though there is no relation between this belief and what women actually look like. On the contrary, the survey found that *almost three-quarters* (72.5 per cent) of victims are veiled.

This brings us to a paradox, which is that Egypt has astonishingly high levels of sexual harassment at a time when women's dress has become markedly more conservative. A little history is necessary here: wearing the veil in its various forms is a recent phenomenon in modern Egypt, where the struggle for women's rights dates back more than a century. The Egyptian feminist Hoda Shaarawi, who was born in 1879, challenged the practice of wearing the veil when she arrived at Cairo's main railway station on her way back from an international conference in 1923. With a fine sense of drama, Shaarawi removed her veil in front of supporters waiting to greet her, beginning a movement that spread among educated women. (She founded the Egyptian Feminist Union in the same year.) By the 1950s, it was rare to see Egyptian women wearing the headscarf outside rural areas, in much the same way that middle-class women abandoned the *burqa* and *chador* in urban centres in Afghanistan and Iran. But in an astonishing turn-around, four-fifths of Egyptian women have gone back to wearing the *hijab* or even adopted the face-veil (*niqab*) in recent years.

Its reappearance is linked to a familiar phenomenon in authoritarian societies, where the absence of the institutions of civil society – free political parties and trade unions – means that opposition often coalesces around extremely conservative religious organisations. In Egypt, the most effective opposition to the corrupt and authoritarian governments of the second half of the 20th century came from the Muslim Brotherhood, a proscribed organisation which survived underground and in the country's grim prisons. Although its leadership renounced violence, the Brotherhood's offshoots included Egyptian Islamic Jihad, which assassinated President Anwar Sadat in 1981, and Jamaat al-Islamiyya, the terrorist group responsible for the massacre of 62 people, mostly European tourists, in Luxor in 1997. While the Brotherhood condemned Sadat's assassination, its leaders have always been uncompromising in their attitudes to women's dress. In interviews, they have accused unveiled women journalists of turning up 'naked', as Mona Eltahawy discovered when she went to interview the Brotherhood's Supreme Guide, Mohammed Mahdi Akef, in 2005. Eltahawy, who wore the *hijab* as a young woman but abandoned it at the age of 25, objected that she was actually wearing a short-sleeved t-shirt and trousers. It made no difference: 'According to God's law, you are naked,' Akef insisted. 'Your arms are naked, your head is naked. There is only one interpretation.'[10] (In November 2011, Eltahawy was arrested near Tahrir Square by riot police, sexually assaulted and had her left arm and right hand broken.)

This question of interpretation is crucial but first it's worth recording that women reported being harassed for not wearing the veil during the 2012 presidential election, which was won by the Muslim Brotherhood's candidate, Mohamed Morsi. A Coptic Christian, Mariz Tadros, wrote in the *Guardian* that women's rights were under attack in Egypt:

> Women, Muslim and Christian, who do not cover their hair or who wear mid-sleeved clothing are met with insults, spitting and in some cases physical abuse. ... And the Islamists have made it worse. A Coptic Christian woman said to me 'we and our Muslim friends who do not cover our hair get yelled at by men passing by telling us "just you wait, those who will cover you up and make you stay at home are coming, and then there will be no more of this lewdness".' It was, she said, as if they were gloating over the fact that we were being pushed off the streets.[11]

Of course 'lewdness' is in the eye of the beholder, who is almost always male. Rhetoric about 'modest' female dress is a cover for the male right to interpretation, which we've already observed in the Supreme Guide's definition of nakedness: if I say you are naked, you *are* naked. (It would be nice to encounter a monotheistic religious leader who insists on stricter dress rules for *men,* just for once. But I'm not holding my breath.) This notion has percolated down from the leadership of the Muslim Brotherhood to young men on the streets, as the BBC correspondent Bethany Bell found when she interviewed a group of young men on the Qasr al-Nil bridge in Cairo, where women often suffer sexual harassment. One of them said:

> If the girls were dressed respectably, no one would touch them. It's the way girls dress that makes guys come on to them. The girls came wanting it – even women in *niqab*.[12]

Another boy joined in, suggesting that any woman who wore a 'tight' *niqab* was 'up for it'. The distinction between a loose and a tight face-veil might seem a fine one to a disinterested observer, but these boys believed completely in their right to make the judgement. So did the Egyptian-born Grand Mufti of Australia, Sheikh Taj din al-Hilali, when he preached a sermon in Arabic at a mosque in Sydney in 2006. Al-Hilali famously compared unveiled women to meat, saying:

> If you take out uncovered meat and place it outside on the street, or in the garden or in the park, or in the backyard without a cover, and the cats come and eat it … whose fault is it, the cats or the uncovered meat? The uncovered meat is the problem … If [the woman] was in her room, in her home, in her *hijab*, no problem would have occurred.[13]

In Australia, al-Hilali's observations caused outrage, but there are many countries where they would have seemed unremarkable. In a limited sense, they perform a useful function, giving clerical authority to the lie at the heart of debates about the veil in its various forms, which is that it protects *women*. We've already seen that it doesn't: the experience of women in many countries, from Egypt and Tunisia to Afghanistan and the Gulf States, is that veiled women are as likely – often *more* likely – to be assaulted than women whose Western dress signals an assumption of autonomy.

Millions of women who believed the lie have discovered its untruth, but then they're told that being groped or raped is *their* fault because they didn't cover sufficiently. In reality, the situation is even worse than that: if the veil were genuinely a sign of profound respect for women, it would be reasonable to expect countries where it's habitually worn to be among the most progressive in the world in terms of women's rights. They're not, and that's easily demonstrated by examining the legal protection afforded to women in countries where it's the dress code for some or most of the female population. That includes most Middle Eastern countries, North Africa, some East African countries, and parts of South Asia. Only three Middle Eastern countries – Egypt, Morocco and Jordan – have laws against domestic violence.[14] Only two, Algeria and Iraq, have laws against sexual harassment.[15] Marital rape is not illegal in a single Middle Eastern country,[16] a particularly significant omission in Tunisia and Morocco where girls are sometimes forced to marry men who have already raped them. As the Lebanese activist Yalda Younes points out, women in many Arab countries suffer from the same problems, which are 'rooted in a similar culture independent from political regimes'.[17] But the lack of laws protecting women *is* a direct result of the low numbers taking part in political decision-making in the Middle East, as either members of parliament or ministers; the region has the lowest rates of female participation in government anywhere in the world.[18] Kuwait did not allow women to vote until 2005 and Saudi women have been permitted to vote, but only in local elections, since 2011. The absence of advocates for women's empowerment from government has other baleful consequences: a quarter of girls in the Middle East aged 17 to 22 have fewer than four years' schooling, and in South Asia the figure rises to 35 per cent.[19] Three countries where the veil is worn in one form or another – Afghanistan, Pakistan and Somalia – were among the five worst places to be born a woman according to a survey published in 2011.[20]

Domestic abuse and sexual violence happen everywhere but the absence of laws against them is a telling commentary on the status of women. In Europe, political Islam has had a degree of success in reinventing the veil as a symbol of resistance to 'Western' values, obscuring the fact that the choice *not* to wear it requires a great deal more courage. In some Middle Eastern and African countries, girls and women risk physical violence and even death if they do not submit to demands to cover. In Saudi Arabia, girls fleeing a fire at a school in Mecca in 2002 were forced back inside the building by religious police because they did not have time to cover themselves, resulting in 15 fatalities.[21] In Afghanistan, women live in fear of the return of the Taliban, who are so paranoid about women's faces and bodies that they will not allow them to be examined by doctors. In Iraq, the removal of a nasty dictatorship has been a setback for women's rights, with Islamist militia kidnapping and murdering prominent women who refuse to observe conservative dress codes. The return of the veil in Iraq was accompanied by a new constitution which gave more power to clerics and religious courts, while practices such as 'temporary marriage' – essentially a form of prostitution – were revived. The Human Rights Office of the UN Assistance Mission to Iraq (UNAMI) reported in 2008 that women had been warned not go to markets on their own. It continued:

> In other cases, women have been warned not to drive cars, or have faced harassment if they wear trousers. Women have also reported that wearing a headscarf is becoming *not a matter of religious choice but one of survival* in many parts of Iraq, a fact particularly resented by non-Muslim women [my italics].

Iraqi women who had been doctors, teachers, journalists and university lecturers were forced by Islamist militias to give up their jobs; also in 2008, UNAMI reported that almost 87 per cent of Iraqi women were not working outside the home. Iraq is by no means the only country where wearing the veil is a matter of survival, not choice, and to pretend otherwise is dishonest.

Since the veil does not protect women from male violence or reflect respect for the female half of the population, what does it actually do? First of all, it signals an acceptance that different and stricter rules apply to women. By wearing it, they cede the right of interpretation of what constitutes female 'modesty' to men – not just male clerics, as we have seen, but to men and boys who assume the right to dictate how women should dress and 'punish' them for supposed infractions. What some claim as a symbol of resistance is thus its opposite, a visual acknowledgement of women's lack of personal autonomy. A garment freighted with such meaning cannot be anything but problematic for anyone who believes that women have the same human rights as men; wearing the veil might not harm individual women who live in societies where their rights are enshrined in law and custom, but it demands acceptance for a practice which restricts the freedom of millions of girls and women elsewhere in the world. I don't doubt that some women in Europe and the US adopt it freely, but they are a minority in global terms, and we know that others come under pressure from clerics and male relatives to adopt it. That isn't to argue that the practice of adults wearing even the most extreme forms of the veil, such as the *niqab* or *burqa*, should be outlawed in Western countries, although it's reasonable to insist that girls under the age of 18 cannot make an informed choice to cover. The French ban on the face-veil is a mistake even though it is supported by some Muslim feminists, including Sihem Habchi, president of the admirable organisation *Ni Putes Ni Soumises*. In democracies, adults are allowed to make bad choices in relation to themselves, as long as they're not being forced to do it against their will.

What they can't expect is to have those choices go unchallenged, excluded from important political debates about rights and values. As Habchi points out, it is hypocritical to condemn wearing the veil in the Middle East and Asia while arguing that it means something quite different in Western democracies. Some Muslim feminists argue that it is merely a modest form of dress, a means of avoiding the sexual display which is a feature of popular culture in the West, but they've rather spectacularly missed the point. Even its least concealing form, the *hijab*, extends the definition of what's explicitly sexual from sites of anatomical difference to human hair, which is common to men and women, but the stricture resulting from it applies only to the latter. Indeed, there's an irony here: the veil is in itself a highly sexualised garment, drawing attention to the very part or parts of the body it's supposed to conceal. For that reason, it's disingenuous of women who cover completely in London or Paris to complain that people stare, just as they would if they spotted someone walking along the street without clothes; the two states, naked and fully veiled, are not that far apart because each of them makes an issue out of sex. When someone ventures out of her home in a *niqab* or *burqa*, whether she's in Birmingham or Kabul, the only information we have about her is that she's female. She might be young or old, a grandmother or a student, stylish or completely uninterested in her appearance, but she has no face, no features, no indication of character. What she does have – in effect, all she has – is gender. Thus a consequence of putting on the *niqab* or the *burqa* is to sexualise the entire body, reducing women to the status of ambulant sex organs. Secularists instinctively understand this, which is why the *niqab* causes such dismay and revulsion: if one woman can be persuaded to sacrifice her individuality in this way, it can and will happen to other women. Obviously this is a much greater risk in countries where Islamist governments are in power but no matter where it happens, the face-veil in its various forms is a dramatic symbol of inequality.

It is no accident that the Arab Spring brought all these matters into sharp focus. Most of the women who went to Tahrir Square to demonstrate against a corrupt, militarised government wore the veil, and they were targeted by men on both sides of the barriers. Let's be clear about this: Egyptian women thought of themselves as *protesters*, asserting their political identity, but they were brutally handled as *women*. That's what the soldiers were doing when they tore off that young woman's *abaya*, dragging her helpless body across the ground and exposing her underwear. No wonder she never came forward: she went to the demonstration believing she had rights, that she was a citizen like anyone else, and the soldiers shattered her illusion. At last we are approaching the core of the problem, which is what the veil represents for *men*. It spares them the necessity of ever having to treat women as equals, at home or in public places. This is the veil's true message, prettied up with excuses about modesty and safety, but it isn't hard to read.

COERCION

POSSESSION

Toby Day was a model husband and father. He was well known in the Leicestershire town where he lived and worked, refereeing football matches in his free time but never really switching off from his job as a police inspector. There were admiring mentions in his local paper – 'Dad detective Toby commended for off-duty arrests' was one headline[1] – while his wife Samantha, herself a former police officer, worked part-time as a nursery teacher. The couple lived in a modern semi-detached house in Melton Mowbray, with a small back garden for the kids: a daughter aged 15, a son of 13 and a second daughter who was six. Day liked to keep fit, running the London marathon one year in memory of a colleague, PC Melissa Ward, who'd been stabbed to death by an ex-boyfriend. At work, things could hardly have gone better, with Day and his team praised by their superiors for 'quite exceptional achievements … in tackling crime and anti-social behaviour'.[2] As Christmas approached in 2011, the two girls were excited when they were chosen to dance in the pantomime *Mother Goose* at Melton Theatre.

Then it all went wrong. On Thursday 8 December, the elder daughter ran bleeding from her parents' house to a nearby school. She had been stabbed several times but managed to escape via the back garden and raise the alarm.

Armed police hurried to the house where they found Day, his wife and the two younger children all suffering from knife wounds. They were rushed to hospital but both adults and the six-year-old died from their injuries. As the press began writing about a 'house of horrors', an even more horrifying fact emerged: the police acknowledged that they were not looking for anyone else in connection with the murders. Inexplicably to neighbours, family and friends, it became clear that Day had tried to slaughter his entire family and then turned the knife on himself. Shocked neighbours described him as 'the perfect neighbour', while the priest at Oakham parish church, who had known the Days for seven years, insisted that they were a 'lovely family' and 'regular worshippers'.[3]

Four days later, on Monday 12 December, four bodies were discovered in a fire-damaged bedroom at a house in Leeds. On this occasion, a father had succeeded in wiping out his entire family, using a knife on his wife and children, one of whom he then smothered to death. Not only that: neighbours recalled seeing Richard Smith washing his car on the Sunday morning, at a time when the police concluded that the rest of his family was already lying dead inside the house. It wasn't until the Sunday afternoon that Smith, who was 37 – the same age as Toby Day – barricaded himself into a bedroom, blocked the window with a mattress and set fire to the room. When police were called to the house they hesitated to go inside, suspecting that some kind of noxious chemical had been released, but they eventually went upstairs to find Smith's wife Clair and one-year-old Aaron dead from stab wounds; Ben, who was 10, had a knife wound in the chest but the actual cause of his death was suffocation. Once again, friends and family reacted with shock and horror, describing the Smiths as a 'perfect family'.[4]

In the days after these murder-suicides, photographs of both families were widely published in the press. What was striking was the way the pictures were posed, sending out the unmistakable message that each family was a loving, harmonious and integrated unit. Toby and Samantha Day had lined up with their children on holiday in the formation child–father–child–mother–child, arms around each other and smiling faces turned towards the camera; a second holiday snap showed Day, naked to the waist and clearly proud of a muscular torso, holding his wife (a little too firmly, with hindsight) and staring into her eyes. There is a disturbing possessiveness about Day, especially in the second photograph, which suggests that this is a man consciously performing the role of husband and father. There is a similar message in a posed picture of Richard Smith and his family in which he is the dominant figure in a father–child–child–mother formation, suggesting a man displaying his wife and children to the world. But the death toll of seven members of these two families in less than a week demonstrates that the carefully constructed impression of normality in the photographs cannot be correct. Not much is known about the dynamics in Richard Smith's family before he killed his wife and children, although detectives suspected he had been having an affair. But Toby Day's life was falling apart: he'd been sacked a week earlier after using the police national computer to check on a man he suspected of having an affair with his wife, and he told acquaintances his savings would last only a couple of months. Friends said he was 'very depressed' following his sacking, which seems to have come as a shock despite the fact that he must have known his behaviour at work was reckless. 'He did not see it coming and he just didn't know what to do,' one said. [5]

In the US, murder-suicides by a family member are known as 'family annihilations' or 'familicide'. They're a subcategory of murder-suicide, which is currently running at a rate of a dozen incidents per week, according to the Violence Policy Center.[6] Seven out of ten of these murder-suicides involve the killing of an intimate partner, and 94 per cent of the victims are women. There are far fewer incidences in the UK, mainly because it's more difficult to get hold of firearms,[7] but they happen on average about five times a year. Since so few perpetrators survive, there are rarely trials in which the circumstances leading up to the massacre can be examined; one of the effects of this is that cases of family annihilation are closed and filed as homicides rather than domestic violence, especially when there isn't a previous record of complaints by the man's partner. That doesn't mean much in itself, given that domestic abuse is so widely under-reported: victims of domestic abuse are more likely to experience repeat victimisation than victims of any other type of crime, suffering an average of 35 incidents before they report it to the police.[8] In cases of family annihilation, the absence of a documented history of violence encourages the popular misconception that the cause is an otherwise normal man 'snapping' under extreme pressure. Some mental health professionals have even put forward the bizarre notion that such men are trying to 'protect' their families, unable to bear the shame of a marriage break-up or losing the family home; in this scenario, the murderer is transformed into a misguided altruist, who tries to 'spare' his family the consequences of events he believes he should have been able to shield them from. It's an implausible theory, if not entirely unexpected in cultures still dominated by patriarchal notions, but the metamorphosis of family-man into family-annihilator requires more rigorous analysis. First and foremost, it needs to be shifted from the category of murder to domestic abuse, where its twisted dynamics shed a revealing light on the wider subject.

The single most striking feature about family annihilation is that it is a highly gendered phenomenon. While there is little difference in the numbers of mothers and fathers who kill children,[9] the vast majority of perpetrators of murder-suicides are men, accounting for 90 per cent of offenders according to the Violence Policy Center.[10] The men involved are often narcissists, keenly conscious of how they are perceived by the outside world, and driven by an abnormal need to maintain control. They may not be physically violent – such behaviour would challenge their view of themselves as perfect husbands and fathers – but they are likely to lay down strict rules for the family in terms of dress, social contacts and behaviour. Women whose partners kill their children often speak of having endured years of what amounts to bullying, and in 2012 the Home Office announced a consultation on whether the definition of domestic abuse should be widened to include what it called 'coercive control'. There has been resistance to the idea of recognising the central role of control in domestic abuse, and for a very straightforward reason: the phenomenon of family annihilation poses a challenge to cherished notions about the nature of family life. The fact that the perpetrator's interest in his family is obsessive, confirmed by an absence of close friends and little external support, gets missed because neighbours and work colleagues are deceived by attitudes they perceive as old-fashioned but certainly not threatening. Indeed, a common factor in murder-suicides is the way in which perpetrators seek to exclude the outside world, building up a family unit which is both idealised and defended against external influence. Such relationships start to break down when the female partner tries to challenge her husband's rules, perhaps by getting a job and having more contact with outsiders, and it is at this point that the man becomes physically violent or pre-existing violence escalates.

Another British case, in which six members of a single family were wiped out, illustrates this process all too well: in October 2006, a taxi driver called Mohammed Riaz killed his wife and four daughters as they slept in the family's terraced house in Accrington, Lancashire.[11] Riaz, who was 49, grew up in a remote area of Pakistan and came to the UK after an arranged marriage. His limited grasp of English reduced his job opportunities but his British-Asian wife Caneze pursued a career in community relations, working with other women from a South Asian background. After the death of her father, who had traditional ideas about gender, Caneze began to widen her circle of friends and encouraged the ambitions of her eldest daughter, Sayrah, who wanted to become a dress designer. Instead of enjoying his wife's success, Riaz became embittered and angry, especially when 39-year-old Caneze took the girls' side in an argument about the practice of arranged marriage.

Late one evening, Riaz made his way through the family's terraced house, sprinkling petrol on the furnishings and setting the building on fire. Caneze woke and tried to save her three-year-old daughter Hannah, who was sleeping beside her, but they were overcome by smoke; so were 16-year-old Sayrah, her younger sister Sophia, 13, and Alisha, who was 10. After killing his wife and daughters, Riaz set light to himself and died a couple of days later from dreadful burns. The couple's 17-year-old son survived only because he was terminally ill in hospital, where he died six weeks after the slaughter of his entire family.

The Riaz and Smith murder-suicides fit the pattern observed in the US by Professor Jack Levin of Northeastern University. He says:

> These are executions. They are never spontaneous. They are well planned and selective. They are not carried out in the heat of the moment or in a fit of rage. They are very methodical and it is often planned out for a long time. There are certain people the killer blames for his problems. If a friend came along, he wouldn't kill him or her. He kills his children to get even with his wife because he blames her and hates her. The killer feels he has lost control. Annihilating his family is a way of regaining control. It is a methodical, selective murder by a rational, loving father.[12]

If this offers a frightening insight into what look to outsiders like 'normal' families, it has to be placed in context. The scale of violence by partners or ex-partners is breathtaking: domestic violence remains the cause of 14 per cent of all recorded violent crime, even though it has come down from a high of 23 per cent in 1997.[13] Nearly one million women experience at least one incident of domestic abuse each year, while two women are murdered each week by a male partner or former partner.[14] Here is a sample of lethal incidents in the UK:

- Horden, County Durham, January 2012. Susan McGoldrick, 47, was shot dead by her partner, a taxi driver called Michael Atherton, who also murdered her sister Alison Turnbull, 44, and her niece Tanya Turnbull, 24. Atherton then killed himself. Susan's 19-year-old daughter was injured but managed to escape through a first-floor window. In November 2012, the Independent Police Complaints Commission criticised Durham police for failing to investigate Atherton's history of domestic violence when deciding whether he should be allowed to own firearms. In 2006, a handwritten note in his file included the words '4 domestics' and 'would like to refuse' in response to his request for a shotgun certificate. The recommendation was ignored and Atherton ended up owning six weapons. In 2008, his guns were seized after another domestic incident but they were later returned without licensing staff carrying out formal interviews with Atherton or members of his family.[15]

- Rochester, Kent, August 2011. Edite Titane, 22, was murdered by her jealous husband Agris Titans, aged 25, with whom she had a three-year-old daughter. The couple had married in Latvia and came to England to work as fruit pickers, but Titans became suspicious about Edite's friendship with a work colleague. Titans had a record of violence and the judge at his trial told him: 'You killed her because you were overcome with rage and jealousy.' Titans was jailed for life, with a recommendation that he should serve at least 13 years.[16]

- Tottenham, North London, April 2011. Nathaniel Brown stabbed his ex-wife to death in front of their two children as they returned from a barbecue in a local park. Brown, 27, stabbed Zandra Maxwell-Nelson, 24, up to 20 times in what a witness described as a 'methodical' manner. In 2007 Brown had been convicted of assaulting his baby son. Maxwell-Nelson left him in 2010, began divorce proceedings and started to build a new life. At the time of her death, she was working part-time in order to fund a university course.[17] Brown was jailed for life and told he would serve at least 21 years.[18]

- Leicester, February 2011. Joy Small, 24, and her two young children were murdered by her husband, Aram Aziz, an Iraqi Kurd, whose body was found shortly afterwards in a nearby country park. Joy had recently got back together with Aziz for the sake of the children, three-year-old Aubarr and Chanarra, aged two, even though she was afraid of him. After the murders, a friend said that Aziz had was extremely possessive and once poured petrol over his wife's head and tried to set her alight. 'He was an abusive monster,' the friend said.[19]

- Lower Ashtead, Surrey, December 2010. Laura Davies Jones was stabbed to death by her husband, Richard Davies Jones, a 34-year-old solicitor and former army officer. When she tried to leave the marriage Davies Jones killed her and stabbed himself. The couple had five children, one of whom wrote: 'Because of what happened, I am scared that he will come and get me, the same as he did my mum.'[20] Davies Jones was jailed for life, with a recommendation that he should serve at least 20 years.[21]

- Nottingham, October 2010. Casey Brittle, 21, was found dying of head injuries after being attacked by her former partner, Sanchez Williams. Brittle, who was the mother of a small child, called the police and asked for help on 11 occasions between September 2008 and August 2010. Williams was jailed for life for her murder. Nottinghamshire police were later criticised by the IPCC, which said she was 'a young mother who was killed by a man well known to local police for his propensity for violence and threatening behaviour'.[22]

- Ascot, Berkshire, October 2010. Joanna Brown was battered to death by her estranged husband, Robert Brown, who buried her body near Windsor Great Park. She was killed a week before her divorce hearing. Her best friend told the court that she was 'constantly' subjected to abuse after leaving Brown, who was a pilot with British Airways: 'He threatened her with a knife, he used to drive slowly past her house. It was intimidation on a scale you can't comprehend.' Brown was cleared of murder but convicted of manslaughter, and sentenced to 26 years in prison.[23]

- Birtley, Gateshead, July 2010. Raoul Moat, a nightclub bouncer who had just been released from prison, shot and injured 22-year-old Samantha Stobbart, the mother of his daughter, and killed her new boyfriend, Chris Brown. Moat, 37, had a history of violence and had beaten up Samantha on several occasions. After Brown's murder, Moat shot and blinded a police officer, PC David Rathband, before going on the run for almost a week; he eventually killed himself after a six-hour stand-off with the police in Northumbria. In his suicide note, Moat blamed Samantha for his rampage, saying: 'This hot and cold thing has pushed me too far and maybe now you will understand just what affect [sic] it's had on me.' Moat had two accomplices, Karl Ness and Qhuram Awan, who were later given long prison terms for their part in his crimes; before being released from jail, Moat threatened Samantha and asked Ness, 26, to go through her bins, check her Facebook page and sit outside her house to find out if she had a new partner. Awan, 23, admitted picking up Ness and Moat from the roundabout where the latter had blinded Rathband, and the two men helped him evade police for several days. Ness was convicted of murder and possession of a firearm with intent to endanger life, while Ness and Awan were found guilty of conspiracy to murder, attempted murder and robbery of a chip shop.[24]

- Southwark, South London, February 2010. Antoinette Say, 44, received a phone call from her estranged husband Jean, who told her: 'I have killed your children. Come and get the bodies.' Say, aged 62 and originally from Ivory Coast, was about to be evicted from his council flat after Antoinette left him, but he had been allowed to have the children to stay on a scheduled visit. Police found the retired concierge sitting next to the bodies of the children, Regina, aged eight, and 10-year-old Rolls, who had suffered knife wounds and blows to the head. He was said to have tormented his wife with violent, jealous and possessive behaviour before she left him, and police believe he killed the children to 'spite' her.[25] Say was sentenced to life in prison and told he would serve at least 30 years.[26]

- Rotherham, South Yorkshire, October 2010. Laura Wilson, 17, was repeatedly stabbed by her boyfriend, 18-year-old Ashtiaq Asghar, who threw her into a canal and stabbed her again in the top of the head when she tried to struggle out of the water. Laura was lured to the isolated spot by Asghar's neighbour Ishaq Hussain, 22, with whom she had a one-year-old child. Three days before the murder, she had told the families of both men that she had had sexual relationships with them. They were both furious and on the day before she died, Asghar sent a text to Hussain in which he said, 'I'm gonna send that *kaffir* bitch straight to hell.' Both men were charged with Laura's murder but Hussain was acquitted. Asghar admitted murder and was told he would serve a minimum of 17-and-a-half years in prison.[27]

- Cardiff, August 2009. Joanna Michael, 25, was murdered by her ex-boyfriend Cyron Williams, 19, in a 'ferocious and frenzied' attack which police compared to a horror movie. She had 74 separate injuries. On the evening of the murder, Williams found Michael in bed with another man and punched her in the face. He left and she called the police, but Williams returned before they arrived and attacked her so brutally that he broke the blade of his knife. He was jailed for life.[28]

• July 2009, Connah's Quay, North Wales. Karen McGraw, 50, was murdered by an ex-boyfriend she'd met on an internet dating site. Trevor Ferguson, 49, from Sale in Manchester, forced his way into McGraw's home and stabbed her with a filleting knife. She managed to escape but was trapped by gates she had installed in an attempt to keep him out, and he finished her off. Ferguson was jailed for life and told he would serve a minimum of 17 years.[29]

• Wombwell, South Yorkshire, May 2008. Tracey Grinhaff, 42, was murdered by her estranged husband. Gary Grinhaff placed a tracking device in his wife's car, suspecting she was having an affair, and bludgeoned her to death while their daughters, aged 13 and three, were asleep in nearby bedrooms. He then parked his car in nearby woods and used an electric drill to kill himself.[30]

• Barnsley, South Yorkshire, November 2007. Jane Lee, 51, was murdered by her estranged husband Robert, also 51, who was on bail for previously trying to strangle her. Jane called the police on the night of the first attack, six weeks earlier, but they arrested her for being drunk and she was locked in a cell until a custody officer noticed marks on her neck. Lee was banned from contact with his wife but he lay in wait for her outside a house where she worked as a cleaner, armed with a baseball bat and two knives. A passer-by tried to intervene when she saw Lee hit his wife with the baseball bat but he threatened her before stabbing his wife repeatedly. He had a history of violence and an earlier relationship ended in 2004 when he was convicted of assaulting his then partner. Lee was jailed for life and told he would serve a minimum of 19 years.[31]

* Arbroath, September 2007. Agnes Raffan, 58, was murdered by her husband Peter, 49, who said he could not face the fact that their house was about to be repossessed. Agnes called the police and was heard pleading with her husband, but she was dead by the time they arrived. He was originally charged with murder but his guilty plea to culpable homicide on grounds of diminished responsibility was accepted by the court. Raffan was sent to prison for eight years.[32]

* Cwmbran, Torfaen, July 2007. Fiona Erickson was killed by her husband Andrew, a 46-year-old taxi driver, who deliberately ran her over after a row. Eyewitnesses watched in horror as Erickson stopped at a roundabout, dragged his wife from their car and aimed it at her. The judge at Erickson's trial described it as a 'brutal killing' but the court accepted his plea of guilty to manslaughter on the grounds of 'provocation'. He was jailed for seven years.[33]

* Cannock, Staffordshire, March 2007. Diane Ingram, 61, was murdered by her ex-husband Harold the day before he was due to pay her £133,000 in their divorce settlement. Ingram, a 63-year-old retired miner, stabbed Diane with a screwdriver and went on the run. When he was arrested, Ingram described the marriage as '38 years of robbery' and said he was furious about the cost of the divorce. He was found guilty of murder and sentenced to life in prison.[34]

◆ Merseyside, June 2007. Monika Szmecht, 21 and originally
from Poland, was kidnapped, held prisoner for four hours
by her jealous ex-boyfriend, stabbed six times in the
stomach and set alight. She somehow managed to stagger
to a nearby house where she named her killer, 27-year-old
Anthony Clarke, before dying from her terrible injuries.
Clarke, who ran a taxi firm after being dishonourably
discharged from the army, was found guilty of murder and
jailed for life. The judge told him: 'Nobody who listened to
the evidence of how Monika died will fail to be horrified.
This murder began by you kidnapping [her] and keeping
her captive for almost four hours. You drove her out to
an isolated spot. You stabbed her six times and you set
her alight with the aid of a petrol can and when you saw
she was still moving, you stabbed her further. Despite
her extreme suffering she somehow walked, or perhaps
staggered, to a nearby house where she collapsed, naked
and smouldering. And she identified you as her attacker to
those who came to her aid.' Clarke's uncle, David Clarke,
and his best friend, Philip Savin, were originally charged
with murder but pleaded guilty to lesser offences. Clarke
was jailed for two years for assisting an offender after
the court was told that he helped his nephew dispose of
evidence and obstructed the investigation into Monika's
death. Savin got four-and-a-half years for assisting in the
kidnap and attempting to destroy evidence.[35]

◆ Cheadle Hulme, Greater Manchester, July 2006. Uzma
Arshad and her three children were battered to death with
a rounders bat by her husband, 36-year-old Rahan Arshad.
Uzma had left her husband but returned to live with him

shortly before the murders. After killing the children – Abbas, eight, Henna, six, and Adam, 11 – Arshad flew off on holiday to Thailand. The bodies were discovered three weeks later when a neighbour called the police. Arshad returned to Britain and was arrested at Heathrow airport, but expressed no regret for the murder of his wife who he described as 'that fucking bitch'. During his trial, he said he had been angered by the fact that his wife had started wearing Western clothes: 'It wasn't right for a mother and someone who came from Pakistan to change the way she dressed all of a sudden.' Arshad was jailed for life and told he would never be released.[36]

There are a number of striking features about these dreadful cases. One is the diversity of the perpetrators, who are male but don't fit single categories of age, class, religion or ethnic background. They range in age from 18 to 63, from manual workers to middle-class professionals, and their ethnic backgrounds include white British, British Asian, West African, Kurdish and Latvian; three are Muslim but religious affiliation, if any, isn't known in a majority of cases. Their victims included wives, partners, ex-partners, children and even other relatives.

There are common factors, however, and principal among them is motive. Jealousy and revenge crop up time and time again, for either leaving or planning to leave relationships, or for exposing a connection that the perpetrator hoped to keep secret. In every single case, the underlying issue is control; these are men responding furiously to profound social changes which mean women expect more equal relationships *and* are able to leave if their partners refuse to treat them decently. It's impossible to overstate how significant a shift this is: for most of recorded history, the way husbands treated their wives was regarded as entirely their own business; for centuries, women who left abusive marriages faced social disapproval, almost certain loss of contact with their children and quite possibly destitution. Even in Western democracies, it was only in the second half of the 20th century that the state began to take on the role of enforcing women's rights, which are now enshrined in a series of international treaties and domestic legislation. Spain's very first Equality minister, Bibiana Aido Almagro, encapsulated the change in a speech in 2009, when she recalled that the first act of the socialist government led by Jose Luis Zapatero on coming to power five years earlier was to pass a law against gender violence. She said that the new law provided a response to the most brutal proof of continuing inequality between the sexes:

> The fact that this was the very first law passed by the Council of Ministers showed not only the Government's concern for the problem, but also that for the first time gender violence would be considered *as a problem of public interest*, that it had stopped being a personal or private matter and had passed to the top of our country's political agenda [my italics].[37]

In 2005, special courts were created in Spain to deal with cases of domestic violence, and within two years almost 70,000 men had been prosecuted; 48,971 were convicted.[38] The law was controversial in a country where the Catholic Church continues to insist that what happens inside the

family unit is not the business of the state, but that didn't
stop victims making use of it: in 2007, 126,293 complaints
of domestic violence were filed.[39] Resistance to the Spanish
law is instructive, demonstrating the enduring nature
of beliefs about the subservient role of women; even in
a modern democracy, there will always be advocates of
turning the clock back. Opposition ranges from political
and religious conservatives to men who are not articulate
but no less convinced of their 'right' to behave as they wish
in the home; modern theories of gender equality appear as
an intolerable challenge to the authority of the father, who
is imagined as a species of benign despot with a superior
understanding of what is best for his wife and children. And
it is here that we begin to see the link between 'mainstream'
domestic violence and so-called 'honour' killings, which
are often treated (wrongly, in my view) as an entirely
separate category. We've already seen, in fact, that some
family annihilators could easily be moved into the 'honour'
killing category: Mohammed Riaz, who killed his wife and
daughters because they were too independent, and Rahan
Arshad, who didn't want his wife to wear Western clothes,
are examples. Here is a short list of other 'honour' killings
planned or carried in the UK:

• Greenford, West London, November 2007. Geeta Aulakh,
  28, was hacked to death with a machete on her way home
  from her job as a receptionist at Sunrise Radio in Ealing.
  Geeta's right hand was severed in the savage attack, which
  happened yards from the house where she was due to pick
  up her sons, aged eight and 10, from their child-minder.
  Geeta had left her 32-year-old husband Harpreet Aulakh

and asked for a divorce, making him so furious that he hacked into her Facebook account and went to her flat, obsessively looking for evidence that she was seeing another man. Then Aulakh recruited two other men, Jaswant Singh Dillon, 30, and Sher Singh, who was only 18 and had come to the UK on a student visa arranged by Aulakh, to kill her; Sher carried out the murder while Dhillon acted as a look-out. Aulakh was sentenced to life in prison and told he would serve a minimum of 28 years. The other two were also jailed for life and given minimum sentences of 22 years. A fourth man, Harpreet Singh, 21, was later convicted of driving the gang's getaway car and jailed for 22 years.[40]

- Iraqi Kurdistan, May 2007. Shawbo Ali Rauf, 19, was taken from her home in Birmingham to Iraqi Kurdistan where she was lured on a picnic and murdered by her husband's family. According to relatives in Britain, the murder was planned after an unfamiliar number was found on her mobile phone.[41]

- Mitcham, Surrey, January 2006. Banaz Mahmod, 20, was raped, strangled and stuffed into a suitcase, which was buried in a garden in Birmingham. Banaz came from a family of Iraqi Kurds who moved to London to escape Saddam Hussein. She was forced to marry a cousin when she was 16 but her husband was violent and she left him, returning home to her parents' house. Her father, Mahmod Mahmod, was furious when she fell in love with another man and Banaz went to the police several times after he threatened her; she even told officers that her mother had received a telephone call from her uncle, Ari Mahmod, threatening to kill her because she had been seen kissing her boyfriend and had supposedly brought 'shame' on the family. An officer interviewed Banaz after she broke a window to escape from her father, who had forced her to drink a bottle of brandy, but dismissed her claims as 'fantasy'. The Mahmod brothers decided to have her killed and employed two cousins, Mohammed Saleh Ali and Omar Hussain, to carry out the attack. The two men subsequently fled to Iraq but were extradited to the UK and found guilty of murder, disposing of Banaz's body, conspiring to kidnap her boyfriend and threatening to kill him. They were jailed for life and given minimum jail terms of 22 and 21 years respectively. The Mahmod brothers were jailed for life for ordering the murder; Banaz's uncle was told he would serve a minimum of 23 years and her father 20 years.[42]

- Southall, Middlesex, April 2005. Samaira Nazir, 25, was murdered in front of her parents by her cousin Imran Mohammed, who was only 17, and her elder brother, Azhar Nazir, a 30-year-old greengrocer. Samaira's family was from Pakistan and disapproved of her Afghan boyfriend, Salman Mohammed, whom she wanted to marry. Azhar Nazir ordered Samaira to come to their parents' house where he confronted her along with her mother, father and cousin; her nieces, aged two and four, were also present. There was a heated argument and then the men attacked Samaira, holding onto her so she couldn't escape. A neighbour heard her screams and knocked on the door but her father claimed she was having a fit, and the assault continued after the neighbour left. Samaira was attacked with four knives, stabbed 18 times and left with three cuts to her throat. The police arrived and Azhar Nazir told them his sister had not wanted an arranged marriage. 'We only allow marriage within the family,' he said. 'My sister wanted to run away from the house and was stopped.' He was jailed for at least 20 years and Imran Mohammed was told he would serve 10 years for his part in the murder. Samaira's father was arrested and bailed but fled to Pakistan. His family claim he died there.[43]

- Warrington, Cheshire, September 2003. A 17-year-old schoolgirl, Shafilea Ahmed, disappeared from home and her body was found in a river in Cumbria five months later. Shafilea was a clever and ambitious girl who wanted to become a lawyer but there were quarrels about her parents' insistence that she enter a forced marriage; not long before her disappearance, she returned from a trip to Pakistan where she drank bleach in a desperate attempt to avoid an unwanted engagement. In 2012, after a trial in which the jury heard graphic evidence of sustained physical abuse, Iftikhar Ahmed, 52, and Farzana Ahmed, 49, were found guilty of suffocating their daughter with a plastic bag in front of their other children. They were each sentenced to life imprisonment with a minimum term of 25 years.[44]

- Woodford Green, North London, January 1999. Tulay Goren, 15, was savagely beaten and murdered by her father, Mehmet Goren. She had run away from home several times before the murder and reported earlier attacks by her father, who had told the police he wanted her to undergo a 'virginity test'. Her body was buried in the garden of the family home before being dug up and disposed of elsewhere. Goren was arrested after his daughter's disappearance but he claimed she had run away again and forced his family to lie to the police. He wasn't charged until 10 years later when his wife Hanim agreed to give evidence against him, providing harrowing testimony about seeing Tulay covered in bruises and tied up on a bedroom floor. In December 2009, Mehmet Goren was convicted of his daughter's murder and told he would serve at least 22 years in prison.[45]

• Punjab, India, December 1998. Surjit Athwal, 27, who worked as a customs officer at Heathrow airport, was lured to a family wedding in India and murdered. The murder was planned by her husband, Sukhdave Athwal, and his mother, Bachan, when they discovered Surjit was having an affair and wanted a divorce. In India, Surjit 'disappeared from the face of the earth' and made no further attempt to contact her children, according to evidence given at Sukhdave and Bachan's murder trial in London in 2007. The trial took place after members of the family came forward and told the police Surjit had been strangled in India. Bachan, who was 70 by the time of the court case, was told she would spend a minimum of 20 years in jail, while her 43-year-old son was given 27 years.[46]

One of the most shocking 'honour' killings occurred not in the UK but Canada, where a couple and their son were convicted in January 2012 of murdering four other members of the same family.[47] Muhammad Shafia, 58, was a wealthy businessman who came to Canada from Afghanistan, bringing with him his wife Rona Amir

Muhammad, who was 52 at the time of her murder. They settled in Montreal but when it became clear that Rona could not have children, her husband married a second wife, Tooba Yahya, in defiance of Canadian law. Tooba gave birth to four children, three girls and a boy. In June 2009, the family was returning from a trip to Niagara Falls when their car was found submerged in a canal with the bodies of Rona and her step-daughters inside. Shafia claimed the accident happened when his eldest daughter Zainab, who was then 19, took the car for a joy-ride with her sisters and step-mother. But forensic evidence showed that the murders had been committed elsewhere and the bodies placed in the car, which was then pushed into the canal. Shafia, his 42-year-old second wife and their son Hamed, 21, were all convicted of murder. The court heard that Shafia dominated the family, laying down strict rules about what his daughters wore, when they could use the internet and who they were allowed to have as friends; when he was absent on business trips, his son Hamed took over as master of the household. Rona wrote in her diary that Shafia beat her and 'made life a torture' while his second wife treated her as a servant. Zainab fled to a shelter in terror of her father while 17-year-old Sahar had to conceal the fact she had a non-Muslim boyfriend. According to telephone intercept evidence, Shafia cursed his daughters after their deaths, calling them whores and invoking the devil to defecate on their graves.

This is an extreme case of multiple perpetrators, which is often cited as the most significant distinguishing feature in 'honour' killings. But the greater involvement of relatives in 'honour' crimes is explained by a difference in family structure: families who have immigrated from traditional societies tend to live in larger groups where a hierarchy of male elders is maintained. As we have seen, younger members of such families may reject the values of their parents and grand-parents, who are more likely to adhere to the pre-modern notion that the family's 'honour' is bound up with the behaviour of its female members. In the UK, the number of 'honour' crimes reported to the police rose rapidly in the first decade of the 21st century, with a 47 per cent increase in one year alone; in London, the figure rose from 235 to 495 between 2009 and 2010, while police in Greater Manchester reported an increase from 105 to 189 in the same period.[48] But the nuclear family is not in itself a guarantee of safety for women and girls, offering an opportunity to abusive men who want keep outsiders at a distance and project an idealised image of themselves. It is not even the case that murderers from secular communities always act alone and on the spur of the moment; both Raoul Moat and the ex-soldier Anthony Clarke were able to enlist friends or family members in either the planning of their crimes or organising a cover-up. The Swedish author and journalist Stieg Larsson made this point in his 2004 essay on where 'honour' crimes fit in relation to the wider problem of violence against women. Examining cases of domestic violence among the white population in Sweden, he concluded that 'surprisingly often … violence is encouraged by individuals in the killer's close circle of friends.'[49]

Indeed, the common factors in domestic abuse, family annihilations and 'honour' crimes are more striking than the differences. In each case the underlying issue is the same: an attempt to regain control over family members –

wives, partners, ex-partners, daughters, sisters – who have broken away or are seeking to escape from male control. As Huma Qureshi wrote in the *Guardian*, the 'senseless motives behind ["honour" crimes] are surely the same as in any other form of domestic abuse and violence against women, involving over-bearing men, hurt prides, wounded egos and uncontrollable, savage tempers.'[50] I would argue that in a significant proportion of cases the men in question *choose* not to control their tempers, but in every other respect Qureshi is right. Patriarchal ideas about a man's 'right' to exercise the power of life and death over his female relatives are overt in traditional families but Toby Day and Richard Smith – men from apparently modern suburban families – felt they were within their rights to slaughter their wives and children. Culture explains some of the differences between individual cases but these are all stories about violence against women and children: criminal, immoral and wrong in every instance. Regardless of a man's background, ethnicity, culture or religion, the simple fact remains that women and children are not possessions.

'TIS PITY SHE'S A WHORE

In the spring of 2012, Ched Evans was an up-and-coming professional football player. At the age of 23, he had played briefly for Manchester City before being sold to Sheffield United for £3m, where he scored 35 goals in the 2011–12 season. He had also appeared for the Welsh national side, scoring the winning goal in his first match in 2008, and played for the team in a dozen more internationals. But there was another side to his character: in a game where casual sexism is rampant, Evans believed he and his friends could have any woman they wanted. 'We're footballers, we're rich and we've got money, that's what girls like,' he bragged.[1] In March 2012, he was named League One Player of the Month; a month later, he was convicted of raping a 19-year-old woman in a hotel in North Wales.

The case against Evans, which was accepted by a jury at Caernarfon Crown Court, revealed a staggering disregard for the welfare of a woman he didn't even know. He appeared in the dock alongside his friend, another footballer called Clayton McDonald, who admitted having sex with the woman but was acquitted of rape. Here is the sequence of events outlined by the prosecution: McDonald, who plays for Port Vale, had been invited to spend a bank holiday weekend in Rhyl by Evans, whose mother lived in the seaside town. Evans booked a room in a hotel for McDonald because there wasn't space for him in his mother's house, and they spent the Sunday evening in bars and a nightclub in Rhyl. They became separated after visiting a takeaway but shortly afterward Evans received a text McDonald saying he'd 'got a girl'. Evans and his friends went to McDonald's hotel, where they found the player in bed with the victim. The two men disagreed about what happened next: McDonald insisted that Evans asked if he could have sex with the woman, while Evans claimed that McDonald invited him to join in. What isn't in doubt is that Evans had sex with the near-unconscious woman, later claiming that she consented and 'was moaning and groaning like she was enjoying herself'. Evans finished and left by a fire escape, later saying he was worried that his girlfriend would call him while he was with the young woman. In a telling commentary on the misogynist culture shared by this group of young men, Evans's brother and a friend watched through a window as he had sex with the victim. The friend even tried to video the encounter on his mobile phone.[2]

The next morning, the woman woke up naked and confused, and feared her drink might have been spiked. 'My clothes were scattered around on the floor. I just didn't know how I got there,' she said. The conclusion of Nita Dowell, senior crown prosecutor in Wales, was damning: 'Ched Evans took advantage of a vulnerable woman who was in no fit state to consent to sexual activity. He did so knowingly and with a total disregard for her physical and emotional wellbeing.'[3] Detective Chief Inspector Steve Williams said the victim had shown 'a great deal of resilience and strength in difficult circumstances'. The judge, Merfyn Hughes QC, told Evans that he had thrown away a successful career. 'The complainant was extremely intoxicated,' he said. 'CCTV footage shows, in my view, the extent of her intoxication when she stumbled into your friend. She was in no condition to have sexual intercourse.'[4] He sentenced Evans to five years in prison.

The judge's view of the seriousness of Evans's offence was not shared by some of his friends and supporters, who took to the internet to express outrage about his conviction. The hashtags #ChedEvans and #JusticeFor Ched appeared on Twitter, and one of the first people to express an opinion was Evans's Sheffield United team-mate, Connor Brown. 'I'm with you geez,' he posted, describing the woman raped by Evans as a 'money-grabbing little tramp' and a 'slag'.[5] Jonathan Cox from Sheffield tweeted her name, sneering she 'isn't a victim she's a whore', while another man from Sheffield, Joshua Laughton, re-tweeted the woman's name and a message claiming 'she's got a massive reputation … for doing similar things.'[6] Other people joined in, despite the fact that rape victims are entitled by law to lifelong anonymity. The police launched an investigation and arrested more than a dozen people on suspicion of committing a criminal offence, while the victim's family said she was 'traumatised, shocked and deeply upset' about being identified.

The use of social media to abuse a rape victim is a relatively new phenomenon. But the problem highlighted by the Evans case is anything but novel. Blaming the victim has always been at the heart of a 'rape culture' which treats women with suspicion and contempt – 'She asked for it' – while their attackers receive apparently endless indulgence, before and after conviction. In the autumn of 2009, celebrities rushed to support the movie director Roman Polanksi, who had finally been arrested in Switzerland after fleeing the US in 1978 to avoid a prison sentence after he admitted the statutory rape of a 13-year-old girl. 'I know it wasn't rape-rape. It was something else but I don't believe it was rape-rape,' declared the actor Whoopi Goldberg.[7] Gore Vidal, doyen of American intellectuals, went even further: 'I really don't give a fuck. Look, am I going to sit and weep every time a young hooker feels as though she's been taken advantage of?'[8] In the rarefied world inhabited by the rich and famous, such views may be commonplace and, regrettably, pass unchallenged. But organisations which work with rape victims and some more enlightened police officers understand their pernicious effects on women.

Reluctance to believe victims was one of the reasons why John Worboys, a former stripper who became a licensed taxi driver in London, was able to prey on women until his arrest in 2008. Worboys drugged and sexually assaulted women who got into his black cab, including victims who went to the police in 2003 and 2007; in the latter case, he was arrested and admitted being at the scene of the assault, but detectives failed to challenge his explanation and let him go. He attacked seven more women before his arrest the following February, when another '80 plus'[9] victims came forward. He was convicted of 19 charges, including rape and sexual assault, but detectives eventually identified a total of 81 offences, making Worboys the country's most prolific sexual offender until the Savile allegations emerged. The Soham killer, Ian Huntley, is another case in point: the Bichard Inquiry heard that an alert police officer, PC Michael Harding, had identified Huntley as a danger to women and girls three years *before* he murdered 10-year-old Holly Wells and Jessica Chapman in Cambridgeshire. Harding was investigating a rape in Huntley's home town, Grimsby, in 1999 and noticed that Huntley had been accused of a string of sexual offences, including three previous accusations of rape, four of sex with under-age girls and an indecent assault on an 11-year-old. Although Huntley had never been tried or convicted, Harding wrote an intelligence report which correctly identified him as a 'serial sex attacker'.[10] The report was later 'weeded' out with other documents, and Huntley was able to get a job as a school caretaker in Soham.

In spite of the publicity surrounding the cases of Huntley and Worboys, critical attention in rape cases still focuses on victims to an extraordinary degree. Their clothes, behaviour, alcohol consumption and sexual history (real or supposed) are minutely scrutinised in a never-ending quest for extenuating factors. According to research carried out for Amnesty International in 2005, more than a quarter of respondents believed a woman was totally or partially responsible for being raped if she wore certain types of clothes, while an even higher proportion (30 per cent) thought it was her fault if she was drunk; one in 12 thought a woman was to blame if she had had numerous sexual partners.[11] There is neither logic nor morality in these assumptions, which make women responsible for their own *and* men's behaviour; it infantilises adult men, treating them as though they're incapable of exercising moral choice or self-control. But there's an even worse effect to consider, which is that fear of being blamed undoubtedly acts as a deterrent when women are deciding whether to seek help or go to the police. In a survey of 1,600 women carried out by the website Mumsnet in 2012, more than four-fifths of respondents who said they'd been raped did not report the attack; over half gave embarrassment or shame as the reason why they were reluctant to go to the police.[12] Another report, compiled for The Havens sexual assault referral centres in London, found that 55 per cent of respondents would be too ashamed or embarrassed to report a rape to the police.[13]

Against this background, the practice of 'monstering' women who claim to have been coerced into having sex without their consent takes on another dimension. It is more than an attack on the individual concerned, although that is bad enough, because it acts as a reminder to the wider female population of what they might be subjected to if they seek redress from the criminal justice system. In the Ched Evans case, discussion of the trial and abuse of the victim were confined to the UK, but there have been others where the status and celebrity of the accused men have created an international outcry. The same sinister theme – that women make allegations of sexual assault maliciously or for gain – emerges in these cases as well, exposing a roiling stew of misogyny and conspiracy theory. Both are so well known that they need little introduction, save to say that one involves the celebrity hacker and WikiLeaks founder Julian Assange, who was accused of sexual assault and rape in Sweden in August 2010; the other centres on the French politician and former head of the International Monetary Fund, Dominique Strauss-Kahn, who was arrested on suspicion of attempted rape in New York in May 2011. Both men were famous at the time of their arrests but their accusers could hardly have been more different: the woman in the DSK case was a hotel employee, an African immigrant who couldn't read or write, while the allegations against Assange were made by two middle-class white women, both of whom happened to be political activists. Nevertheless, the treatment they received in the media and on the internet was remarkably similar, amounting to a sustained campaign of character assassination. DSK's allies in the Parti Socialiste, then the French opposition party, accused right-wing opponents of setting him up to spoil his chances of defeating the sitting President and UMP candidate, Nicolas Sarkozy, in the 2012 presidential election, while Assange's supporters detected a plot to get him to Sweden where he would be extradited to the US and face the death penalty for treason. Neither claim stood up to much scrutiny: Assange was arrested in the UK, whose own extradition treaty with the US is regularly lambasted for being too generous towards requests from American prosecutors, while his extradition from Sweden would require the consent of both the Swedish *and* British governments. DSK's support began to fall away when other claims of brutish behaviour towards women surfaced.

The two cases exist at opposite ends of the spectrum of assault allegations. Both men admit having sex with the women who accused them, but insist it was consensual. That is just about all the cases have in common, for the complaint against Assange turns on an adult's right to refuse unprotected sex while DSK was accused of a violent sexual attack, including oral rape. In the Assange case, the women initially agreed to sex but say they changed their minds when he was reluctant or refused to use condoms. The allegations against him are set out in the European Arrest Warrant,[14] which refers to the women as AA and SW, and lists one count of unlawful coercion, two counts of sexual molestation, and one of rape. AA's witness statement gives more detail and was summarised by the High Court in these terms:

> AA said in her statement that she had offered the use of her apartment to Mr Assange from 11–14 August 2010 when she was away. She had returned on 13 August 2010 earlier than planned and then met him for the first time. They went out to dinner and returned to her apartment. As they drank tea, he started to fondle her leg which she welcomed. Everything happened fast. Mr Assange ripped off her clothes and at the same time broke her necklace. She tried to put her clothes on again, but Mr Assange had immediately removed them again. She had thought that she really did not want to continue, but it was too late to tell Mr Assange to stop as she had consented so far. Accordingly, she let Mr Assange take off all her clothes.[15]

At this point, AA and Assange went to bed, with AA on her back and Assange on top. The encounter continued:

> Mr Assange wanted to insert his penis into her vagina, but she did not want him to do that because he was not using a condom. She therefore squeezed her legs together in order to avoid him penetrating her. She tried to reach several times for a condom which Mr Assange had stopped her from doing by holding her arms and bending her legs open and

trying to penetrate her with his penis without a condom. Mr Assange must have known it was a condom AA was reaching for and he had held her arms to stop her. After a while Mr Assange had asked AA what she was doing and why she was squeezing her legs together; AA told him she wanted him to put on a condom before he entered her. Mr Assange let go of AA's arms and put on a condom which AA found for him. AA felt a strong sense of unexpressed resistance on Mr Assange's part against using a condom.[16]

AA used her hand to check that Assange had put on the condom. They had sex, then Assange pulled out of her and did something with the condom. He entered her again, ejaculated and pulled out. When he removed the condom, AA saw it was empty and felt semen trickle out of her vagina. She told the police she believed that Assange had deliberately broken the condom when he pulled out of her and then continued with sex until he ejaculated.[17]

Clare Montgomery QC, who represented the Swedish Prosecuting Authority during an extradition hearing in London in July 2011, observed that 'it is one thing to consent to unprotected sex and another thing to consent to protected sex.'[18] She claimed both women had described circumstances in which they 'were coerced either by physical force or by a sense of having already been trapped in a position where they had no choice and therefore submitted to Mr Assange's intentions'.[19] In the case of the second woman, there was 'absolutely clear' evidence that 'she had been penetrated while asleep – furthermore being penetrated in a way which is absolutely clear she did not consent to, namely unprotected from disease or impregnation'.[20] Assange's lawyer, Ben Emmerson QC, made little attempt to defend his client's behaviour and adopted a respectful tone towards AA and SW. He said:

> Nothing I say should be taken as denigrating the complainants, the genuineness of their feelings of regret, to trivialise their experience or to challenge whether they felt Assange's conduct was *disrespectful, discourteous, disturbing or even pushing at the boundaries of what they felt comfortable with* [my italics].[21]

Assange's own version of his encounter with SW featured in an interview he gave to Marie Colvin in the *Sunday Times*.[22] Assange told Colvin that SW arrived at a lunch in a 'revealing' pink sweater, flirted with him and took him home. Assange stayed the night and SW awoke to find him having sex with her, immediately asking if he was wearing anything. 'I am wearing you,' he told her. Assange claimed to Colvin that the two women became angry when they realised he had slept with both of them in quick succession – it seems he was already trying to establish the 'revenge' theme to discredit them – but he made an interesting admission: the women's initial concern, he believed, was to force him to take a test for HIV. This aside was eclipsed, unsurprisingly, by what he went on to tell Colvin about how he came to find himself in this predicament: 'Sweden is the Saudi Arabia of feminism. I fell into a hornets' nest of revolutionary feminism.'

Assange didn't actually claim to have seen Swedish men wearing head-to-toe veils or travelling to work with female 'guardians'. But he was pitching an appeal to an audience which, while not supporting his political activities, would find common cause in his hostility to feminism. Here is how the *Daily Mail* described AA in a lengthy article published towards the end of 2010:

An attractive blonde, [AA] was already a well-known 'radical feminist'. In her 30s, she had travelled the world following various fashionable causes. While a research assistant at a local university, she had not only been the protégée of a militant feminist academic, but held the post of 'campus sexual equality officer'. Fighting male discrimination in all forms, including sexual harassment, was her forte.[23]

The article asked whether Assange was the victim of a 'honeytrap', a suggestion also made by his first lawyer, Mark Stephens, who claimed 'dark forces' were at work against his client.[24] (Assange later fell out with Stephens in a row about legal fees.) AA's background in left-wing politics made her a surprising choice for a CIA-backed 'dirty tricks' campaign but a similar allegation surfaced in an article for the CounterPunch website, written by Paul Bennett and Israel Shamir, a WikiLeaks supporter who has been described by *Searchlight* magazine as a 'Swedish anti-Semite'. The article characterised Assange as a superhero, Captain Neo, who found himself entrapped by a sinister organisation known as 'the Matrix' in 'Blonde Land':

the Matrix plays dirty and lets loose a sex bomb upon our intrepid Neo. When you can't contest the message, you smear the messenger. Sweden is tailor-made for sending a young man into a honey trap. Sweden has particularly thorny anti-rape legislation, where a conviction might be secured from something as thin as an anonymous accuser's allegation.[25]

The suggestion that accusers are 'anonymous' in Swedish rape trials is nonsense: their identities are protected by law but they are known to both legal teams and their allegations are subject to rigorous scrutiny in court. In any case, both women in the Assange case were quickly identified on the internet. Here is an extract from an anti-feminist Canadian blog called 'Dick Freeman' – that's Free-man, for anyone who hasn't got the reference – which named AA and subjected to her to vicious abuse:

Assange's 'victim' is a twisted, man-hating bitch who was bent on revenge for getting played. She fabricated a rape charge within two days of having sex. [AA's real name] is a sick puppy whose petty act of vengeance will damn an innocent man. This is the feminazi little darling.[26]

The blog then published a photograph of AA, accompanied by this barely literate tirade:

Julian Assange's rape accusers are nothing more than lying feminist slags ... Men alike must make a definitive case as to how feminazis have destroyed modern society, and familys [sic], children as their mentally disturbed feminazi groupies not only make false rape accusations. We must hang this albatross around the feminists' necks and give them a blow that they will never recover from.

Besides smearing his alleged victims, some of Assange's supporters habitually misrepresented the case against him, denying that he was accused of rape and demanding that he should be questioned in London or by video-link. In fact, the Swedish authorities wanted to question and if necessary *arrest* him prior to trial, which they clearly couldn't do by video-link, but his supporters would not tolerate anything short of adulation of their hero. On one occasion, after writing about the case in the *Independent*, I received an email from an Assange supporter who accused me of being a 'stupid paid-to-post neocon WHORE'.

Assange's campaign to avoid extradition was supported by an array of celebrities, including the socialite Jemima Khan, the film-maker Michael Moore and the journalist John Pilger. (Khan eventually became disenchanted with Assange and suggested he was in danger of becoming 'an Australian L. Ron Hubbard', a reference to the founder of Scientology.)[27] He could have put an end to the protracted proceedings at any time by acknowledging that he was subject to due process, like any other citizen, and returning to Sweden. But his lawyers went to court time after time until he finally lost his fight in the UK's Supreme Court in the summer of 2012. With no other legal avenue open to him, Assange broke his bail conditions – and landed friends who'd stood bail for him with a bill running into thousands of pounds – by seeking asylum in the Ecuadorean embassy in Knightsbridge. At the same time, his supporters redoubled their efforts to deny that what he had done amounted to rape. The recently elected Respect MP for Bradford West, George Galloway, led the charge in a now-notorious video broadcast. Galloway said:

Even taken at its worst, if the allegations made by these two women were true, 100% true, and even if a camera in the room captured them, they don't constitute rape. At least not rape as anyone with any sense can possibly recognise it. And somebody has to say this.

Woman A met Julian Assange, invited him back to her flat, gave him dinner, went to bed with him, had consensual sex with him, claims that she woke up to him having sex with her again. This is something which can happen, you know. I mean, not everybody needs to be asked prior to each insertion.[28]

It's a little surprising to hear a woman compared to a slot machine, and Galloway's 'insertion' remark surely deserves its own footnote in the history of sexual politics. But he was wrong in law: the notion of 'perpetual consent' in English law only ever applied to married couples, and it ended in 1991 when the House of Lords upheld the conviction of a man who had been jailed for attempting to rape his estranged wife. Even so, Jemima Khan's brother, the financier Ben Goldsmith, supported Galloway in a tweet, declaring: 'I'm with @georgegalloway on Assange. Trumped up Swedish "rape" charges are a ruse to get him to an American jail. Scary stuff.'[29] Celebrity endorsements continued, with the rapper M.I.A. and the singer Lady Gaga turning up at the Ecuadorean embassy to show their support for a man who was now a fugitive from justice. Critics pointed out that Assange appeared to have come to share the expectation of impunity which WikiLeaks denounced so fiercely when it was exercised by governments, as well as denying his accusers the opportunity to have their allegations tested in court. But it was also a textbook example of rape culture, in which some supporters of a self-appointed crusader for human rights saw no contradiction in unleashing a torrent of abuse against his alleged victims.

The encounter between Dominique Strauss-Kahn and a woman called Nafissatou Diallo in a suite at the Sofitel in New York on 14 May 2011 was brief. Prosecutors established the time she entered his suite from her room-access card, while DSK's phone records showed he made a call to his daughter between seven and nine minutes later; this short time span was one of the factors which led investigators to conclude that the encounter was unlikely to have been consensual. The politician's biographer, Michel Taubmann, later offered a version of events from the DSK camp, saying it was drawn from half a dozen conversations he had with the politician while writing his book. The most startling passage describes the moment DSK emerged naked from the shower to find Diallo in his suite and 'she ostentatiously looked at his penis', according to Taubmann's version of events.[30] Although he didn't speak to her, DSK immediately jumped to the conclusion that this total stranger wanted to have sex with him:

> The flesh is weak. Dominique Strauss-Kahn saw this as a proposition. Rarely in his life has he ever refused the possibility of a moment of pleasure. He did not resist the temptation of oral sex.[31]

This account prompted a pithy headline in *New York* magazine: 'Ladies Look at DSK and Instantly Want to Do Sex, Says DSK Biography'.[32] Diallo's version is very different:

she says she apologised for disturbing the naked guest and tried to leave the suite.[33] But she claims that DSK then came towards her, clutching at her breasts, and wrestled her onto the bed. He tried to push his penis into her closed mouth and she managed to get away, but he caught her and pulled up her uniform dress. He ripped down her tights, grasped her vagina with his hand and forced her onto her knees. This time he succeeded in pushing his penis into her mouth. She tasted something wet and sour and spat it out. She ran out of the suite into the corridor, still spitting semen, and hid round a corner. Moments later, she saw the man leave the suite and get into a lift. Not long afterwards, her supervisor noticed she was in a state of distress and asked what was wrong. Diallo asked: 'If somebody try to rape you in this job, what do you do?' After some discussion involving security staff, the hotel called the emergency number 911 and Diallo was examined at St Luke's Roosevelt Hospital. Diallo was 'in tears', according to medical records, and told staff that a man grabbed her vagina, leaving a red mark, and forced her to have oral sex. It was later revealed that the hospital record stated 'Cause of the injuries: assault. Rape'.[34] Diallo's account was considered sufficiently credible to justify DSK's arrest at JFK airport, where he had boarded a plane to Paris.

The detention of such a powerful and well-connected man caused a sensation. In France, friends and political allies rallied to defend him, including the Socialist politician and former Culture Minister Jack Lang, who wondered why DSK had not been released immediately since 'nobody died in that hotel room'.[35] Another supporter, magazine editor Jean-Francois Kahn, characterised DSK's encounter with the hotel employee as a *troussage de domestique*, a phrase which describes a master stripping or having non-consensual sex with a servant.[36] But it was the philosopher Bernard-Henri Levy who offered the most impassioned defence of his old friend, writing shortly after charges were filed:

> the Strauss-Kahn I know, who has been my friend for 20 years and who will remain my friend, bears no resemblance to this monster, this caveman, this insatiable and malevolent beast now being described nearly everywhere. Charming, seductive, yes, certainly; a friend to women and, first of all, to his own woman, naturally, but this brutal and violent individual, this wild animal, this primate, obviously no. it's absurd.[37]

BHL appeared totally oblivious to his own patriarchal attitudes, but he was unhappy with the spectacle of his friend being treated like any other defendant. He raged:

> This morning, I hold it against the American judge who, by delivering him to the crowd of photo hounds, pretended to take him for *a subject of justice like any other* [my italics].

In his home country at least, DSK was already being portrayed as the victim of a politically correct justice system which had failed to recognise the status of such an important man, reigniting Franco-American hostilities which dated back to the run-up to the Iraq war in 2003. It took only four days for the French press to identify Diallo, whose name had not at that point been mentioned in the American media, and from then on her anonymity was blown worldwide.

In this febrile atmosphere, the high attrition rate in cases of alleged rape – the proportion that never come to court – was overlooked, as if the fact that DSK had been charged meant he was bound to face trial. This was far from being a certainty: according to Professor Joanna Bourke, author of a magisterial history of rape, defendants who end up being convicted of rape in a court of law 'must regard themselves as exceptionally unlucky'.[38] Bourke says that the 'typical' rape victim in the US is a young, poor black woman, yet African-American women are less likely to be believed than white complainants *and* are assumed to be sexually voracious. Both of these assumptions came into play as the criminal investigation ground on, creating a web of half-truths and outright lies which combined with Diallo's disadvantages as a witness to undermine her credibility. On 1 July, the District Attorney, Cyrus Vance Jnr, called a surprise hearing to acknowledge that the prosecution team had doubts about Diallo; their anxiety was *not* about the alleged rape but discrepancies in her recollection of what she did immediately afterwards, and lies she had told about her life in Guinea and her application for asylum in the US. Vance did not seek to withdraw the charges at this point but DSK's bail was refunded and he was released from house arrest, signalling a significant shift in the respective positions of complainant and defendant.

Whatever Vance's intention, the effect on Diallo's case was disastrous, opening her up to a series of attacks in the media. Her chief tormentor was the *New York Post*, a mass-market tabloid owned by Rupert Murdoch, which had already insinuated, within days of the alleged attack, that she might be HIV-positive.[39] On that occasion, the paper referred to her with the slighting phrase 'IMF gal' and the claim, which Diallo denied, was clearly intended to suggest she had had numerous sexual partners. But the paper's hostile coverage really took off with the 1 July hearing, beginning with a huge headline: 'DSK case bombshell. Maid's "lies" and "drug links" leave DA no good witness'. The 'drug links' were tenuous, referring to associates of Diallo rather than the woman herself, but the paper had a more direct slur up its sleeve. It returned to the attack the following day, introducing a new allegation that Diallo had worked as a prostitute and 'took care' of hotel guests 'on the side'.[40] By 3 July, the *Post*'s accusation had developed into a scenario in which Diallo made the rape allegation after DSK refused to pay her for sex, along with an improbable claim that she 'saw johns while in DA protection'.[41] There was no evidence for the allegation that Diallo had worked as a prostitute, which certainly didn't feature in the DA's summary of events, but it had a hugely influential effect on public opinion. Diallo sued the *New York Post* for libel, but the damage had already been done as the paper's lurid headlines were seized on by racist and anti-feminist bloggers. In a matter of six weeks, she had gone from being the anonymous victim of an alleged sex attack to a 'lying black whore', according to one website.[42] 'Don't all you white knights who rushed to this tart's defense feel just a little foolish?' the author demanded.

Towards the end of August 2011, Vance finally asked a judge to dismiss the charges against the politician. In the document submitted to court, he used an ambiguous formulation: 'The nature and number of the complainant's falsehoods leave us unable to credit her version of events beyond a reasonable doubt, *whatever the truth may be about the encounter between the complainant and the defendant*' [my italics].[43] It sounded as if prosecutors thought that Diallo's account of the alleged rape might well be true but wouldn't stand up in court because of what the defence would say about her character. It was an unsatisfactory outcome for both sides: 'Dismissal does not mean he is innocent, simply that the District Attorney doesn't believe the case can go to trial', observed a French lawyer, Pierre Hourcade.[44] Anticipating this turn of events, Diallo's lawyers had already initiated civil proceedings against DSK, but the politician was told he was free to return to France. There was even talk of his entering the contest to become the Socialist candidate in the 2012 presidential election, as though his troubles were behind him. Meanwhile the *New York Post* resumed its attack on Diallo, calling for her to be deported in an editorial with the headline 'No longer welcome':

Nafissatou Diallo, the self-proclaimed 'victim' in the sordid saga of a hotel maid's *false rape claim* against former International Monetary Fund head Dominique Strauss-Kahn, needs to be on an airplane back to her native Guinea as soon as the paperwork can be completed [my italics].[45]

DSK's relief was short-lived. If Diallo's history had blocked her access to American justice, the politician's own sordid past was about to catch up with him. Shortly after his arrest in New York, a young French writer called Tristane Banon accused him of trying to rape her in 2003. Banon had mentioned the alleged attack once before, during a TV debate, but DSK's name was bleeped out. Now she named him and described an encounter in an apartment in Paris where she went to interview him and he allegedly leapt on her like a 'rutting chimpanzee'. She said:

> It finished badly ... very violently ... I kicked him. When we were fighting, I mentioned the word 'rape 'to make him afraid, but it didn't have any effect. I managed to get out.[46]

Banon said she had been dissuaded from going to the police in 2003 by her mother, Anne Mansouret, who was herself a Socialist politician. (Mansouret is said to have told police she once had sex with DSK at the OECD office in Paris when they were working together and she did not find it a pleasant experience, recalling that 'he took me with the vulgarity of a soldier'.[47]) DSK angrily denied Banon's accusation but French prosecutors opened an investigation into the attempted rape claim. In October 2011, his credibility suffered a huge blow when a public prosecutor ruled that there was *prima facie* evidence of a lesser offence, sexual assault. The inquiry was dropped because the alleged offence fell outside the statute of limitations[48] but Banon declared that she felt vindicated. DSK ended an action against her for defamation, but he was soon fighting on another front.

When French police began investigating an alleged prostitution ring based at the Carlton Hotel in Lille, in northern France, it was not long before DSK's name came up. It was claimed that orgies had been held at upmarket hotels in Lille and Paris, where prostitutes were supplied for customers. The Lille police chief, Jean-Christophe Lagarde, was said to have organised an eight-person orgy for DSK at a hotel in Paris in 2010, while a businessman from the city, David Roquet, was accused with three other men of providing prostitutes for the head of the IMF in the hope of gaining political favours. At least five women told the police they had had sex with DSK and one, who said she had taken part in 11 orgies with him, said she 'got the feeling he liked rough sex'. Roquet and Lagarde were even alleged to have flown prostitutes to the US to take part in an orgy with DSK on 13 May 2011, the day before the alleged attack on Diallo.[49] Faced with these allegations, DSK did not deny taking part in orgies arranged by 'friends' but claimed he did not know that the women he had sex with worked as prostitutes. 'At these parties, people were not dressed, and I defy you to tell the difference between a naked prostitute and other naked woman,' one of his lawyers protested. Another lawyer failed to explain why his client believed that so many young women wished to have sex with a portly man in his 60s, but argued that DSK's behaviour was 'simple libertine activity'.[50] French prosecutors were unconvinced: they believed that DSK was actively involved in procuring women for sex and in March 2012 they brought preliminary charges of 'complicity in pimping in an organised vice ring', which carries a sentence of up to 20 years in prison. For a time, the politician was also facing charges of gang rape involving a Belgian woman in a Washington hotel, but they were dropped in October when the alleged victim withdrew her statement. In December, however, DSK's French lawyers failed in a bid to have the pimping charges dismissed. A week earlier, he settled out of court in New York with Nafissatou Diallo. The settlement remained confidential but was reported to involve a payment of millions of dollars, in return for Diallo dropping her civil lawsuit over the attempted rape allegation. It was a costly outcome for a man who had always maintained his innocence.[51]

Rape is a serious accusation. The proper place for it to be examined is in court, not in lurid headlines or abusive posts on social networking sites. But too few cases get to trial, allowing rape myths and abuse of victims to flourish, and even women whose attackers have been tried and convicted in a court of law suffer as a result. In November 2012, the Appeal Court turned down an attempt by the rapist Ched Evans to challenge his conviction and sentence. In the same week, nine people appeared in court in Wales, admitted naming his victim on Facebook and Twitter and were each ordered to pay £624 compensation.[52] They included Evans's cousin Gemma Thomas, his friend Benjamin Davies and a 25-year-old biology teacher, Holly Price. Twenty-six-year-old Paul Devine from Sheffield not only named the victim but suggested to other users of Twitter that they should find out her address. In court, Devine said he was angry because he supported Sheffield United and they had just lost to MK Dons; presumably Devine thought his team would have played better with a convicted rapist in its ranks, but it's not much of an excuse. District judge Andrew Shaw didn't mince his words, observing that the defendants had posted the comments 'with deliberate malice'. He told them: 'Your actions have re-victimised this woman.'[53] Shortly after the case, a detective revealed that the woman had had to move from her home and be given a new identity to protect her from what he described as 'keyboard warriors'.[54] Bullied on line, driven from her home, forced to change her name: all of this happened in a supposedly equal country to a 19-year-old victim of sexual violence who was brave enough to demand justice. This relentless abuse of women who say they've been raped is a form of terrorism, and it has to stop.

BUYING POWER

Here are two stories about the way prostitution operates in the UK in the 21st century. The first focuses on a British girl known as 'Suzie', the second a young Ukrainian woman I'm going to call 'Sonya'. I haven't met Suzie but she is the main case study in a report published in September 2012 by the Safeguarding Children Board in Rochdale, a town in Greater Manchester. In dry language, the report describes how Suzie first came to the attention of the authorities:

> When Suzie turned 15, there were already signs that she was a troubled and vulnerable young person. In the course of that year Suzie disclosed on two separate occasions and to two different agencies that she had been the victim of serious sexual assaults by a number of adults who were linked to takeaway premises in the area.[1]

The police carried out an investigation but 'the possibility that [Suzie] was being sexually exploited was not recognised'. Social workers, meanwhile, also failed Suzie:

> At that time, professional focus was on providing individual support services for Suzie and on assisting her parents to set boundaries to keep her safe. It seems, however, that these actions had little impact on Suzie's circumstances:

she remained at risk of sexual harm, compounded by her abuse of alcohol and possibly drugs. Whilst still a teenager Suzie became pregnant.[2]

I doubt whether anyone would guess from this summary that Suzie had been forced into child prostitution with dozens of men. Her ordeal began in the summer of 2008 when another teenage girl took her to a takeaway food shop where she was given free food, cigarettes, alcohol and taxi rides. One night, after members of the gang had gained her trust, she was encouraged to drink vodka until she was 'dead drunk', taken upstairs and raped by the 55-year-old leader of the prostitution ring. He ignored her protests, telling her she had to pay him back for all the 'gifts' he'd given her, and soon she was being passed around other members of the gang.[3] Suzie became so distressed that she lashed out, smashing the counter of the takeaway, and found herself arrested on suspicion of criminal damage. At the police station, Suzie spent six hours telling the police what gang members were doing to her on a daily basis, but she was released and the abuse continued. In one four-month period, she was driven between houses and flats in a taxi and forced to have sex with up to five men a night.[4] At the beginning of 2009 Suzie made another complaint to the police and arrests followed in connection with suspected offences against her and other girls. But the Crown Prosecution Service decided that Suzie would not make a good witness and did not proceed with charges.[5]

A few months later she went to the police again, but it was only in November 2010 that the police launched an inquiry known as Operation Span. At long last, detectives uncovered a child prostitution ring which had been operating in Rochdale for more than two years after Suzie first raised the alarm. It was not just Suzie's case which should have triggered a much earlier investigation: between 2004 and 2010, an NHS team providing sexual health services to vulnerable young people made 83 referrals to Rochdale borough council about girls they believed were being exploited or were vulnerable to sexual exploitation.[6] In court, the prosecution focused on five children, including a 13-year-old girl who became pregnant and had an abortion, but police believe there may have been as many as 47 victims. In May 2012, nine men from Rochdale and Oldham were convicted on charges including rape, sexual assault, conspiracy to engage in sexual activity with a child and trafficking.[7] The ringleader, who could not be named at the time because of a pending trial, received a sentence of 19 years; he was later identified as Shabir Ahmed, aged 59, after being convicted of 30 child rapes in a separate case involving a young Asian girl and given a 22-year sentence.[8] It seems probable, though, that many other men who happily abused under-age girls were never apprehended. After the trial, Suzie said: 'What they did to me was evil. They ripped away all my dignity and all my last bit of self-esteem. By the end of it I had no emotion whatsoever.'[9]

Suzie's story is about a vulnerable girl being 'groomed' and internally trafficked into child prostitution in the north of England. Sonya, whom I met after she was rescued from an East European sex-trafficking gang, was tricked into coming to the UK and forced by her captors to have sex with thousands of men. When I talked to her, Sonya was in her early 20s and trying to recover from spending two years and three months in forced prostitution in flats up and down the country.[10] In a set of circumstances which is far from unusual, she was trafficked by her father and a family friend after she finished college in Ukraine and couldn't find a job.[11] The family friend told her he could help her go to England to study, assist in getting a visa from the British embassy in Kiev and provide a coach ticket to London. Her father told her she would be picked up at the coach station in London by 'kind people' who would show her how to register at college. She told me:

> They took me to a nice house and treated me well. In the first week they gave me a tour of London. I was very happy. After a week I asked when I could start studying. They said: 'You didn't come here for studying. We spent a lot of money on your travel to the UK.' They said I have to work and give them the money back. They said I have to do prostitution.
>
> I was crying. I said I can't do that. I said I can do any other job to pay the money back. They were beating me and treating me very bad. The next day they took me to a flat, to work there. An Englishwoman provided me with clothes, shoes, cosmetics.
>
> The first client attended the place. I was told to go with him. I worked all day, maybe 12 hours. In the evening, someone came to collect me from the flat. She gave me an envelope with money and a list of clients and the services I gave. After that they took me to another flat. There were many girls from different countries, all Eastern European. We were sleeping on the floor, covered with coats. I was working seven days a week. Every day a different place.

Sometimes there were two or three girls, sometimes eight or ten. We were not allowed to speak to each other.

I was thinking I was in London but one time a client asked me how I liked [a northern city]. I thought, am I in this place? I was forced to pretend I'm fine and like the job, otherwise I'd be beaten. I couldn't keep my money, not even tips, which were paid to me by clients. I was searched after every job. I was beaten on many occasions, very badly, kicked and punched.

Sonya discovered that the traffickers in the UK had bought her from a Ukrainian gang for £3,500. They took away her passport and told her she had to pay the money back. Extreme violence was the norm and she once witnessed another young woman being assaulted and held under water until her eyes haemorrhaged. On one occasion, when Sonya's eye was damaged in a beating, she was given an eye patch and forced to go on working. She tried to escape through a first-floor window but the traffickers caught her. She recalled:

They were saying I'm illegal and they could kill me because I didn't exist here. They said if the police checked me they would put me in prison for two years. They said I'm their property, I will be with them for the rest of my life – I'm not human, just something that can be bought.

After she was rescued, doctors told Sonya she would never fully regain the sight in her damaged eye. When I met her, she was finally attending college and hoping to stay in the UK. 'I think I've lost my country and I can't go back,' she said sadly. 'It's still affecting my life but I'm trying to make it work.'

Campaigners for legalised brothels claim that sex-trafficking is an entirely separate phenomenon, as though there's a 'fair trade'[12] form of prostitution which is free from harm. They make a distinction between men who want to pay for sex without intimacy and a supposed minority of 'problem' punters who want to humiliate, hurt or even murder women; they argue that most of the damage to women who work as prostitutes is caused by its illegal status, which obliges them to work on the streets or in unlicensed brothels. There is an obvious weakness in this proposition, which is that no one forces men to abuse women they pick up for sex on the street; they do it because they like it. Campaigners admit as much when they argue that legal brothels are safer: why would women need protection if a substantial proportion of 'punters' weren't violent and abusive in the first place? And the operative word here is safer: according to one academic study, two-thirds of women working as prostitutes have experienced 'client violence' and women working indoors still face 'physical, economic and sexual violence from their clients, including serious assaults'.[13] Another study which looked at the experience of prostituted women in five countries suggests that 'sexual and other physical violence is the normative experience for women in prostitution'.[14] Crucially, it found that prostituted women continue to suffer rape and assault *regardless of the legal status of prostitution*. More recently, the *British Medical Journal* reported that standardised mortality rates for women who work as prostitutes are *six times* those seen in the general population and *18 times* higher for murder – the highest for any group of women.[15] Some of this excess mortality is accounted for by drug use and sickness, including infection with HIV, but that's because so many women enter prostitution to fund a drug habit or find the life so awful that they develop one. What this suggests is that abuse is *integral* to prostitution, not a side-effect of illegality, and that most of the men who use prostituted women are looking for something other than simple sexual gratification.

History bears out this proposition. In the Victorian period, when sex outside marriage was not an option for 'respectable' women, prostitution could be regarded as an outlet for men who didn't otherwise have access to sex. When I first thought about prostitution, I assumed it was a relic of repressive attitudes towards sex and would wither away as a consequence of the sexual revolution. Until that happened, it seemed reasonable to suggest that the dwindling – as I imagined – population of women who sold sex for a living should be able to operate in legal off-street premises. What changed my mind was the realisation that quite the opposite was happening: the commercial sex industry actually *expanded* in the late 20th century, despite the fact that sex between consenting adults had become freely available in Western culture. That trend has continued into the 21st century; for men, at least, it has never been easier to get sex without paying for it. Yet the proportion of men in the UK who admit to buying sex has risen dramatically; between 1990 and 2000, the figure doubled from one in 20 to almost one in 10.[16] Nor are these men drawn principally from a group who are single, lonely and unable to get sex by other means: research cited by the Home Office in 2009 concluded that 'clients tend to be married, employed, and more educated than the prostitutes they are visiting, and to come from all ages and classes.'[17] At the same time, the stigma associated with using prostituted woman has diminished, and it's now regarded as normal in some circles for groups of men to visit brothels together. Demand has risen so much that the supply of local women voluntarily providing sexual 'services' cannot keep up, and increasing numbers of foreign women and under-age girls are being tricked into working as prostitutes by pimps and traffickers.

In that sense, sex-trafficking exposes the lie about the essentially 'benign' nature of prostitution, which is such a horrible 'job' – let's have no more nonsense about its being a 'profession' – that it has to be staffed by criminal methods. In 2003, the Home Office suggested there were 4,000 women trafficked for prostitution in the UK, and in 2009 the Home Affairs select committee raised the estimate to at least 5,000.[18] In 2010, a report from the Association of Chief Police Officers went some way towards revealing the effect of rising demand, estimating that 17,000 of the 30,000 women involved in off-street prostitution in England and Wales were migrants. The report suggested that only 2,600 of these women had definitely been trafficked but its methodology was flawed – the researchers entered brothels in London to talk to women without interpreters – and it acknowledged that another 9,200 women in the off-street trade were 'vulnerable migrants' who might well be victims of trafficking. These figures are almost certainly under-estimates: the ACPO researchers didn't find a single African victim of trafficking, even though Anthony Steen, chair of the Human Trafficking Centre and a former Conservative MP, pointed out that 'accommodation units for trafficked women are entirely taken up with women from Africa.'[19] In addition, these statistics relate only to victims of *external* trafficking, including women like Sonya, but they don't include victims of *internal* trafficking.

Most of these individuals are under-age girls, and in 2005 the children's charity Barnardo's estimated that 1,000 children were at risk of sexual exploitation in London alone.[20] But it wasn't until 2011, when *The Times* published the results of its own investigation into child prostitution in the north of England,[21] that the scale of this problem began to become apparent – and in controversial circumstances. What made headlines was the ethnic background of most of the perpetrators, who tended to be British Asian men, and the paper found evidence that they had 'groomed' under-age girls in a string of northern towns: Leeds, Keighley, Blackpool, Oldham, Blackburn, Sheffield, Manchester, Skipton, Nelson, Preston, Rotherham and Derby. Dozens of men had been charged with rape and prostitution offences and sent to prison but many more, who were happy to pay in money or favours for sex with very young girls, were never apprehended. And while the trials concentrated out of necessity on small numbers of victims, it was clear that hundreds, and possibly thousands, of girls had been abused; in Blackpool alone, police believed around 60 girls were groomed by workers at takeaway food shops.[22] (Two girls who had been deemed vulnerable to sexual exploitation, 14-year-old Charlene Downs and 15-year-old Paige Chivers, went missing in Blackpool and are believed to have been murdered.) In another notorious trial, nine men from Derby were convicted in three separate trials involving girls as young as 12; one young victim described an assault involving at least eight men.[23]

Race played a sensational but confusing part in these cases. It's true that many of the perpetrators came from a rural – and patriarchal – South Asian culture which does not value women and girls. More significant than their ethnicity, however, was the fact that they were unskilled men who worked in the night-time economy. Taxi drivers and takeaway workers have access to vulnerable children who come from chaotic backgrounds or are in local authority care. They also have the cash to impress teenagers with expensive cars, alcohol and drugs, cynically exploiting their longing for love. In other cases of 'grooming' which have ended up in court, the perpetrators were white and the deputy children's commissioner, Sue Berelowitz, has pointed out that perpetrators and victims come from all ethnic groups.[24] (A study published by her office confirmed that thousands of children were being sexually abused each year, identifying 16,500 from across England who were 'at high risk' between April 2010 and March 2011 alone.[25]) The testimony of women rescued from traffickers suggests that men who use brothels come from a wide range of backgrounds: Sonya's 'clients' included men from different ethnic groups and they didn't ask if she was working voluntarily in prostitution, even when she was bruised from beatings and wore a patch on her damaged eye. The fact that so many men are prepared to pay for sex with women and children who have been coerced into prostitution speaks volumes; men who use 14-year-olds or terrified African women for their enjoyment regard women as objects, to be used and discarded, without regard for the consequences. Their attitudes would not change if they were able to use legal brothels, and indeed the experience of countries which have relaxed prostitution laws is that it leads to a big increase in the number of legal *and* illegal brothels.

In Australia, the first state to legalise brothels was Victoria in 1984, with the intention of reducing illegal prostitution, police corruption and harm to women. But this isn't what happened, according to an article in *The Age* newspaper,[26] which claimed that illegal brothels outnumbered legal ones in Victoria four to one (there were 400 illegal establishments, according to police and owners of legal brothels). Something similar happened in Amsterdam when prostitution was legalised there in 2000: the city soon experienced a big increase in the number of brothels *and* women trafficked into the Netherlands by gangsters. Six years later, the city council refused to renew the licences of 37 prostitution businesses, arguing that many had connections with organised crime.[27] Three years after that Amsterdam's mayor, Job Cohen, announced plans to reduce the number of brothels and regenerate the city's red light district. He said legalisation 'didn't bring us what we hoped and expected. We want in part to reverse it, especially with regard to the exploitation of women in the sex industry.'[28]

If there appears to be a paradox here – that legalisation of prostitution promotes growth in the illegal trade – the reasons are not hard to find. Legal brothels provide cover for traffickers by making it harder for the police to distinguish between women who are working voluntarily and those who have been coerced into prostitution. In addition, they eliminate risk for 'punters' and normalise the practice of paying for sex, sending the message that it's a perfectly acceptable part of male behaviour. In a recent study of 116 countries, researchers found that countries where prostitution is legal tend to experience higher levels of trafficking than those where it's prohibited. One of the authors, Professor Eric Neumayer, outlined the findings:

One theory is that legalised prostitution reduces demand because legally residing prostitutes are favoured over trafficked ones after legalisation. However, our research suggests that in countries where prostitution is legalised, there is such a significant expansion of the prostitution market that the end result is larger reported inflows of human trafficking.[29]

Neumayer believes legalisation has 'potential benefits' but appears to 'boost the market for this fast-growing global criminal industry'. Thus Germany experienced a sharp increase in reports of human trafficking after legalisation in 2002, while the number of trafficking victims in Denmark, which decriminalised prostitution in 1999, is four times higher than in Sweden where buying sex is a criminal offence.[30]

At the same time, countries where prostitution is legal also have high numbers of sex tourists to other parts of the world, usually trafficking and prostitution hubs in Asia. Legal brothels will never be able to cater to all the demands of men who pay for sex, some of whom are prepared to go abroad to get what they want: under-age girls, in the case of the convicted paedophile Gary Glitter, or unsafe forms of sex. Others seek out unlicensed establishments which exist alongside legal brothels, providing unprotected and anal sex or physically dangerous practices such as 'fisting'. This, in turn, puts pressure on women working legally to lower prices and offer 'services' that endanger their health. Humanity in Action, an organisation which is broadly in favour of legalisation, acknowledged as much in a post about the situation in Amsterdam:

> With the influx of migrant workers from around the world, and trafficked workers from various parts of Eastern Europe including Bulgaria, Romania and Lithuania, prostitutes are faced with heavy competition amongst each other. This creates an environment in which women have become more willing to perform acts that they would not normally do. For example, many women are asked if they would be willing to have sex without the use of a condom for extra money; money which they might be obliged to take after renting a window, paying taxes and in some cases, paying a pimp. Other acts may include fist and anal sex which in most cases would be turned down, but in the current situation … many of these workers will accept for fear of losing clients to other prostitutes willing to perform those acts.[31]

In the Australian state of Victoria, a 1998 study found that 40 per cent of clients refused to use condoms and in 2011 a woman even reported that she had been threatened with a gun when she wanted to use one.[32] Nor is it only at the cheaper end of the market that women face demands for unsafe sex. In 2008, the case of the Governor of New York, Eliot Spitzer, offered a rare insight into the behaviour of a man who habitually used an expensive prostitution service. Spitzer resigned after it was revealed that he had used something called the Emperors Club VIP, which charged clients $1,000 per hour. He used the pseudonym 'James' and a woman who supplied him with prostitutes recalled that he had a 'condom problem. James didn't want to use one ... and he'd be a real weasel about it too. He just couldn't seem to take no for an answer.'[33]

It should be clear by now that what happens to women and girls in prostitution, whether or not it's legal, constitutes a spectrum of abuse. In the UK, after the Rochdale child prostitution scandal, there was much hand-wringing over the fact that under-age girls had been subjected to rape and violence in the town for such a long period without effective intervention from the authorities. Official investigations focused on those failures but they also revealed astonishing assumptions within the local authority about relationships between vulnerable girls and older men. Case files stated that children were considered to be 'making their own choices' and 'engaging in consensual sexual activity'.[34] The council's review of what went wrong contains this breathtaking sentence:

Social work practitioners and managers wholly over-estimated the extent to which Suzie could legally or psychologically consent to the sexual violence being perpetrated against her.[35]

These words have implications which go far beyond the Rochdale case. It is nonsense to suggest that an under-age girl can 'consent' to abuse, either morally or in terms of the law. Where children are concerned, the legal situation is clear: it's a criminal offence under the Sexual Offences Act 2003 for an adult to pay for sexual services with someone under the age of 18, and payment is defined as discharge of an obligation or provision of services, not just an exchange of money. If the child is under the age of 16, the adult can be sent to prison for 14 years; the maximum sentence if she's under 13 is life imprisonment. But the ethical issue is just as unequivocal, as Barnardo's pointed out more than a decade ago in a report which skewered 'the myth that girls could be consenting prostitutes, walking the streets at night'.[36]

In fact, the notion that *anyone* can consent to sexual abuse is problematic, especially when so many girls and women enter prostitution after experiencing homelessness, violence and sexual assault within their families. A Home Office consultation paper published in 2004[37] suggested that as many as 85 per cent of prostitutes have suffered physical abuse *before* starting to sell sex and 45 per cent have experienced familial sexual abuse; many have a history of poor school attendance and homelessness, and 70 per cent have spent some time in local authority care; Barnardo's has even collated evidence suggesting that children's homes are deliberately targeted by pimps.[38] The Home Office paper highlighted common factors which drive children and adults into prostitution:

As research makes clear, a high percentage of adults first became involved in prostitution at an early age. And for those who became involved as adults, the route is markedly similar. Vulnerability is the key – although for adults economic vulnerability is likely to play as significant a part as emotional vulnerability. This is particularly the case for those involved in off-street prostitution where research has found the 74 per cent cited the need to pay household expenses and support their children as the prime motivating factor.[39]

Once a child or adult has entered into a life of selling sex, it isn't easy to leave. The paper pointed out the difficulties facing women who wanted a way out of prostitution:

Debt and drug addiction play a major part in driving people into prostitution. They are also significant factors, along with the threat of violence from pimps/partners, in making it difficult to leave. Those involved in prostitution can be particularly difficult to reach, claiming that prostitution is their choice and that they don't want to leave – through a combination of fear, the process of normalisation or in an effort to maintain their dignity.[40]

It's not surprising that adults who sell sex for a living find psychological mechanisms to make it bearable. It's also worth noting that it's in the interest of people with a financial investment in the trade – pimps and owners of legal brothels – to make the lifestyle sound as harmless and indeed glamorous as possible. But it should be clear by now that significant numbers of women in prostitution are *habituated* to abuse before they enter the life, and find themselves unable or too frightened to escape from it. For them – and they're almost certainly the majority of women working as prostitutes – the issue of 'choice' is as meaningless as it was for Suzie and Sonya. Legalising prostitution might improve conditions for a minority but it doesn't even begin to address the entrenched misogyny of men who pay for sex, whether they're using women and girls as a commodity or acting out a deep loathing of women. In 1998, the Swedish government cut through the old arguments about prostitution and passed ground-breaking legislation which focused on the problem of *demand*. It declared:

> In Sweden prostitution is regarded as an aspect of male violence against women and children. It is officially acknowledged as a form of exploitation of women and children and constitutes a significant social problem, which is harmful not only to the individual prostituted woman or child, but to society at large ... Gender equality will remain unattainable so long as men buy, sell and exploit women and children by prostituting them.[41]

The new law came into force on 1 January 1999. In a reversal of the old system, it is now illegal to *buy* or attempt to buy sexual services in Sweden – the offence is punishable by fines or up to six months in prison – but not illegal to sell it. It's an approach which requires an exit strategy and resources to help women leave prostitution but it also means that the men who cause the problem are targeted, rather than their victims. In 2010, the Swedish government's first evaluation of the policy suggested that levels of street prostitution in Sweden had halved since 1999; according to the National Criminal Police, the ban on the sale of sexual services also 'acts as a barrier to human traffickers and procurers considering establishing themselves in Sweden'.[42] In 2009, the British government took tentative steps towards adopting the Swedish approach, making it a criminal offence to pay for the sexual services of anyone who has been exploited or subjected to force by a third party. In 2011, French MPs started on the same road, passing a non-binding resolution which would make paying for sex punishable by fines or prison. The following year, President Hollande's new government backed repeal of laws criminalising prostituted women and declared its support for legislation imposing penalties on clients. 'My objective, like that of the Socialist Party, is to see prostitution disappear,' declared Najat Vallaud-Belkacem, Minister for Women's Rights.[43]

It's a huge and welcome ideological shift. For centuries, prostitution has been fought over by puritans who blame its victims on the one hand, and libertines who regard access to the bodies of women and children as a right on the other. In the second half of the 20th century, feminists were caught somewhere in between, reluctant to ally themselves with anti-sex campaigns but disturbed by the levels of verbal abuse and physical violence suffered by prostituted women. Both sides made the mistake of thinking it was all about sex but innovative feminist thinking places prostitution in the broader context of violence against women and children. It's becoming clear that the central issue raised by prostitution isn't sexual freedom: men who pay for sex are in reality buying power over other human beings. Suzie and Sonya had no power, no choice and no way out, unlike the men who used their 'services'. Most men don't use prostituted women but the ones who do cannot be tolerated in societies based on equality and human rights.

THE WITCHES OF PERUGIA

On 22 February 1445, a woman called Santuccia da Gualdo Tadino[1] was arrested in Umbria on suspicion of witchcraft. Santuccia was taken to the nearby city of Perugia where she faced grave charges: the secular authorities claimed she was a *faturaja* or sorceress who had bewitched her neighbours and murdered 50 infants by drinking their blood. Contemporary archives do not record whether Santuccia was tortured, which was common practice in other jurisdictions, but she was speedily tried, convicted and sentenced to death. On 6 March, she was publicly humiliated by being forced to ride through Perugia on a donkey, facing backwards and wearing a mitre bearing images of two demons; on arrival in the city's Campo della Battaglia, she was burned to death. Santuccia's execution predated publication of the *Malleus Maleficarum* by four decades, but she was not the only supposed witch to face a hideous death in Perugia at this time. The Archivo di Stato di Perugia contains records of four more cases between 1455 and 1501,[2] and one modern authority[3] describes the city as the 'epicenter' of 15th-century witch trials.

Such was the history of the forbidding walled city which was to become the setting for one of the most sensational murder trials of the early 21st century. In the second half of 2007, two young women from different continents made their way to Perugia to study; sheer chance – the sister of the younger woman spotted an Italian student putting up a notice about a room to let – brought them together as flatmates. Meredith Kercher arrived first, towards the end of August, and moved into a stone cottage in Via della Pergola on the outskirts of the city. The cottage was divided into two flats, one on each floor: Kercher was to share the upstairs apartment with two Italian women in their mid-20s, Filomena Romanelli and Laura Mezetti, who were old friends and training to become lawyers. Kercher was 21, a student at the University of Leeds whose family came from Coulsdon in Surrey. A month later, the apartment's fourth bedroom was rented by Amanda Knox, an American student whose family lived in Seattle. Knox was only 18 months younger than Kercher and in the first few days they socialised and got to know each other, but they were not cut out to be close friends. Kercher was studious and a little reserved, while Knox was sporty, outgoing and noisy, with a disconcerting habit of slipping into yoga positions in the middle of a conversation. She arrived from Seattle with condoms and a vibrator in her toilet bag, which she left in one of the shared bathrooms, and her standards of hygiene were trying for her English flatmate; Kercher complained that Knox didn't always ensure the toilet was clean, even when she was menstruating. Both women acquired boyfriends in Perugia; by the end of October, Kercher had begun a relationship with one of the male students who lived in the cottage's downstairs apartment while Knox had just met Raffaele Sollecito, 23, a student from a small town north of Bari in southern Italy. Although he was often described as Knox's long-term or steady boyfriend,

Sollecito had been seeing her for just 10 days when tragedy engulfed everyone who lived in the upstairs apartment.[4]

In a sequence of events distorted by rumour, sloppy forensic work and lurid sexual fantasies, it is not always easy to sift out uncontested facts. One is that at some point on the night of 1 November 2007, while Kercher was alone in the cottage, someone gained access to the apartment on the upper floor and brutally assaulted her. She was left dying on the floor of her bedroom with cuts to her throat in a scene which might have come from a horror film: her body almost covered by a quilt, her underwear and smeared blood on the floor, a bloody print from a knife on the bedding. There were traces of blood in the bathroom Kercher shared with Knox and unflushed faeces in the flat's other bathroom. Glass from a broken window in Romanelli's bedroom suggested a break-in, although police would quickly dismiss evidence of an apparent burglary as staged from inside. There was no doubt about the ordeal Kercher had suffered before her death: a post-mortem established that she had died from asphyxiation as her lungs filled up with blood, and one of the experts testified that she might have struggled for life for as long as 10 minutes. Sexual activity had taken place shortly before she died but despite bruising in her vagina, the medical witnesses were unable to say for certain whether or not she had been raped. Even so, the late-night murder of a young woman who happened to be alone in an isolated apartment had all the markings of a sexually motivated assault. It also pointed to a male perpetrator, since it is undeniable that men commit the vast majority of such crimes.

The second fact in this case is that, within 15 days of the murder, the prosecution had copious forensic evidence incriminating Rudy Guede, a young man of 20 or 21 – accounts vary – who had left traces of himself all over the murder scene. Guede was originally from Ivory Coast, had had a troubled childhood and was estranged from his father who lived on the plain below Perugia. In his teens, Guede had been unofficially adopted by one of the city's wealthiest families but it didn't stop him dropping out of college courses and failing his exams. In the months before Kercher's murder, he had embarked on a string of petty crimes, including a burglary in Perugia in September when he accidentally woke a bar owner, Cristiano Tramontano, and threatened him with a knife. Shortly afterwards, a nursery school in Milan was burgled and petty cash taken from a cashbox; three weeks later, the owner turned up on a Saturday morning for an appointment with a plumber and found Guede in her office. She called the police, who searched his bag and found a large knife which had been stolen in the earlier break-in. They also found a laptop and a mobile phone which had been stolen from a lawyer's office in Perugia on 13 October. Guede refused to answer questions and the Milan police let him go.

It quickly emerged that Guede knew both Knox and Kercher slightly, and had spent at least one evening in the apartment on the lower floor of the cottage in Via della Pergola in the weeks before the murder. He had met Knox briefly in Le Chic, the bar where she sometimes worked for another African-Italian, Diya 'Patrick' Lumumba from Zaire, and they later coincided in the downstairs flat when Guede was visiting the four young men who lived there. Guede recalled smoking joints with the male students and discussing which of the women upstairs they would like to have sex with; he said he would like to 'screw'[5] Knox and moments later she came downstairs, causing embarrassed laughter. Not long after that Kercher came down as well. Guede later said he found her attractive and spent a couple of hours talking to her until the women went back to their own apartment around 4.30a.m. Guede passed the rest of the night in the downstairs flat, stumbling into the toilet where he fell asleep after failing to flush away his faeces. At no point in the evening did he go into the upper apartment.

On 16 November, just over two weeks after the murder, forensic scientists in Rome told the police in Perugia that a bloody partial palm print on a pillow in Kercher's bedroom in the upstairs flat belonged to Guede. His name hadn't previously come up in the investigation but the evidence against him was compelling: as well as the palm print, his DNA was found on a swab from Kercher's vagina, on toilet paper in the unflushed lavatory in the second bathroom, mixed with Kercher's blood inside her shoulder bag, and on the left sleeve of her sweatshirt. After his arrest, it would quickly be established that a footprint in the flat matched the Nike trainers Guede was wearing on the night of the murder – and not, as earlier thought, a shoe worn by one of three suspects who were already in custody. In other circumstances, this series of discoveries might have marked a breakthrough in the case, persuading the investigators that their initial idea that several people had been involved in the murder was simply wrong. Far from it: they issued a warrant for Guede's arrest but it doesn't seem even to have crossed their minds to abandon their outlandish conspiracy theory. They simply reconfigured their supposed cast of murderers to include Guede, bringing the supposed number of killers to four until one of the other suspects provided an unbreakable alibi. It turned out that Guede had left Perugia shortly after the murder, but he was tracked down in Germany and arrested on 20 November. Not long after that, the Italian authorities had the man who should have been their chief suspect in custody in Perugia.

Under interrogation, Guede admitted that he was in the upstairs apartment on the night of the murder. He denied taking part in the attack, saying he was in the flat at Kercher's invitation after running into her at a Halloween party the previous evening. In this version, he arrived to keep the rendezvous with Kercher and started having sex with her in the sitting room, but broke off to use the lavatory; Guede blamed the killing on a stranger who supposedly entered the apartment while he was in the toilet. The single-assailant story wasn't what investigators wanted to hear and Guede changed his story several times, implicating various individuals. But his defence team could not argue with the forensic evidence and he opted for a fast-track trial, appearing separately from the other suspects charged with the murder. On 28 October 2008, almost a year to the day since Kercher was killed, Guede was convicted of sexual assault and murder. He was sentenced to 30 years in prison.

To anyone familiar with sex attackers – their gender, age profile, background and *modus operandi* – the identification of Guede as Meredith Kercher's killer is unproblematic. He knew both Knox and Kercher by sight, he knew where they lived and it is entirely credible that he either knocked on the door or broke into the flat in the hope of having sex with one or other of them. That Kercher was willing to have sex with Guede in such circumstances is implausible, but his presence at the scene of the crime is beyond doubt. With such an obvious contender for the role of chief suspect, what is astonishing about this case is the prosecution's unshakable conviction that he was merely a bit player in a sinister conspiracy; for four years, police and prosecutors held stubbornly to the notion that the savage murder of Meredith Kercher was initiated and orchestrated by someone other than Guede, and that the individual concerned was a young *woman*. Flying in the face of both statistical probability and forensic evidence, the prosecution decided that this young woman was the prime mover in a plot to force Kercher to take part in a *pesante gioco sessuale* or 'heavy sex game'.[6] Not only that: she was supposedly so manipulative that she was able to persuade two young men who hadn't previously met to assist her in this shocking criminal enterprise. That woman was Amanda Knox, and the prosecution's far-fetched scenario left unanswered questions all over the case: how, in little more than a month, had Knox developed such a loathing of her flatmate that she was prepared to hold her down while a male accomplice sexually assaulted and stabbed her? How did she persuade Sollecito, whom she had known for just a week-and-a-half, to take part in the attack? Why was there so little evidence placing Knox and Sollecito at the scene of the crime – none at all, in fact, as we shall see later in this chapter – while the man accused and convicted of the murder had left so much? Above all, why did the prosecution insist that a classic sex crime pointing to an easily identified male perpetrator was actually a conspiracy instigated by a young woman with no motive and no history of violence? Sollecito made this point when he spoke in his own defence in December 2009, arguing that the prosecution had portrayed him as 'a sort of dog on a leash'[7] who would do anything Knox told him to do. 'If Amanda had asked me to do something I didn't agree with, I would have said no,' he insisted. 'Let alone if she had asked me to do something as terrible as killing a girl.'

That, however, is precisely what prosecutors believed. More than two years earlier, and within days of the murder, they had cast Knox in the role of a jealous, drug-crazed, party-loving hedonist who dominated Sollecito and murdered her flatmate for kicks. Knox herself described most of what was said about her by the prosecution as 'pure fantasy' and the nature of that fantasy can be summed up in two damning words which would be repeated in just about every sensational article on the case: 'Foxy Knoxy'. The damning nickname appeared on Knox's MySpace page, and the myth of the murderous student from Seattle took hold with astonishing speed. Like many young people who've grown up with social media, Knox probably didn't give a moment's thought to the way it might be used in hostile circumstances but its implications – that she was predatory, amoral and cunning – proved irresistible to reporters; her family's protests that it was a childhood nickname, derived from her style of playing soccer, were simply ignored. Detectives and the chief prosecutor, Giuliano Mignini,[8] were disconcerted by Knox from the start, regarding almost every aspect of the young American's behaviour – especially on the morning after the murder – as suspicious. What is certain is that Knox returned to the apartment from Sollecito's flat late that morning and found the front door open. The police were incredulous that she went on to have a shower in the bathroom she shared with Kercher, ignoring traces of blood – she later said she thought one of the other women was having a period – and returned to Sollecito's flat as if nothing had happened. (Knox's attitude to menstrual blood was strikingly matter of fact, in contrast to the mystical role it was allotted in mediaeval superstition, as we shall see later in this chapter.) Just after noon, she called her flatmate Filomena Romanelli who, unknown to Knox, had tried and failed to speak to Kercher by phone. Knox told Romanelli what she'd seen at the apartment and said she was starting to feel scared, whereupon Romanelli tried Kercher again on her English and Italian mobiles. She still couldn't get through and called Knox, telling her to go back to the apartment to make sure that everything was all right. Even at this point, it does not seem to have occurred to either woman to call the police; Knox returned to Via della Pergola with Sollecito, calling back at 12.34p.m. to say she'd found broken glass in Romanelli's bedroom and faeces in the second bathroom. 'We've had burglars,'[9] she exclaimed. Romanelli promised to meet her at the flat and urged her to call the police. What Knox actually did was revert to being a scared little girl in a foreign country: she called her mother in Seattle, where it was still the early hours of the morning, and told her someone had been in the flat. She also said that Kercher's bedroom door was locked. At the same time, Sollecito was on the phone to his sister, who was an officer in the military police, and after asking her advice he called the emergency number for the *carabinieri*.

To detectives and the magistrate, Mignini, Knox's behaviour on the day after the murder wasn't just thoughtless and self-absorbed; it signalled, beyond any doubt in their minds, her involvement in the crime. That she was young for her age, entranced by a new boyfriend and living in a student flat where people came and went at all hours, doesn't seem to have occurred to them as a less melodramatic but equally likely explanation of her delay in contacting the authorities. In the days following the discovery of the body, the police interviewed Knox and Sollecito many times, barely allowing them time to sleep; the interviews were carried out without lawyers and at a time when Knox had to rely on interpreters to translate both the police's questions and her answers. (Her Italian later became fluent in jail.) Crucially, she was not told that her status had changed from witness to suspect, not even during a gruelling interrogation which began late on the evening of 5 November and carried on until the following morning. Isolated and exhausted, Knox was devastated when her interrogators suddenly announced that Sollecito had destroyed her alibi, claiming she left his apartment for several hours on the night of the murder. At 1.45a.m., and still without legal advice, she signed a statement in Italian in which she said she met her employer, Lumumba, on the night of the murder and went with him to the apartment on Via della Pergola; she couldn't remember whether Kercher was there or arrived later, but Lumumba had sex with her. 'I remember confusedly that he's the one who killed her,' she agreed.[10] That was enough for the police: just over an hour later they went to Lumumba's apartment, woke him and brought him to the police station. Around midday on 6 November, Lumumba, Knox and Sollecito were all charged with Kercher's murder.

In theory, this unlikely explanation for the tragic death of a vivacious young woman should have begun to unravel almost as soon as it was proposed. Knox's 'memory' of being in the flat when Kercher died was full of gaps; she couldn't even say whether Sollecito, who steadfastly denied any involvement, was present in the apartment during the murder. Within 12 hours of her 'confession', Knox asked for pen and paper and wrote her own account of the evening, admitting she couldn't remember it clearly because of the marijuana she smoked with Sollecito – an admission of law-breaking which she had understandably wanted to keep from the police. To an outside observer, the unreliability of her 'confession' leaps from the page: within hours she was writing frankly that she didn't know whether the things she had told the police were real or a 'dream' she'd come up with under the pressure of 'stress, shock and extreme exhaustion'.[11] From the point of view of the prosecution, things rapidly got worse; after being taken to Capanne prison, which is half an hour's drive from Perugia, Knox finally got a night's sleep and her memory started to come back. Away from the investigators' barrage of questions, she came up with a more confident account of her movements on the night of 1 November; she recalled that she spent the evening at Sollecito's apartment where they lay in bed talking, had sex and eventually went to sleep until the following morning. Like an earnest student doing her best to make up for past mistakes, Knox even apologised to the Italian authorities: 'I'm sorry I didn't remember before and I'm sorry I said I could have been at the house when [the murder] happened. I said these things because I was confused and scared.'[12] But she also told her lawyers she'd been hit twice by a female police officer before she accused Lumumba of involvement in the murder. One of them, Luciano Ghirga, dismissed it as a 'cuff on the head' and decided it wasn't worth bringing up in Knox's defence.[13]

The prosecution's dramatic theory was by now based on a retracted confession from a suggestible young foreigner, and supported by nothing in the way of evidence. Prosecutors had made up their minds *before* getting the results of forensic tests on material found at the crime scene and it wasn't until 15 November, two weeks after the murder, that Mignini was told that forensic investigators in Rome had found minute traces of Knox's and Kercher's DNA on a kitchen knife taken from Sollecito's apartment. (Almost four years later, an independent expert discredited even this claim, confirming that there was no trace of Kercher's blood on the knife and no DNA evidence on a clip from her bra, which the police had attributed to Sollecito.[14]) The very next day, 16 November 2007, the prosecutors received the news that much more significant forensic evidence had been discovered against Guede, and Mignini issued a warrant for his arrest. By then, though, the prosecution's lurid original version of events had already been in the public domain for a week. On 9 November an investigating judge, Claudia Matteini, signed a 19-page order in which she laid out the prosecution's scenario that Knox had agreed to help Lumumba meet Kercher on the night of the murder. Kercher supposedly went to her room with Lumumba and then 'something went wrong' – probably Sollecito trying to join in, according to the judge – and the young woman refused to do what the two men wanted. When Kercher struggled, she was threatened with a knife and stabbed in the throat. Matteini wrote confidently:

> As far as the juridical aspect of the case, there are no doubts at this moment in presuming this to be correct: that there was an initial wish of the three youths to try a new sensation, above all for the boyfriend and girlfriend, while for [Lumumba] the desire to have carnal relations with a girl he liked and who was refusing him, and in the face of a denial from the victim, they did not have the presence of mind to desist, but tried to force the will of the girl using a knife that Sollecito always carried with him.[15]

When sections of Matteini's report appeared in the press, it was a gift to Knox's critics. On 8 November, the *Daily Mail* had already informed its readers that one of Kercher's friends claimed Knox 'brought a string of "strange" men back to the flat' they shared,[16] but now journalists could say more or less what they liked. The following day, the *Daily Mail* quoted unnamed sources in the Italian police to the effect that Knox had 'held Meredith down during deadly sex attack', pressing so hard on the victim's face that 'she left an imprint of her fingers on the skin'.[17] There was no evidence for either claim but Knox's reputation was in the process of being thoroughly shredded. Two days later the *Daily Telegraph* asked a loaded question in a headline: 'Good girl gone bad, or innocent in mourning?'[18] It did cross the paper's mind to wonder how Knox had turned from 'an apparently sweet, caring, athletic girl ... into a promiscuous, sexual deviant who played an active part in a sex-for-kicks killing'. But it quoted anonymous sources to the effect that 'Knox was the leader in her pursuit of exciting sex and was, in the words of one insider, "up for it".' Sollecito was barely mentioned as reporters hurried to discover acquaintances and anecdotes that would bolster this reading of Knox's character. A month after the murder, the *Daily Mail* unveiled what its headline called 'the wild, raunchy past of Foxy Knoxy',[19] reporting that she had arrived in Perugia with 'a dangerous appetite for drink, drugs and sex'. The paper incorrectly claimed that Knox cultivated marijuana plants in the apartment she shared with Kercher; the plants actually belonged to the male students in the downstairs flat and it was Kercher, not Knox, who was asked to water them while the boys were away for a weekend. The paper also got a much more significant fact wrong, reporting that Knox's bloody handprint had been found in the dead woman's bedroom. The tenor of the article may be gauged from its account of her farewell party in a student house she shared with other young women in Seattle, which was supposedly 'like a scene from Baghdad'. A scandalised but anonymous guest told the paper:

> Some people were naked inside the bedrooms. There were people draped over each other. I've been to a lot of student parties in my time, but I've never been to a party like that. Everyone just wanted to get drunk, get high and get laid. There was also a lot of violence because everyone was so pumped up.

In fact, neighbours called the police when some male students began throwing stones and empty beer cans outside

the student house, and officers arrived to find Knox com-
forting a distressed friend. She politely assured them that
she would persuade the drunken youths to go home, and
clubbed together with four women friends to pay a fine of
$269. But that wasn't nearly as appealing a story as the
unfounded suggestion that the American student was no
stranger to kinky sex and 'violence' long before her arrival
in Perugia.

This was not, nor should it ever have been, a case that
hinged on Knox's character. She was slow to realise the
significance of what she'd seen at the flat in Via della
Pergola on the morning after the killing but so were other
people, including Romanelli and Sollecito; in any case, until
the locked door to Kercher's room was broken down, the
disorder seemed to point to a burglary rather than murder.
But the fact that the investigation focused so quickly on
Knox, and continued to do so even when the evidence
identified Guede as the prime suspect, speaks volumes
about the Italian authorities' beliefs about women. They
looked at a naïve, unselfconscious 20-year-old, a foreigner
who was fond of parties and curious about her sexuality,
and saw an amoral *femme fatale* who had led her weak
male accomplices into committing a sensational murder.
The American author and journalist, Nina Burleigh,
understood this process better than most. In her book on
the case, she wrote:

Scampering around Perugia, [Knox] was only doing what
liberated, athletic, self-absorbed young American girls do:
having fun. And that fun – boisterous, brazen maybe – was
read by Italian men like Rudy and the others, including

Mignini and the police, in the only context by which they had to understand female behaviour: she was the witch, the deliberate player of men.[20]

In reality, there was another context for the prosecution's misogyny. Under the premiership of Silvio Berlusconi, a sleazy media baron with an insatiable appetite for younger women, public life in Italy deteriorated into an embarrassing sexual farce. The prime minister's *bunga bunga* parties were notorious, and he would eventually face sordid allegations about paying for sex with women who worked as prostitutes, including an under-age Moroccan girl. Berlusconi's control of the Italian media flooded the country with crude, sexualised images of women, setting back the cause of gender equality by many years. Many Italians were disgusted by their prime minister's behaviour but Berlusconi's antics confirmed age-old prejudices about women's sexual allure and untrustworthiness, with disastrous consequences for Knox. The professional entertainers and women from the commercial sex industry who swarmed around the prime minister, appealing to his monumental vanity, could hardly have been more unlike the young American who arrived from a country where the women's movement had fought for decades against such sexist nonsense. When Knox was wrongly told in prison that a blood test had shown she was HIV-positive, she willingly provided a list of the seven men she had had sex with; it was a lifetime total, but in no time at all the media were reporting that Knox had had seven lovers during her month in Italy.[21] If any single object symbolised Knox's matter-of-fact approach to sex, it was the vibrator in her toilet bag; Knox's generation grew up in the wake of *Sex and the City*, where owning a 'rampant rabbit' was a jokey statement of women's sexual autonomy. But in a country torn between grotesque prurience and conservative Catholic attitudes to sex, Knox felt she had to stand up in court during her trial and explain that a friend in the US had given her the harmless sex toy as a present. The result was more sensational stories, not just in Italy but also in the UK. The *Sun* had already published a bizarre headline to the effect that Knox had 'no pants on in jail'[22] and it later featured the vibrator in a headline loaded with innuendo: 'Why I had a rabbit sex toy at murder house'.[23] In *The Times*, Libby Purves seemed to have the vibrator in mind when she published a comment piece two days after Knox and Sollecito were convicted. Attacking the notion that Knox could be described as 'sexually adventurous', Purves wrote:

Adventurous? Come off it! These people are not Sir Ranulph Fiennes or Captain Scott. They are just randy and needy, and afraid or incapable of love. ... They think that it is OK to objectify other human beings as sex toys, and throw them away afterwards.[24]

In an atmosphere so censorious of female sexuality, it is not surprising that the prison terms handed down at the two trials punished Knox more harshly than anyone else: she got 26 years, Sollecito 25, while Guede's sentence was cut on appeal to 16.

At the same time, Burleigh's suggestion that ideas about witchcraft warped perceptions of the case was spot-on. She argued that the magistrate, Mignini, 'always included witch fear in his murder theory, and only reluctantly relinquished it'. In her book, Burleigh recalled that Mignini told a court in October 2008 that the murder was premeditated, 'a sexual and sacrificial rite' which should have been 'celebrated on the night of Halloween' but had to be delayed for 24 hours because Knox's flatmates held a dinner party on 31 October.[25] But the most direct accusation of witchcraft was made by a lawyer, Carlo Pacelli, who had been retained by Lumumba in his action against Knox for defamation. By a quirk of the Italian legal system, this civil suit was heard alongside the murder charges, offering Pacelli a platform he was not slow to exploit. In November 2009, during the original trial, Pacelli stood up in the Perugia courtroom and launched a no-holds-barred attack, characterising Knox as 'diabolical'. He asked:

Who is Amanda Knox? Is she the angelic person we see here? Or is she really a diabolical she-devil, an explosive concentrate of sex, drugs and alcohol? She is both. But the latter is the Amanda we saw on 1 November, 2007.[26]

These lurid accusations were very much in the minds of Knox's defence team. At the end of her trial in 2009, one of her lawyers, Maria Del Grosso, pointed towards her client. 'Is this the witch you're going to burn?' she demanded.[27] Pacelli was unembarrassed; two years later, during Knox and Sollecito's appeal, he returned to exactly the same theme. He described Knox as a 'witch of deception', making a contrast between the 'angelic' aspect of her character and a side that was supposedly 'Lucifer-like, demonic, satanic, diabolic'. His comments caused widespread astonishment but to anyone familiar with the history of medieval witch-hunts, they had an uncomfortably familiar ring. When the supposed witch Santuccia di Gualdo Tadini was burned to death in Perugia in 1445, a Franciscan friar, Giacomo della Marca, turned up to cheer on her execution. There was clearly some anxiety in the city that ordinary people might feel sympathy with the accused woman, and the monk duly preached a sermon urging doubters to look into Santuccia's face. They would instantly be reassured as to her diabolical nature, he claimed, because they would see that the devil 'dwells in her at all times'[28] – the very accusation Pacelli made against Knox. Nor did the parallels end there. Two weeks after Santuccia's execution, three of her male 'accomplices' were brought before the authorities. Santuccia had been accused of using consecrated hosts obtained from priests to bewitch her victims, and all three of the men who'd been arrested were in holy orders. Two were accused of holding regular meetings with Santuccia and being sorcerers themselves, while the third was apprehended in a convent which was forbidden territory to men. Their sentences, however, were strikingly different from the one imposed on poor Santuccia; two were given prison sentences while the third escaped with a fine.[29]

But it is another witch trial in Perugia, 10 years after these grim but ludicrous events, which reveals how much power the Umbrian *streghe* or witches were assumed to enjoy – and the overtly sexual nature of that power. Filippa da Citta della Pieve was arrested and executed in 1455, and the city records contain a detailed account of the accusations against her.[30] She is supposed to have created a 'love potion' from her own menstrual blood, powerful herbs and semen, and used it to force at least four men to fall in love with her. Filippa's supposed mentor was an older *strega*, Clarutia Angeli, and the two women were accused of killing young children together by sucking their blood. Naturally they were believed to be in league with the devil, although Filippa seems to have been a somewhat demanding acolyte; one of the most vivid details has her stripping naked before dawn, promising herself to him body and soul and demanding, in return, that he 'carry me where I tell [him]'.

In 15th-century Italy, such accusations appealed to superstitious beliefs about women and quickly led to a death sentence. Five and a half centuries later, a young American who revelled in the equality enjoyed by women of her generation was to spend four years in prison for a crime she did not commit, along with her supposed accomplice. Knox and Sollecito won their appeal against their murder convictions in October 2011, but there was a curious coda to the case. Within minutes of the verdict being announced in Perugia, the *Daily Mail* published an article on its website claiming that Knox had lost her case: 'Guilty: Amanda Knox looks stunned as appeal against murder conviction is rejected', the paper's headline announced. It described a wholly fictitious scene in the courtroom as Knox 'sank into her chair sobbing uncontrollably while her family and friends hugged each other in tears'.[31] Nothing of the sort happened and the *Daily Mail* corrected its account of the verdict after 90 seconds, but the paper was later censured by the Press Complaints Commission for the fake report.

After four years as victims of an egregious miscarriage of justice, Amanda Knox and Raffaele Sollecito were finally free. The real killer, Rudy Guede, was serving a (surprisingly short) prison sentence. Justice for his victim, Meredith Kercher, had been delayed and her family had had to endure a lengthy and flawed judicial process. But that wasn't quite the end of the matter. The Italian authorities smarted over their failure to keep Knox and Sollecito in jail and announced their own intention to appeal. In the UK, meanwhile, the *Daily Mail* was still struggling to reconcile itself to the idea that Knox was innocent after all. 'What is it about Amanda Knox that so chills the blood?'[32] a headline demanded. Its columnist Amanda Platell was ready with an answer:

> In the coming months we'll get to see a lot more of Foxy Knoxy as she sells her story for millions and helps write the script for her Hollywood movie. She will no doubt portray herself as a cross between Mother Theresa and Angelina Jolie – a sexy saint. The question is, will anyone believe it.

It wasn't just in Italy that a confident young woman aroused deep-seated fears about a supposed link between sexual power and duplicity. Foxy Knoxy, the media's quintessential bad girl, was simply too tempting to give up.

CONCLUSION: WOMEN'S RIGHTS ARE HUMAN RIGHTS

It shouldn't need to be said in the 21st century. The proposition should be so obvious, so clear to everyone, that it doesn't have to be pointed out. The theory of inalienable human rights, which became the foremost ethical doctrine of the second half of the 20th century, was not developed and codified solely for the benefit of *men*. Yet I've just written a book about what's happening to half the human race in the 21st century and I feel like shouting from the rooftops: *women's rights are human rights*. I know that men are oppressed and killed by unpleasant regimes and in terrorist attacks. I've spent years opposing censorship, torture and the death penalty, regardless of the victims' gender. But there is a problem. I was once invited to introduce the then Foreign Secretary, Robin Cook, before he made a big speech about human rights in the grand surroundings of the Locarno room in the Foreign and Commonwealth Office in London. The audience consisted of ambassadors and journalists, and was overwhelmingly male. When I made the point that women's rights are human rights, I could tell that they didn't really understand what I was saying. Women? Human rights? What's the issue? The answer to that question is very simple, and a consequence of the confusion that's been at the heart of human rights discourse throughout its more-than-200-year history.

For centuries, the concept of a 'human being' was synonymous with that of 'man'. When political philosophers began drawing up lists of rights and drafting conventions, the beneficiary they had in mind appeared and sounded male. Simone de Beauvoir understood the elision and expressed it succinctly in *The Second Sex*, where she wrote that 'humanity is male and man defines woman not in herself but as relative to him'.[1] In the 1970s, when feminists began to think about language, they didn't object to the use of the word 'man' to include woman merely as an exercise in semantics. They understood that language has an impact on the way people think, in this case reinforcing the idea that men provide the standard by which normal human behaviour should be defined. The consequences are far-reaching, as a brief history of our present subject demonstrates.

The notion of natural rights which are common to all human beings emerged around the time of the French Revolution. In the very first summer of the revolution, August 1789, the National Constituent Assembly debated a ground-breaking document which was described as a Declaration of the Rights of Man and of the Citizen. Because women could not be citizens, their exclusion from the document was clear, and it infuriated the playwright and polemicist Olympe de Gouges. De Gouges was born Marie Gouze in Montauban, south-west France, in 1748; she married a caterer from Paris at the age of 18, had a son and was rescued from this unhappy relationship – she said she regarded her husband with 'repugnance' – by his early death. She moved to Paris with her son and reinvented herself as Olympe de Gouges, embarking on a series of relationships with men outside the protection, insofar as it existed, of marriage. Painfully aware of women's lack of legal rights, she produced her own Declaration in September 1791, pointedly rewriting the clauses of the original. De Gouges insisted that women had a role to play in public life:

> Woman has the right to mount the scaffold, so she should have the right equally to mount the rostrum, provided that these manifestations do not trouble public order as established by law.[2]

De Gouge's Declaration of the Rights of Woman and the Female Citizen demanded equal rights under the law, denounced marriage as 'the tomb of confidence and love' and challenged the 'barbarous prejudice' against unmarried women having children. Centuries ahead of her time, she understood that rights mean little if they can't be enforced and came to the very modern conclusion that the state needs to be involved as a guarantor: 'The safeguard of the rights of woman and the female citizen requires public powers.'[3] Sadly, when De Gouges stuck to her principles and spoke out against the increasing savagery of the revolution, she was tried and condemned; she died on the guillotine on 3 November 1793 at the age of 45. Two weeks later, when women wearing red bonnets protested publicly against the banning of women's political clubs, the extreme Jacobin Pierre Gaspard Chaumette denounced them and held up De Gouges as a warning. The terms of his denunciation are chilling but also instructive:

Remember this virago, this woman-man, this shameless Olympe de Gouges who was the first to set up women's clubs, who abandoned her household duties, wanted to take part in politics and committed crimes. ... All these immoral creatures have been annihilated by the vengeful fire of the law; and you would like to imitate them? No, you should surely feel that you are only interesting and worthy of appreciation when you are that which Nature wanted you to be.[4]

Chaumette himself went to the guillotine five months later. The right of French women to full citizenship was not recognised until 1944, when they finally got the vote. But even as De Gouges died for her principles, a new champion of women's rights had joined the struggle in the form of the English writer Mary Wollstonecraft. She shared De Gouges's radical views on marriage, describing it as 'legalised prostitution' in her most famous work, *A Vindication of the Rights of Woman*, which appeared in 1792. Wollstonecraft was vilified as 'that hyena in petticoats'[5] but her contribution to the debate about human rights was as significant as De Gouges's had been in France. She widened the theory to include subjects such as education, arguing that it was essential if girls were to stop being helpless dependants of their male relatives.

Confusion about the relationship between human rights and gender continued for the next century and a half. In 1947, a committee was tasked by the UN with drawing up a new declaration of human rights to prevent a repetition of the horrors of the Second World War. The committee's composition reflected its time, with nine members chosen to represent countries and continents, including not just the US and UK but Russia, Lebanon and China. The US representative, Eleanor Roosevelt, was the only woman. They worked on the document until the end of the following year, 1948, when it was accepted by the UN General Assembly. In many ways a fine piece of work, the Universal Declaration of Human Rights begins with a high-minded preamble which insists upon 'the equal and inalienable rights of all members of *the human family*' [my italics]. But things start to go awry in the very next paragraph, which talks about the 'conscience of *mankind*'. It takes only one more paragraph for the word 'man' to appear instead of 'human being'. I don't suppose for one moment that Roosevelt and her co-authors intended to exclude women from the protection offered by the declaration, but it sometimes appears as if it has had – and is still having – that subliminal effect.

Declarations and conventions do not prevent wars and atrocities. Human rights abuses have occurred in many countries since 1948, from military coups in Latin America and civil wars in former Yugoslavia to the Rwandan genocide. But declarations of rights achieve two things: they establish values which the signatories agreed to defend and they challenge the impunity which was enjoyed by torturers and murderers for centuries. Chile's General Pinochet was astonished when an agreeable shopping trip to London, which he had enjoyed on many previous occasions, ended with him under house arrest on the orders of a Spanish judge; the former President of Liberia, Charles Taylor, was found guilty at The Hague of war crimes and crimes against humanity and sentenced to life imprisonment.

Economic and sporting sanctions were instrumental in ending the apartheid era in South Africa, while military interventions in Sierra Leone, the Balkans and Libya aimed to protect civilians and get rid of unpleasant regimes. Yet it is a striking fact that world leaders sometimes behave as though the offence is in a lower register if most or all of the victims of a regime are female. Saudi Arabia operates a blatant form of gender apartheid but Western governments treat the Saudi government as a favoured trading partner. The Taliban closed girls' schools and forced women to leave their jobs in Afghanistan, but the regime achieved pariah status only when Mullah Omar made the mistake of sheltering Osama bin Laden. Western leaders worry about Iran's nuclear programme but have less to say about the daily lives of Iranian women, who are denied basic freedoms and threatened with barbaric punishments for 'offences' such as adultery. (It's only the most egregious cases, such as that of Sakineh Mohammadi Ashtiani, an ethnic Azeri woman sentenced to death by stoning, which prompt international condemnation.) In 2012, when the England cricket team went on an official tour of Sri Lanka, their trip coincided with a Channel 4 documentary which revealed evidence of massacres during the civil war, including footage of government soldiers joking over the bodies of Tamil rape victims.

Time after time, the response of the international community suggests that human rights abuses against women are simply not as visible as those against the general population of a given country. The situation is made worse by the nature of modern conflict, which is asymmetrical and creates massive civilian casualties, most of whom are women and children. Research by Amnesty International confirms this proposition:

> Women and girls are uniquely and disproportionately affected by armed conflict. In modern warfare, an estimated 90% of the casualties are civilians, and 75% of these are women and children.
>
> Women are 80% of all refugees and displaced persons. Rape and sexual violence targeting women and girls are routinely used not only to terrorize women, but as strategic tools of war and instruments of genocide.[6]

Despite their over-representation among victims of war and genocide, women are vastly *under*-represented in the process of ending conflict. No woman has ever been appointed chief or lead negotiator in UN-sponsored peace talks, and research by Womankind Worldwide shows that in 25 years only one in 40 peace treaty signatories has been female.[7] Yet many of the crimes committed against women and girls are gender-related, whether they happen during a conflict or are carried out by troops from the winning side. It's only in recent years that the truly staggering extent of rape by German and Soviet troops in the Second World War has been exposed, while the wars in former Yugoslavia provided shocking evidence of the use of 'rape camps' to humiliate Muslim women. In Sierra Leone, thousands of girls were forced to become child prostitutes by rebel soldiers, while women and girls in the Democratic Republic of Congo have been repeatedly raped while trying to flee to neighbouring Uganda. Even when women and children reach the supposed 'safety' of refugee camps, they remain vulnerable to rape and sexual assault. These are huge violations of human rights yet it's only recently that rape in war has started to be treated with the gravity it deserves. It did not feature in the first three Geneva Conventions, making its first appearance only in 1949 when the Fourth Convention prohibited wartime rape and enforced prostitution. Even then, rape and sexual enslavement did not become crimes against humanity until 2001.

In terms of gender, there is always a risk of defining human rights too narrowly. When I chaired the Writers in Prison Committee of English PEN, most of the imprisoned and threatened writers I dealt with were male. Some had undergone dreadful forms of torture in countries like Syria and Uzbekistan and fully deserved any support we could offer, but the fact that so few women featured on our lists of prisoners was troubling. In many countries, women have neither sufficient education nor access to forms of publication to allow them to exercise their right to free expression. Literacy is essential for anyone who wishes to take part in civil and political society, yet two-thirds of the world's almost 800m illiterates[8] are women. Only 39 per cent of rural girls attend secondary school, according to global figures from the UN,[9] and the problem is exacerbated by early marriage. In cultures where girls habitually marry below the age of 18, they are unlikely to finish their education and pass on illiteracy to their daughters. The problem is particularly acute in South Asia: 43 per cent of children in Afghanistan are married before the age of 18, and the figure for Bangladesh is 69 per cent. In Pakistan, one survey of adults aged 25 to 29 revealed that 37 per cent of the girls had actually been married below the legal age, which was 16 at the time. Even in India, almost half the country's children are married before they reach 18.[10] (In England and Wales, for comparison, early marriage is rare; only 2,710 women married under the age of 20 in 2010.)[11] Marriage in the early teens usually means forced marriage, for participants of both sexes are too young to give informed consent, but the physical impact on girls is much greater. They face repeated pregnancies at an age when their bodies are not sufficiently developed, which is why child marriage is the leading cause of young women aged 15 to 24 dying in pregnancy.[12] Yet a discussion paper prepared for UNICEF points out that early forced sex where a girl is married 'has not been recognized as a form of sexual abuse except where warlords or traffickers have recruited girls as sexual slaves'.[13] It's an astonishing omission but, as we have already seen, gender-specific issues have often been overlooked in human rights law and discourse.

From its 18th-century beginnings, human rights theory has concentrated on the fairer redistribution of economic and political rights among a category of people – namely men – which already enjoys them. It has not been imaginative enough to challenge the *specific* oppression of women and girls, who are still second-class citizens in many countries. But I believe there is another sense in which human rights theory has failed the female half of the population. The men whose names are most closely associated with human rights abuses in the late 20th century are well known: Saddam Hussein, Robert Mugabe, Kim Jung-il, Slobodan Milosevic, Colonel Gaddafi, Hafez and Bashar al-Assad. Their crimes against men, women and children are on a grand scale, and they could not have survived so long without the support of a cadre of willing torturers and killers. Yet there is another class of men, whose names will never appear on lists issued by international tribunals, who also need to be considered human rights abusers. You've encountered some of them in this book, where I've written about men who slaughter their wives and children, who rape women when they're drunk and vulnerable, who buy sex with victims of trafficking because they don't want to treat women as equals. I don't believe they're representative of all men, any more than I think every man is a Milosevic under the skin, but I can see a common thread. Rapists, domestic abusers, men who commit 'honour' crimes: they're capable of doing terrible things because they've dehumanised their victims. They're not, for the most part, desperate refugees fleeing war zones where they've been brutalised, although that's the case with a tiny minority. They think of themselves as regular guys, but the truth is that control matters more to them than seeing their victims as human beings.

If you see another person as basically the same as yourself, with the same feelings, you can't beat, rape or sell her to the highest bidder. If you accept that the sexes are equal, with exactly the same rights, you can't lie, humiliate and hurt women on a daily basis. You can't do any of these things if you believe that women are fully human, and it's that failure which lies at the heart of the problem I've laid out in this book. It's been going on for centuries but it's become more visible in recent decades, because women have become more visible. In the Introduction, I noted many ways in which women's lives have improved in developed countries over the last century. Education, the professions and the whole span of civic society have opened up to women, and our lives are better for it. But our visibility in the public world has highlighted the fact that a minority of men is uncomfortable with what we've achieved. Instead of embracing equality and the opportunity to have relationships with women who aren't dependants, they feel women's achievements as a loss. Each time a man threatens his wife, hits his partner or goes to a night club to shout abuse at a pole dancer, he's revealing a gnawing anxiety about his masculinity. He's showing that he feels diminished, unable to live in the modern world, and his coping mechanism is to deny the fact that women are as human as he is.

I promised in the Introduction that I would finish this book with a new Declaration of the Rights of Women. It draws on the work of women I admire, including Olympe de Gouges, Mary Wollstonecraft and Simone de Beauvoir, and addresses subjects whose importance has been demonstrated by recent events, such as the right to enjoy public space. Its purpose is to help women flourish as human beings, not to take anything away from men, and I hope they will find much they can support. As we've seen, the notion that the state should act as a guarantor when human rights are infringed was first raised by De Gouges more than two centuries ago, and some European politicians have begun to realise she was right. The public woman is first and foremost a human being. Our rights are human rights. It's time to tell the world's leaders we will accept nothing less.

DECLARATION OF
THE RIGHTS OF WOMEN

I

Women are born free and equal to men. All human beings
have the same rights; they have a responsibility to ensure
that those rights are enjoyed by everyone,
regardless of gender.

II

Women and girls have the same right bodily integrity as men
and boys. No one should be expected to tolerate physical
or sexual abuse, sexual harassment or any form
of genital mutilation.

III

Women have a right to safe contraception and abortion.
They should be able to live with any children they bear until
the child reaches the age of 16, except in cases of abuse.

IV

Girls are entitled to the same level of education as boys.
Literacy is essential to enable women to participate in civil
and political society.

V

No one, whether male or female, should be married under the age of 16; in some circumstances, 18 may be preferable. Adults have an absolute right to choose partners of either sex or live alone.

VI

Women and girls have an unconditional right to use and enjoy public space, for both social and political purposes. They have the right to exercise, take part in sport and observe it on the same terms as men.

VII

The law should not dictate how adults dress, except in circumstances where safety or identification requires it. Children cannot give informed consent and should not be required to adopt religious forms of dress.

VIII

Women have a right to equal working conditions and pay, and to transparency in pay structures so that it can be enforced.

IX

Women should enjoy the same property and inheritance rights as men.

X

Abuse on grounds of gender is as abhorrent as racism.

XI

Law should be secular and apply equally to men, women
and children. Separation of church and state is essential to
protect human beings from discrimination on grounds of
belief or absence of it.

XII

The state has a moral obligation to ensure that women and
girls are free to enjoy these rights, and to guarantee them
when they are denied.

NOTES

INTRODUCTION

1   UCAS final end of year figures for 2011.

BRITAIN'S GOT NARCISSISM

1   *Being Jordan: My Story – From the Very Beginning* (John Blake, 2005).
2   Ibid., p. 7.
3   Ibid., pp. 41–2.
4   'Katie Price: I haven't got body dysmorphia', NOWdaily website, 31 July 2010.
5   *Being Jordan*, p. 90.
6   First published 1949; Penguin translation by H. M. Parshley, 1972, p. 295.
7   *Being Jordan,* p. 59.
8   Ibid., p. 91.
9   Ibid., p. xvii.
10 'Drop the cougar act, Demi. It's time for an old codger in a cardigan', Mail Online, 30 Sept. 2011.
11 'Katie Price: I'm a minger who looks like a market trader!', NOWdaily website, 19 Oct. 2012
12 'A bra is not enough! Katie Price keeps her newly enhanced assets in check … by wearing a leather harness', *Daily Mail*, 14 Nov. 2012.

POLAR DISORDER

1   Tim Hodgdon, *The Chicago Women's Liberation Union: On the Cutting Edge of Protest Against Sexual Objectification* (2000), p. 2, CWLU Herstory website.
2   'Life Lessons from the 1968 Playboy Bunny Club Manual', The Hairpin website, 28 April 2011.
3   Jennifer Hayashi Danns with Sandrine Leveque, *Stripped: The Bare Reality of Lap Dancing* (Clairview, 2011), p. 105.
4   Ibid., p. 30.
5   Website of Diamonds Gentlemans Club [*sic*], Staines.
6   Website of Secrets, Hammersmith.
7   Teela Sanders, Kate Hardy and Rosie Campbell, *The Regulatory Dance: Sexual Consumption in the Night Time Economy* (University of Leeds, 2012), summary of final findings.

8 'Sex in the City: Spearmint Rhino pulls bankers bearing bonuses', *Guardian*, 20 Feb. 2011.

9 'Stringfellows's laps up profits', *Evening Standard*, 6 Aug. 2008.

10 'Bare facts: you can bank on dance, says Peter Stringfellow', This is Money website, 8 May 2009.

11 'Exposed: Stringy's £200k strippers', *The Sun*, 12 Oct. 2010.

12 '£200,000-a-year stripper "was forced to give nude lap dances to Peter Stringfellow's friends for free"', Mail Online, 18 Nov. 2011.

13 'Stringfellows lapdancer loses unfair dismissal case … then gets compared to a church organist', Mail Online, 21 Dec. 2012.

14 Julie Bindel, *Profitable Exploits: Lap Dancing in the UK* (Glasgow City Council, 2004), p. 49.

15 'Sex sold at Spearmint club', *Evening Standard*, 2 Sept. 2003.

16 Kat Banyard and Rowena Lewis, *Corporate Sexism: The Sex Industry's Infiltration of the Modern Workplace* (Fawcett Society, 2009), p. 13.

17 Bindel, *Profitable Exploits*, p. 52.

18 Ibid., p. 31.

19 Danns and Leveque, *Stripped*, p. 55.

20 Ibid., p. 76.

21 'Stringfellow's: the last dance saloon?', *Independent*, 13 Aug. 2006.

PERFORMANCE

1 'Amy Winehouse remembered by Mark Ronson', *Observer*, 11 Dec. 2011.

2 Mark A Bellis, Karen Hughes, Olivia Sharples, Tom Hennell and Katherine A. Hardcastle, 'Dying to be famous: retrospective cohort study of rock and pop star mortality and its association with adverse childhood experiences', *BMJ Open,* Dec. 2012.

3 'Amy Winehouse remembered by Mark Ronson', *Observer*, 11 Dec. 2011.

4 Quoted in 'Amy's not-so-glamorous poolside display of tattoos and scars', Mail Online, 18 May 2007.

5 'Amy Winehouse wins court ban on paparazzi at her home', *Guardian*, 1 May 2009.

6 '"Amy was so ashamed of being an alcoholic, she wouldn't even drink in front of me"', Mail Online, 4 Nov. 2011.

7 'Tony Bennett: I wish I could have helped Amy Winehouse', Mirror Online, 6 Oct. 2011.

VAGINA CANTATA

1 'Church employee says Pussy Riot show has given her "unceasing pain"', Interfax website, 31 July 2012.

2 Closing statement, 8 Aug. 2012.

3 Ibid.

4 Sigmund Freud, *On Sexuality*, tr. James Strachey (Pelican Freud Library, 1977), vol. 7, p. 354.

5 'The Todd Akin school of Christian thought on abortion and rape', *Guardian*, 20 Aug. 2012.

6 'Todd Akin's rape comment was bad, but his abortion views are much

worse', *Daily Beast*, 20 Aug. 2012.

7   Ibid.

8   'Richard Mourdock: even pregnancy from rape something "God intended"', CBS News, 23 Oct. 2012.

9   Quoted in *Daily Beast*, 20 Aug. 2012.

10   'Rep Steve King: I've never heard of a girl getting pregnant from statutory rape or incest', TPM website, 21 Aug. 2012.

11   'Rush Limbaugh's "personal attack" on Sandra Fluke? More like 20 attacks', *Washington Post*, 3 May 2012.

12   'Lawmakers banned from speaking on House floor after using the words "vagina" and "vasectomy" during abortion bill debate', *Daily Mail*, 15 June 2012.

13   'Lisa Brown, silenced on the Michigan House floor, helps read "Vagina Monologues" on statehouse steps', *Washington Post*, 19 June 2012.

14   Website of Harley Medical Group.

15   Website of Gynecosmetics.

16   Consultingroom.com.

17   *WHO Fact Sheet*, 241 (WHO, 2012).

18   Charlotte Feldman-Jacobs and Donna Clifton, *Female Genital Mutilation/ Cutting: Data and Trends* (Population Reference Bureau, update 2010).

19   Sumanta Roy, Dr Patricia Ng and Ikamara Larasi (Imkaan) with Efua Dorkenoo OBE (Equality Now) and Professor Alison Macfarlane (City University, London), The Missing Link: A Joined up Approach to Addressing Harmful Practices in London (Imkaan, 2011).

20   Nayra Atiya, *Khul-Khaal: Five Egyptian Women Tell their Stories* (American University in Cairo Press, 1984), p. 41.

21   Ibid.

22   'Islamist parliamentarian demands abolition of Egypt's ban on FGM', Desert Flower blog, 29 March 2012.

23   Mariatu Kamara with Susan McClelland, *Bite of the Mango* (Bloomsbury, 2009), p. 89.

24   Ibid., p. 87.

25   'Meeting Pussy Riot', interview by Henry Langston for vice.com website.

26   Ibid.

QUEEN WAG

1   'And what do you DO? Queen wants Kate Middleton to get charity job to counter claims she is workshy', Mail Online, 24 Aug. 2008.

2   'The Queen tells the Duchess of Cambridge to curtsy to the "blood princesses"', *Daily Telegraph*, 24 June 2012.

CALM DOWN, DEAR

1   Her sole Conservative predecessor was Florence Horsbrugh, who served in 1953–4. The first female Cabinet minister was the Labour MP Margaret Bondfield, who took office in 1929.

2   Margaret Thatcher Foundation article archive: 'Falklands: "The Sphinx and the curious case of the Iron Lady's H-Bomb"', *Sunday Times*, 20 Nov. 2005.

3   Ibid.

4   'The forging of the Iron Lady', *The Lady*, 6 Jan. 2012.

5   'It's that woman or us, wife told Major', Mail Online, undated.

6   'Exclusive: Cabinet is worth £70m', *Daily Telegraph*, 27 May 2012.

7   *The Impact of Austerity on Women* (Fawcett Society policy briefing, March 2012), p. 5.

8   Ibid., p. 12.

9   Ibid.

10   Ibid., p. 9.

11   Ibid., p. 6.

12   Ibid.

13   Ibid.

14   'Yvette Cooper: Coalition cuts are an "assault" on the family', *Guardian*, 27 Sept. 2010.

15   Fawcett Society, *Impact of Austerity*, p. 3.

16   'David Cameron makes joke at MP Peter Bone's wife question', BBC News Northampton, 27 June 2011.

17   'Nadine Dorries storms out of Commons to schoolboy laughter after Cameron quips that she is "extremely frustrated"', Mail Online, 8 Sept. 2011.

18   'PMQs review: Cameron's anger boils over', *New Statesman*, 25 April 2012.

19   'Labour fury as David Cameron tells Angela Eagle: "Calm down, dear"', *Guardian*, 27 April 2011.

20   'Cameron like bully Flashman, says Miliband', BBC News Politics, 11 May 2011.

21   'Leaked memo on support from women for the coalition government', *Guardian*, 13 Sept. 2011.

22   'Conservative support among women: little change since the general election', Ipsos-MORI, 4 Oct. 2011.

23   Fawcett Society, *Impact of Austerity*, pp. 7–8.

24   Ibid., p. 11.

25   Ibid., p. 25.

26   'Women's Institute warns Government against rail staff cuts', Telegraph Online, 9 Aug. 2012.

27   'Ian Duncan Smith exposes and condemns Labour's record on the family', Centre for Social Justice, 19 Jan. 2010.

28   Home Office, 2011.

29   Fawcett Society, *Impact of Austerity*, p. 19.

30   Jude Towers and Sylvia Walby, *Measuring the Impact of Cuts in Public Expenditure on the Provision of Services to Prevent Violence Against Women and Girls* (Lancaster University, Northern Rock Foundation and Trust for London, 2012), key findings.

31   All figures from Towers and Walby, *Measuring the Impact*.

32   'Equality: Coalition is missing the point about women', *Observer*, 12 Feb. 2012.

33   'David Cameron axes equality assessments in war on "red tape"', *Guardian*, 19 Nov. 2012.

34   Fawcett Society, *Impact of Austerity*, p. 40.

KEEPER OF THE FLAME

1 'Three in four news journalists are men, study finds', *Press Gazette*, 4 March 2011.
2 I gave evidence to the Inquiry on 21 Nov. 2011. Six months earlier, officers from the phone hacking inquiry, Operation Weeting, showed me evidence suggesting that my mobile phone had been hacked in 2004. In Jan. 2012, I accepted damages of £27,500 from News International, parent company of the *News of the World*, which also paid my legal costs.
3 Brooks's evidence to the Leveson Inquiry, 11 May 2012.
4 'Untangling Rebekah Brooks', *Vanity Fair*, Feb. 2012.
5 Brooks, Cudlipp lecture.
6 'Profile: Rebekah Brooks, ex-News International chief', BBC News Politics, 24 July 2012.
7 Ibid.
8 Piers Morgan, *The Insider: The Private Diaries of a Scandalous Decade* (Ebury, 2005), p. 39 (entry for 5 July 1994).
9 Graham Johnson, *Hack: Sex, Drugs, and Scandal from Inside the Tabloid Jungle* (Simon & Schuster, 2012), p. 174.
10 'Pottergate: we publish the secret tapes', *Daily Telegraph*, 6 Sept. 2002.
11 '"Up to £1m payout" for Sharon Shoesmith', *Independent*, 27 May 2011.
12 Text message from Brooks to Cameron, 7 Oct. 2009, revealed by Brooks at Leveson Inquiry.
13 'The woman who could bring down Cameron', *Daily Beast*, 9 May 2012.
14 Johnson, *Hack*, pp. 171–2.
15 Freud, 'Some psychical consequences of the anatomical distinction between the sexes', *On Sexuality*, p. 334.
16 'Sun editor admits row "got out of hand"', Mail Online, 4 Nov. 2005.
17 '"Fat, jealous" Clare brands Page 3 porn', *The Sun*, 27 July 2007.
18 'Rebekah Brooks, the schmoozer hated by Murdoch's wife and daughter', Mail Online, 17 July 2011.
19 'Soap star Ross to marry girl from Warrington', *Warrington Guardian*, 26 July 1996.
20 '"Shut up, you homophobic cow"', *Evening Standard*, 7 July 2011.
21 *Tatler*, July 2009, quoted in 'Rebekah's world: lunch in Venice, dinner at Wiltons, weekends with the Oxfordshire set', *Guardian*, 5 July 2009.
22 On 15 May 2012, Brooks was charged with three counts of conspiring to pervert the course of justice. On 2 Aug. 2012, she was charged with three counts of conspiring to intercept communications. On 19 Nov. 2012, she was further charged with conspiracy to commit misconduct in public office. Brooks vigorously denied all the charges.

VEILED MESSAGES

1 'Egyptian general admits "virginity tests" conducted on protesters', CNN, 31 May 2011.
2 'One brave woman's fight against virginity-test ordeal in Tahrir Square', *Guardian*, 28 Oct. 2011.
3 Nazra, 'Testimonies on the recent sexual assaults on Tahrir Square vicinity',

Feminist Studies (13 June 2012), pp. 6–7.

4   Ibid., p. 3.
5   Ibid., p. 4.
6   Ibid., p. 2.
7   Ibid., p. 2.
8   'Talk is cheap: addressing sexual harassment in Tunisia', tunisia-live.net, 14 April 2012.
9   Rasha Mohammad Hassan, *Clouds in Egypt's Sky, Sexual Harassment: From Verbal Harassment to Rape,* a sociological study, with scientific revision by Dr Aliyaa Shoukry, supervised by Nehad Abul Komsan (Egyptian Centre for Women's Studies, 2008).
10 'I will stand up for the Muslim Brotherhood', Mona Eltahawy, Forward.com, 21 Sept. 2007.
11 Mariz Tadros, 'Egypt's women have had enough of being told to cover up', *Guardian*, 29 May 2012.
12 'Egypt's sexual harassment of women "epidemic"', BBC News Middle East, 3 Sept. 2012.
13 'Muslim leader blames women for sex attacks', *The Australian*, 26 Oct. 2006.
14 UN Entity for Gender Equality and the Empowerment of Women, *Progress of the World's Women, 2011–2012: In Pursuit of Justice* (UN, 2012), annex 4: Violence against Women.
15 Ibid.
16 Ibid.
17 'More Arab females join women's rights movement to demand equality', Al Arabiya News, 9 Oct. 2012.
18 UN, *Progress of the World's Women*, annex 1: Women's political rights.
19 Ibid., p. 107.
20 Research by Thomson Reuters Foundation, reported in the *Guardian*, 'Afghanistan worst place in the world for women, but India in top five', 15 June 2011.
21 'Saudi police "stopped" fire rescue', BBC News Middle East, 15 March 2002.

POSSESSION

1   *Melton Times*, 27 Feb. 2003.
2   'Police inspector who murdered wife and daughter may have probed similar case', *Mail on Sunday*, 11 Dec. 2011.
3   Ibid.
4   'The Leeds man who turned on his "perfect family"', *Guardian*, 14 Dec. 2011.
5   *Mail on Sunday*, 11 Dec. 2011.
6   Marty Langley, *American Roulette*, 4th edn (Violence Policy Center, 2012).
7   Ibid. Out of 313 murder-suicide incidents in the US in 2011, 280 (89.5 per cent) are known to have involved the use of firearms.
8   'Domestic violence: the facts, the issues, the future', speech by Keir Starmer QC, Director of Public Prosecutions, 12 April 2011.
9   Child homicide statistics, NSPCC, Jan. 2012. On average, 56 children in England and Wales are killed by another person each year, and most of these

are under the age of 5. Killings of children by natural parents are committed in roughly equal proportions by mothers (47 per cent) and fathers (53 per cent). Where the child is killed by someone other than a natural parent, males 'strongly predominate'.

10 *American Roulette*, 4th edn (2012).

11 'Father killed family for being too western', Telegraph Online, 21 Feb. 2007.

12 'Fathers who kill their children', *Observer*, 5 Nov. 2006.

13 Starmer, 'Domestic violence'.

14 Ibid.

15 'Horden shootings: IPCC highlights Durham Police failings', BBC News Tees, 19 Nov. 2012.

16 'Agris Titans sentenced to 13 years in jail for strangling young wife', *Huffington Post*, 31 Jan. 2012.

17 'Nathaniel Brown found guilty of Tottenham murder', BBC News London, 31 Jan. 2012.

18 'Nathaniel Brown jailed for life for murdering Zandra Maxwell-Nelson', *Brent and Kilburn Times*, 3 Feb. 2012.

19 'Muslim convert wife and children "killed by abusive monster"', Telegraph Online, 14 Feb. 2011.

20 'Solicitor convicted of wife's murder', *Independent*, 27 July 2011.

21 'Cheating Ashtead lawyer sentenced to 20 years for wife's murder', This is Local London Online, 27 July 2011.

22 'Casey Brittle murder: IPCC criticises domestic abuse care', BBC News Nottingham, 18 Oct. 2011.

23 'Joanna Brown's family and friends call for court reform', BBC News Berkshire, 25 Nov. 2011.

24 'Raoul Moat warned ex-girlfriend before shooting spree', Telegraph Online, 5 Sept. 2011; 'Raoul Moat accomplices guilty of murder and conspiracy to murder', *Guardian*, 11 March 2011.

25 'Jean Say murdered children to spite estranged wife', Telegraph Online, 8 Dec. 2011.

26 'Father who slit children's throats to spite wife is jailed for life', Mail Online, 12 Dec. 2011.

27 'White teenage mother stabbed to death and dumped in canal "after her married Asian lover rejected her child"', '17.5 year sentence for the murder of Laura Wilson', CPS, 21 Dec. 2011.

28 'Woman murdered by boyfriend "would have survived but for 999 blunder"', Telegraph Online, 12 March 2010; 'Man jailed for killing ex-partner at her Cardiff home', BBC News, 11 March 2010.

29 'Jilted lover who murdered mother-of-four Karen McGraw is jailed for life', *Western Mail*, 5 Dec. 2009.

30 'Jealous husband murdered wife and killed himself with electric drill after she ended marriage on Facebook', Mail Online, 11 Feb. 2009.

31 'Husband stabbed wife to death just weeks after getting bail for trying to strangle her', Mail Online, 13 May 2008.

32 'Debt fears led man to kill wife', BBC News, 18 Jan. 2008; 'Wife killer to serve eight years', BBC News, 13 March 2008.

33 'Taxi driver killed wife after row', BBC News, 3 Nov. 2008.

34   'Miser knifed wife day before due to give £133,000 divorce payout', Mail
     Online, 7 Nov. 2007; 'Life for OAP who murdered his wife', *Derby Evening
     Telegraph*, 18 Nov. 2007.

35   'Jailed for life: man who stabbed and set his girlfriend on fire but was caught
     out by her dying accusation', Mail Online, 3 May 2008.

36   'Life for taxi driver who murdered wife and children', *Guardian*, 14 March
     2007; 'Rahan Arshad: profile of a killer', *Manchester Evening News*, 13
     March 2007.

37   Speaking at meeting of Committee on Elimination of Discrimination Against
     Women, UN General Assembly, 23 July 2009.

38   'Fight against domestic violence in Spain only strong on paper', Womensphere
     website, 22 May 2008.

39   Ibid.

40   'Geeta Aulakh killing: a brutal murder ordered by a jealous husband',
     Guardian, 3 Dec. 2010; 'Geeta Aulakh murder: getaway driver jailed', *Ealing
     Gazette*, 18 April 2011.

41   'Shawbo Ali Rauf, a 19 year old victim of "honour" killing in Kurdistan',
     Kurd Net website, 24 May 2007.

42   '"They're following me": chilling words of girl who was "honour killing"
     victim', *Guardian*, 22 Sept. 2012; 'Banaz Mahmod "honour" killing cousins
     jailed for life', BBC News London, 10 Nov. 2010. A documentary about the
     murder premiered at the Raindance film festival in 2012. *Banaz: A Love
     Story* was produced by the Norwegian human rights activist and music
     producer, Deeyah.

43   '"You're not my mother any more," shouted Samaira. Then her family killed
     her.' *Guardian*, 15 July 2006.

44   'Parents of Shafilea Ahmed sentenced to 25-years after being found guilty of
     her "honour" killing', Telegraph Online, 3 Aug. 2012.

45   'Honour killing: father convicted of murder of Tulay Goren', Telegraph
     Online, 17 Dec. 2009.

46   'Mother-in-law "lured a cheating wife to her death"', Mail Online, 2 May
     2007; 'Mother and son jailed over "honour" killing', *Guardian*, 19 Sept. 2007.

47   'Canadian jury finds Afghan family guilty of "honour killings"', *Guardian*,
     30 Jan. 2012.

48   '"Honour" crimes against women in UK rising rapidly, figures show',
     Guardian, 3 Dec. 2011.

49   Stieg Larsson, *The Expo Files*, tr. Laurie Thompson (Maclehose Press, 2011),
     133.

50   '"Honour" crimes are domestic abuse, plain and simple', *Guardian*, 21
     March 2012.

'TIS PITY SHE'S A WHORE

1   'Ched Evans trial: player "could have had any girl he wanted" detectives
     told', *Daily Post*, 17 April 2012.

2   'Sheffield United and Wales striker Evans jailed for five years after being
     found guilty of rape', Mail Online, 20 April 2012; 'Footballer rape trial:
     Ched Evans jailed five years, Clayton McDonald cleared', BBC News Wales,

20 April 2012; *Daily Post*, 17 April 2012.

3   Mail Online, 20 April 2012.

4   Ibid.

5   '"Money-grabbing little tramp": Ched Evans' team-mate in foul-mouthed Twitter rant after rape conviction', Mirror Online, 21 April 2012.

6   'Ched Evans' teammate suspended over Twitter comments about rape conviction', Mail Online, 23 April 2012, updated 18 May 2012.

7   'Polanski was not guilty of "rape-rape", says Whoopi Goldberg', *Guardian*, 29 Sept. 2009.

8   'A Conversation with Gore Vidal', *The Atlantic*, Oct. 2009.

9   Independent Police Complaints Commission report, Jan. 2010. The IPCC investigation into the Worboys case found 'missed opportunities due to individual errors of judgement as well as more systemic issues.' Two detective inspectors, a detective sergeant and two detective constables were disciplined as a result.

10   'How the police lost track of Ian Huntley', Telegraph Online, 23 June 2004.

11   Sexual Assault Research Summary Report, prepared by ICM for Amnesty International UK, 12 Oct. 2005, posted on Amnesty website 21 Nov. 2005.

12   Mumsnet, rape and sexual assault survey results, Feb.–March 2012. The website subsequently launched a campaign 'We Believe You' to support victims of sex attacks.

13   'Wake Up to Rape Research', compiled for The Havens by Opinion Matters

14   Julian Assange v Swedish Prosecution Authority, High Court (Divisional Court), Summary to assist the media, 2 Nov. 2011.

15   Judgment, between Julian Assange and Swedish Prosecution Authority, High Court of Justice, Queen's Bench Division, Divisional Court, 2 Nov. 2011, paragraph 74.

16   Ibid., paragraph 74.

17   Ibid., paragraph 93.

18   'Julian Assange accused of "roughing up" alleged sexual-assault victim', *Independent*, 14 July 2011.

19   'Julian Assange accusers felt trapped, prosecutors claim', Telegraph Online, 13 July 2011.

20   *Independent*, 14 July 2011.

21   'Julian Assange tries "silent" strategy in court fight to beat extradition', *Guardian*, 12 July 2012.

22   'Accuser snapped me in the nude', *Sunday Times*, 26 Dec. 2010.

23   'The Wikileaks sex files: how two one-night stands sparked a worldwide hunt for Julian Assange', Mail Online, 6 Dec. 2010.

24   'Dark forces at work to take Julian Assange to US, says lawyer', *Evening Standard*, 8 Dec. 2010.

25   Paul Bennett and Israel Shamir, 'Assange: the amazing adventures of Captain Neo in Blonde land', CounterPunch, 27–29 Aug. 2010.

26   Dickfreeman.blogspot.com, 7 Dec. 2010.

27   'Jemima Khan on Julian Assange: How the Wikileaks founder alienated his allies', *New Statesman*, 6 Feb. 2013

28   'George Galloway wades into Julian Assange row – and creates a storm', *Guardian*, 20 Aug. 2012.

29 'Friend of Julian Assange names "sexual assault victim" on live television', *Evening Standard*, 21 Aug. 2012. The same article covers a row on BBC2's Newsnight programme the previous evening when I challenged a former British ambassador who named one of Assange's accusers during a live broadcast.

30 Michel Taubmann, *The DSK Affairs, the Counter Inquiry* quoted in 'Book details Strauss-Kahn version of the scandal', *Le Figaro*, 1 Dec. 2011.

31 'My "weak flesh" has cost me everything, says DSK', *Independent*, 2 Dec. 2011.

32 30 Nov. 2011.

33 Diallo gave a detailed account of alleged events in the Sofitel in 'The Maid's Tale', *Newsweek*, 25 July 2011.

34 'Leaked "rape" report sparks new Strauss-Kahn furor', Reuters, 16 Aug. 2011.

35 'Dominique Strauss-Kahn: why French women put up with it', Telegraph Online, 22 May 2011.

36 'Feminists' anger at chauvinism of Strauss-Kahn affair', *Independent*, 23 May 2011.

37 'Bernard-Henri Levy defends accused IMF director', *Daily Beast*, 16 May 2011.

38 Joanna Bourke, *Rape: A History from 1860 to the Present* (Virago, 2007), p. 389.

39 'Hotel maid in HIV shock', *New York Post*, 18 May 2011.

40 'DSK maid a hooker', *New York Post*, 2 July 2011.

41 'Cheap trick', *New York Post*, 3 July 2011.

42 mens-rights.net, 2 July 2011.

43 'Dominique Strauss-Kahn: prosecutors ask judge to dismiss sex charges', *Guardian*, 22 Aug. 2011.

44 Ibid.

45 24 Aug. 2011.

46 'Dominique Strauss-Kahn to countersue writer over attempted rape claim', *Guardian*, 4 July 2011.

47 'Dominique Strauss-Kahn had brutal sex with me too, says mother of "attack victim"', *Evening Standard*, 19 July 2011.

48 'Strauss-Kahn sex case: French inquiry dropped', BBC News Europe, 13 Oct. 2011.

49 'He's just a "simple swinger": DSK had no idea orgy girls were pimped prostitutes, says lawyer', Mail Online, 27 March 2012.

50 'DSK under formal investigation over pimping charges', Telegraph Online, 26 March 2012.

51 'Strauss-Kahn reaches settlement with hotel maid who says former IMF boss sexually assaulted her in hotel suite', Mail Online, 10 Dec. 2012.

52 'Ched Evans: nine admit naming rape victim on social media', BBC News North East Wales, 5 Nov. 2012.

53 'Ched Evans rape case: nine fined over naming of footballer's victim', *Guardian*, 5 Nov. 2012.

54 'Ched Evans rape victim "relocated and given new identity" after being named on Twitter', Wales Online, 11 Dec. 2012.

BUYING POWER

1 *Review of Multi-Agency Responses to the Sexual Exploitation of Children* (RBSCB, Sept. 2012), p. 6.

2 Ibid., p. 6.

3 'Rochdale grooming trial: how the case unfolded', Telegraph Online, 8 May 2012.

4 Ibid.

5 RBSCB, *Review of Multi-Agency Responses*, p. 6.

6 'Rochdale police and council "repeatedly warned" about sex abuse risk in town', *Guardian*, 27 Sept. 2012.

7 'Rochdale grooming trial: nine men jailed', BBC News, 9 May 2012.

8 'Rochdale grooming gang leader gets 22 years for child rape', *Guardian*, 2 Aug. 2012.

9 Telegraph Online, 8 May 2012.

10 My interview with 'Sonya' appeared in an article in *The Times*, '"They said I wasn't human but something that can be bought"', 14 Oct. 2004. All quotes are from my notes and the article.

11 In countries where patriarchal attitudes prevail, young women like Sonya are sometimes regarded as a valuable 'asset' by male relatives.

12 Thanks to Natasha Lewis for this formulation.

13 Marina Barnard, Graham Hart and Stephanie Church, *Client Violence Against Prostitute Women Working from Street and Off-Street Locations: A Three City Comparison* (ESRC, 2002), key findings.

14 Melissa Farley, Isin Baral, Mereb Kiremire and Ufuk Sezgin, 'Prostitution in five countries: violence and post-traumatic stress disorder (South Africa, Thailand, Turkey, USA, Zambia)', *Feminism and Psychology*, 8 (1998).

15 'Protection of sex workers', 334/52 (11 Jan. 2007).

16 National Centre for Social Research: Bob Erens, Sally MacManus, Julia Field, Christos Korovessis; Royal Free and University College Medical School: Anne Johnson, Kevin Fenton; London School of Hygiene and Tropical Medicine: Kaye Wellings, Nov. 2001, *Second National Survey of Sexual Attitudes and Lifestyles (NATSAL)* (2001).

17 Home Office, *Tackling the Demand for Prostitution: A Rapid Evidence Assessment of the Published Research Literature* (Home Office, Research Report 27, 2009), p. 4.

18 Home Office, *Human Trafficking: UK Responses* (Standard Note, House of Commons Library, 16 March 2012), pp. 4–5.

19 Emily Dugan and I listed shortcomings in the ACPO report in an article in the *Independent on Sunday*, 'Police report into brothels dismissed as "amateurish"', 15 Aug. 2010.

20 Quoted in Barnardo's, *Whose Child Now?* (Barnardo's, 2009), p. 7.

21 'Revealed: conspiracy of silence on UK sex gangs', *The Times*, 5 Jan. 2011.

22 'Police "hid" abuse of 60 girls by Asian takeaway workers linked to murder of 14-year-old', Mail Online, 7 April 2011.

23 'Derby sex gang convicted of grooming and abusing girls', BBC News Derby, 24 Nov. 2010.

24 'Report: child exploiters "come from all ethnic groups"', ITV, 21 Nov. 2012.

25 Office of the Children's Commissioner, *'I thought I was the only one.*

The only one in the world': Interim Report, the Office of the Children's Commissioner's Inquiry into child sexual exploitation in gangs and groups (Stationery Office, Nov. 2012), p. 9.

26 'It's time to get serious about sex trafficking in Australia', *The Age*, 13 Oct. 2011.

27 Julie Bindel, 'Window brothels get the red light', *Standpoint*, Oct. 2012.

28 'Amsterdam to clean up red light district', CBS News, 11 Feb. 2009.

29 Eric Neumayer, Seo-Young Cho and Axel Dreher, 'Does legalised prostitution increase human trafficking?', *World Development* (Jan. 2013).

30 Ibid.

31 Joshua Cruz and Swaan van Iterson, *The Audacity of Tolerance: A Critical Analysis of Legalised Prostitution in Amsterdam's Red Light District* (Humanity in Action, n.d.).

32 *The Age*, 13 Oct. 2011.

33 'Former NY governor Eliot Spitzer sex secrets laid bare', *The Australian*, 16 Feb. 2009.

34 RBSCB review, p. 9.

35 Ibid., p. 19.

36 Anne Van Meeuwen, Sara Swann, Diana McNeish and Susan S. M. Edwards, *Whose Daughter Next? Children Abused through Prostitution* (Barnardo's, 1998).

37 Home Office, *Paying the Price: A Consultation Paper on Prostitution* (Home Office, July 2004), p. 11.

38 Ibid., p. 28.

39 Ibid., p. 31.

40 Ibid., p. 39.

41 Ministry of Industry, Employment and Communications, Sweden, *Prostitution and Trafficking in Human Beings*, fact sheet (Ministry of Industry, April 2005).

42 'Evaluation of the prohibition of the purchase of sexual services', presented to the Swedish Government by Anna Skarhed, Chancellor of Justice, 2 July 2010.

43 'French minister wants prostitution to "disappear"', France 24, 25 June 2012.

THE WITCHES OF PERUGIA

1 Santuccia's case is mentioned in the Diary of Graziani, *Magic, Ritual, and Witchcraft*, 1309–1491. A fuller account of the charges against her appears in Richard Kieckhefer, 'Mythologies of Witchcraft in the Fifteenth Century', *Chronicles of Perugia* , 1/1 (University of Pennsylvania Press, Summer 2006).

2 Kieckhefer, 'Mythologies', p. 81.

3 Ibid., p. 88.

4 As well as extensive newspaper reports, there are detailed and unsensational accounts of the murder in two excellent books. One is John Follain, *Death in Perugia: The Definitive Account of the Meredith Kercher Case from her Murder to the Acquittal of Raffaele Sollecito and Amanda Knox* (Hodder, 2011); the other is Nina Burleigh, *The Fatal Gift of Beauty: The Trials of Amanda Knox* (Broadway, 2011).

5   Follain, *Death in Perugia*, p. 39.
6   Burleigh, *Fatal Gift*, p. 274.
7   'Knox: I'm no murderer', *Seattle Times*, 3 Dec. 2009.
8   Mignini is a controversial figure. In 2006, before he became chief prosecutor in the murder of Meredith Kercher, he was charged with abuse of office in another sensational case, the investigation into a serial killer known as the Monster of Florence. In Jan. 2010, he was convicted by a court in Florence and given a 16-month suspended prison sentence. In Nov. 2011, the conviction was overturned on the grounds that the court did not have jurisdiction.
9   Follain, *Death in Perugia*, p. 64.
10   Follain, *Death in Perugia*, p. 135.
11   Ibid., p. 144.
12   Ibid., p. 153.
13   Ibid., pp. 166–7.
14   'Forensic experts discredit evidence against Amanda Knox', Reuters, 29 June 2011.
15   'How the sex game went wrong: judge's report', Telegraph Online, 9 Nov. 2007.
16   'Meredith: Foxy Knoxy "brought strange men back to the house"', Mail Online, 8 Nov. 2007.
17   'Foxy Knoxy "held Meredith down during deadly sex attack", say police', Mail Online, 9 Nov. 2007.
18   Telegraph Online, 11 Nov. 2007.
19   Mail Online, 3 Dec. 2007.
20   Burleigh, *Fatal Gift*, p. 304.
21   Ibid., p. 220.
22   *The Sun*, 31 Oct. 2008.
23   *The Sun*, updated 12 Jan. 2011, original date unknown.
24   'Fantasy world fuelled by sex, drink and drugs', *The Times*, 7 Dec. 2009.
25   Burleigh, *Fatal Gift*, p. 213.
26   Follain, *Death in Perugia*, p. 351.
27   Burleigh, *Fatal Gift*, p. 4.
28   Kieckhefer, 'Mythologies', p. 90.
29   Diary of Graziani.
30   Kieckhefer, 'Mythologies', p. 87.
31   'Daily Mail censured for fictional story about Amanda Knox verdict', *Guardian*, 9 Dec. 2011.
32   5 Oct. 2011.

CONCLUSION

1   De Beauvoir, *Second Sex*, p. 16.
2   Declaration of the Rights of Woman, 1791, art. X.
3   Ibid., art. XII.
4   Speech in Paris, 17 Nov. 1793; published in *Le Courrier Republicain*, 19 Nov. 1793.
5   The phrase appears in a letter written by Horace Walpole, 4th Earl of Oxford

and a Whig politician.

6   *Women, Peace and Security, Our Work: Women as a Force for Peace,* Amnesty International USA website.

7   'Put women at the heart of peace', Womankind Worldwide website.

8   UN, 'Literacy vital for beating poverty and disease and reinforcing stability', 8 Sept. 2011.

9   UN, *Facts and Figures on Rural Women* (UN, 2012).

10 'Early Marriage in South Asia: a discussion paper compiled from a study by Mira B Aghi', UNICEF.

11 ONS Statistical Bulletin: Marriage in England and Wales, 2010

12 Ibid.

13 Ibid.